CW01083178

COGNITIVE
HYPNOTHERAPY

NEW DIRECTIONS IN COGNITIVE-BEHAVIOR THERAPY

A Series of Books Edited By

Robert L. Leahy

Cognitive Therapy
Basic Principles and Applications
Robert L. Leahy

Practicing Cognitive Therapy
A Guide to Interventions
Robert L. Leahy, Editor

Cognitive Behavioral Treatment of Adult Survivors of Childhood Trauma
Imagery Rescripting and Reprocessing
Mervin R. Smucker and
Constance V. Dancu

Cognitive Hypnotherapy
E. Thomas Dowd

COGNITIVE HYPNOTHERAPY

E. Thomas Dowd, Ph.D., ABPP

JASON ARONSON INC.
Northvale, New Jersey
London

This book was set in 11 pt. Berkeley by Alpha Graphics of Pittsfield, NH, and printed and bound by Book-mart Press, Inc. of North Bergen, NJ.

Library of Congress Cataloging-in-Publication Data

Dowd, E. Thomas.
    Cognitive hypnotherapy / E. Thomas Dowd.
        p. cm.
    Includes bibliographical references and index.
    ISBN 0-7657-0228-2
    1. Hypnotism—Therapeutic use. 2. Cognitive therapy. I. Title.
    [DNLM: 1. Cognitive Therapy. 2. Hypnosis. WM 415 D745c 1999]
    RC497.D69 1999
    616.89'162—dc21
    DNLM/DLC
    for Library of Congress   99-14701

Printed in the United States of America on acid-free paper. For information and catalog write to Jason Arson Inc., 230 Livingston Street, Northvale, NJ 07647-1726, or visit our website: www.aronson.com

Contents

Foreword

When I began developing Cognitive Therapy more than thirty years ago, I had no idea how it would develop or how comprehensive the model would become. Since then, Cognitive Therapy has become a major system of psychopathology and psychotherapy and is widely considered to be a powerful integrative theory. Although I originally developed it as a treatment for depression, my colleagues and I later extended the model to anxiety and phobias, personality disorders, substance abuse, bipolar disorders, eating disorders, and marital problems. Recent work has shown this approach to be useful in the treatment of obsessive compulsive disorder, hypochondriasis, and even schizophrenia.

Now, Tom Dowd has taken the theory and practice of Cognitive Therapy one step further. He has integrated it with hypnosis and hypnotherapy and has produced the first-ever book on that topic. Cognitive Therapy has always had an imagery component, and he has systematically developed and expanded that side of it in an imposing manner. A scholar and practitioner who has studied and written on both topics for many years, Dr. Dowd has authored an excellent book that should stand as the definitive work for some time. In addition to integrating Cognitive Therapy and hypnotherapy, he has also integrated science and practice in a way that is truly impressive.

The book is appropriate for those who know something about Cognitive Therapy and hypnotherapy but who wish to extend their knowledge and integrate the two into their practice. Especially interesting and informative are the numerous case examples and hypnotic routines that illustrate how to conduct cognitive hypnotherapy. While not a substitute for experiential workshops and training programs, this book is an excellent first step for practitioners who wish to extend their knowledge into a relatively unknown area.

I have known Dr. Dowd for twenty years and he has been involved in the Cognitive Therapy network for at least that long. As founding editor of the *Journal of Cognitive Psychotherapy* he has stimulated an enormous expansion of the burgeoning field of Cognitive Therapy. I have a great regard for his theoretical and clinical ability, and I recommend this book highly for anyone interested in another important extension of the Cognitive Therapy model.

Aaron T. Beck, M.D.
University of Pennsylvania
School of Medicine
December 1999

Acknowledgments

Writing a book such as this demands not only energy and tenacity but also the combined wisdom of "those who went before," as well as support and encouragement from other people. In that spirit I'd like to acknowledge those individuals who were instrumental, one way or another, in helping me create and finish this book. First, I'd like to mention Robert Leahy, Ph.D., Series Editor for Jason Aronson, who first encouraged me to write this book and kept encouraging me when I wasn't sure I could or wanted to. Let me also mention the late David S. Kuypers, Ph.D., who first taught me hypnosis in the 1970s and whose energetic and creative spirit has been with me since. Next, let me acknowledge my deep debt to two creative giants of the therapeutic world who provided me the theoretical, empirical, and clinical material with which to construct this book: Aaron T. Beck, M.D., and Milton H. Erickson, M.D. I've been privileged to know the former for 20 years and have benefited enormously from his constantly evolving knowledge and wisdom and I treasure the conversations we've had. A very special thanks, Tim, for all you have given me and others. I never met the latter, but I have been impressed for years by his tremendous insight into the human condition and his unusual and creative ability to foster change and growth in people. Indeed, the more I read of him and about him, the richer and farther-seeing his ideas appear.

Next, I want to offer a special thanks to Ms. Penny Caldwell, an undergraduate student who came along and offered her help at a time when my energy was flagging. Her positive enthusiasm for the subject matter and this book was absolutely contagious. She read and offered comments on the entire book and wrote drafts of some of the case examples. She consistently went well beyond what I expected of her and some of her spirit can be found in these pages.

I also want to thank my daughter, Kathleen; my son, Michael; and my son-in-law, Jonathan who by their presence constantly reminded me of what life is really all about. It isn't about work and occupation—it's about relationships and love. No one ever said at death, "Gee, I wish I'd spent more time at the office!"

Finally, I want to offer very special thanks to my wife of 32 years, Therese M. Dowd, Ph.D., who has never lost confidence in my ability and ultimate success. An academic professional in her own right, she has helped to create the conditions and the home life that fostered my growth and development. She has been there for me—at times when I could appreciate it and at times when I couldn't. She has provided a balance between critique and support. It has been said that life circumstances, not native ability, luck, or academic preparation, are what really separate those who are successful from those who aren't. By her creation of positive life circumstances for me, she has helped to foster whatever success I have enjoyed. Therese, I hope that I have helped you half as much as you have helped me.

So, I dedicate this book to Drs. Beck, Erickson, and Dowd, each of whom has fostered my growth and development in very different ways. This book breathes the spirit of all of you.

E. Thomas Dowd
December 1999

1

Introduction

Although it has been known as such only a little over a century, hypnosis as a phenomenon has existed for hundreds of years. Kroger (1977) has described what are undoubtedly hypnotic phenomena throughout the ages—from royal or priestly "laying on of hands" (p. 1) through bodily stroking to magnetic and astral healing. Indeed, it is likely that activities such as priestly exorcism of demons, religious mysticism, and demonic possession itself are at least partly hypnotic in nature. Such psychological phenomena as hysterical conversion reactions and deep relaxation may be partly hypnotic as well.

The first description of what we now call *hypnosis*, however, was provided by an Austrian physician named Franz Anton Mesmer. Mesmer argued that these effects were caused by "animal magnetism," which he thought was analogous to physical magnetism. He used metal objects with which to "magnetize" people and was able to obtain some phenomena, such as convulsions and hallucinations that today we would call *trance behavior*, and obtained some relief of somatic symptoms that might be attributable to hysterical conversions. Mesmer's claims were investigated by a French commission in 1784 which concluded (in an unusually far-seeing decision) that his cures were obtained by the power of unconscious suggestion rather than by animal magnetism. Although Mesmer was then discredited, he gave his name to the activity that for years was called *mesmerism*. Furthermore, all sorts of lurid tales were developed around mesmerism, as exemplified in some of the stories of Edgar Allan Poe. Thus the stage was set for hypnosis's later inclusion among magic and occult phenomena, as well as its tacit association with vampirism. The novel *Dracula*, as well as other vampire stories, effectively presents hypnosis as a method by which vampires overcome their victims. A strong sexual undercurrent to vampire stories has also been present in hypnosis at times.

What we now call modern hypnosis began with the Scottish physician James Braid (Crasilneck and Hall 1985). Braid rejected animal magnetism as an explanation for mesmerism and instead emphasized suggestion as an explanation. Unfortunately, Braid also coined the term *hypnosis* (from the Greek *hypnos*, meaning *sleep*), thus condemning future generations of hypnotherapists to explain repeatedly that hypnosis really isn't sleep.

Later, the French neurologist Jean Marie Charcot investigated hypnosis and considered it to be similar to hysteria and therefore pathological rather than a normal phenomenon. However, others such as Liebeault and Bernheim argued that hypnosis was based on suggestion (Crasilneck and Hall 1985). Somewhat later, Josef Breuer found that suggestions for direct symptom removal were often not effective with patients (e.g., the famous Anna O.). Breuer, with his younger colleague Sigmund Freud, found that the process of *abreaction* (the emotional and cathartic recollection of a repressed memory) was facilitated by hypnosis.

Freud initially embraced hypnosis enthusiastically. Later, however, he came to feel that it interfered with the transference reaction, which was emerging as a cornerstone of his developing psychoanalysis. Second, he was not always successful in hypnotizing patients deeply enough to work with them in trance, and the posthypnotic suggestions he used for symptom removal often had only temporary effects. He began instead to use his newly developed technique of free association with these patients (Crasilneck and Hall 1985). Furthermore, he came to believe that symptoms often served a protective function for the ego and should not be removed indiscriminately (Crasilneck and Hall 1985, Kroger 1977). He also felt that hypnosis removed important patient defenses (Kroger 1977). More significantly, perhaps, he felt that the use of hypnosis tended to "sexualize" the relationship, a conclusion he arrived at after a female patient threw her arms around him after coming out of a trance. For these reasons he gradually abandoned hypnosis as a therapeutic tool and his influence was sufficiently great so that its use declined thereafter. Nevertheless, Freud discovered several important aspects of hypnosis, such as individual differences in hypnotizability, that still influence the way it is and should be used in psychological therapy.

During the first decades of the twentieth century, hypnosis was rarely used or investigated. The exception was the experiments conducted by Clark Hull in the 1930s and the training he provided for future hypnotherapists, among them Milton Erickson. Since the end of World War II, however, hypnosis has once again been in the ascendency. Several scientific and professional societies, such as the American Society of Clinical Hypnosis (ASCH), the Society for Experimental and Clinical Hypnosis (SECH), and the Milton Erickson Foundation, have been formed. Hypnosis is taught in medical and other schools and many books and articles are written about it each year. Numerous continuing education activities in hypnotherapy are also sponsored. Not only is the practice of hypnosis taught, but experimental investigations of hypnotic phenomena are also conducted. While this activity is to be welcomed, there is also a danger. The history of hypnosis has demonstrated that claims for its efficacy have often exceeded the ability of hypnosis practitioners to deliver cures. We can see this at work today, with some hypnotherapists claiming to be able to cure smoking in one or two sessions or to enable people to lose weight effortlessly by hypnosis. One can still find hypnosis publications in bookstores filed under the heading *Magic and the Occult*. I hope this book will contribute to an increase in the usefulness and accessibility of this important technique while encouraging therapists to recognize its limitations.

It is important to understand at the outset that hypnosis is not by itself a therapy; it is an adjunctive technique to be used *within* an existing therapy *as appropriate* (Dowd 1996). Thus dentists may use hypnosis in certain situations within their scope of practice for pain control; physicians, for anesthesia or other medical purposes; and psychologists, within their scope of practice, for the relief of depression, anxiety, and other forms of psychological distress. A point of some current contention is the appropriate use of hypnosis by laypersons, who are often individuals trained in other areas. For example, could sports coaches use hypnosis to enable athletes to relax and focus? Perhaps the question should be, "Is hypnosis being used appropriately within the professional's scope of practice, in which he or she has been trained?" For example, dentists may appropriately use hypnosis for pain control but not for depression.

Even within psychology itself, however, there can be differences in the appropriate use of hypnosis by psychologists of differing theoretical orientations. Thus, for example, behavioral psychologists may use hypnosis in the behavioral treatment of such problems as phobias and obesity; psychoanalytic psychologists, for uncovering repressed memories and interpreting dreams; and psychologists following a cognitive orientation, for cognitive restructuring (Dowd 1993).

One should be wary of hypnotists with no formal training in medical, psychological, or other established professions who claim to be able to cure such entrenched habits as overeating and smoking in one or two sessions. Such individuals prey on the universal human desire for quick and easy relief from their distress, relief that involves little or no effort on the part of the hypnotized. They take advantage of the common misconception that hypnosis is somehow magic in its effects. It takes little time and effort to teach someone how to enter, or help others to enter, a hypnotic trance, but considerably more training and experience to know how to use trance behavior effectively and appropriately. Responsible professionals know how to use hypnosis within the context of a total plan of therapy and in conjunction with other techniques. Hypnosis, even by trained professionals, is rarely used alone.

Cognitive (behavior) therapy began in the early 1970s, in part as a reaction to what was seen as the inadequacy of the behavioral model to explain complex human activity. Donald Meichenbaum, originally trained as a behaviorist, first developed cognitive behavior modification around the discovery that people talk to themselves. Simultaneously (but unknown to each other), Albert Ellis and Aaron T. Beck, each originally trained in psychoanalysis, developed their own brands of cognitively oriented therapy. While they differed in significant ways, all three had in common an assumption that human activities and emotions are mediated by cognitive activities, such as cognitive interpretive errors, self-statements, irrational thoughts, and the personally unique, idiosyncratic meanings we often use to explain phenomena (Dowd 1997a). Humans are meaning-makers and will assign their own idiosyncratic meaning to events if none are obvious. In keeping with its behavioral roots, the cognitive (behavioral) therapy model placed great emphasis on current cognitive activity, often ignoring the background and historical antecedents to that activity.

Beginning in the early 1980s with the work of Vittorio Guidano and Giovanni Liotti in Italy and later Michael Mahoney in America, cognitive therapy assumed a more developmental flavor, as past events and relationships with other people were investigated in the search for the origins of dysfunctional cognitions (Dowd 1997a). Constructivism, or the theory that humans actively construct their own reality out of their personal experiences rather than passively apprehending a uniform reality, emerged as an important theoretical development. The impact of core cognitive rules and assumptions, what are called *tacit memory structures*, on human cognitive activity was also investigated (Dowd and Courchaine 1996). There is evidence that tacit knowledge is often more comprehensive, detailed, and rich than explicit knowledge. Much human learning may be implicit in nature (i.e., not explicitly learned), and early life experiences are especially likely to be implicitly learned. Thus the identification of tacit cognitive themes that are personal to each individual may be particularly important in the therapeutic process. The identification of these personal cognitive themes enables the therapist to personalize hypnotherapy—a procedure made difficult by the individual's lack of awareness of these themes (by the very definition of *tacit*) and resistance to drastically modifying these core meaning structures.

Cognitive therapy, with its new developmental concepts, has, by a curious and ironic recursiveness, now come full circle. By its investigation of past influences on current cognitions, emotions, and behaviors, it resembles Freudian psychotherapy in its focus on the importance of early childhood experience. Furthermore, in the incorporation of cognitive tacit schemas (J. S. Beck 1995, Dowd and Courchaine 1996) as legitimate areas of investigation, cognitive therapy has also approached the Freudian notion of the unconscious. However, cognitive therapy, even with its incorporation of developmental concepts and core tacit schemata, is a much more parsimonious and data-driven system of therapy. Whereas Freudian therapy was grounded in a nineteenth-century scientific mechanistic worldview, heavily hydraulic in nature, cognitive therapy is based on significant findings in experimental psychology and newer theories of the mind. Cognitive therapy does not include such metaphorical constructs as mental layers (id, ego, superego), drive reduction theory, or sublimated sexuality. It is based more on universal processes of cognitive activity rather than on what have become seen as culturally specific concepts. Nevertheless, current cognitive therapists owe a great debt to Sigmund Freud, who created a highly original, though admittedly imperfect, theory and set of therapeutic procedures. His influence is still felt today.

This book combines applications of cognitive therapy and hypnotherapy into a unified approach to psychotherapy. Imagery is increasingly being used in a variety of cognitive therapies, so it seems especially timely. First, the various models of cognitive therapy are described, followed by models of hypnotherapy and methods of hypnotic induction described in sufficient detail for the reader to implement the procedures, including samples of hypnotic dialogue. The major portion of the book examines the cognitive hypnotherapy model and procedures in the amelioration of a variety of psychological disorders, including its use in the reconstruction of memories (which are influenced by core cognitive schemata), a useful, though controversial, technique in childhood abuse and posttraumatic stress disorder. Next, the cognitive hypnotherapy model is applied to the enhancement of life by overcoming common blocks to effective performance. Finally, cognitive hypnotherapy is applied to overcoming the inevitable resistance that accompanies any attempts at significant psychological change.

Part I

Background

2

Cognitive Therapy

HISTORICAL DEVELOPMENT

The recursive nature of human cognitive activity is a constant. Ancient proverbs express this well. One can never, it has been said, step into the same river twice, nor does a bicycle wheel ever touch the same road again. These folk proverbs point to a universal attribute of the human mind: its ability to classify and reclassify inchoate sensory data into successive conceptual categories that are different, yet similar. Furthermore, humans often use metaphors to describe concepts that are difficult to express directly. The evolution of the cognitive therapies illustrates this fundamental attribute and has been described in more detail by Dowd (1997a).

Sigmund Freud was the first modern thinker to develop an organized and comprehensive system of human cognition and behavior. Philosophically, he was a biological determinist as well as a dualist who saw human activities as genetically constrained, developmentally challenged, and bound by opposing forces (opponent processes). He was also deeply pessimistic about the possibility of significant human change. His model, consistent with nineteenth-century mechanics, was the hydraulic system wherein unacceptable impulses, via repression and resistance, were prevented from entering consciousness. According to this model, symptom change alone was illusory and ephemeral; symptoms denied expression in one situation would only occur elsewhere. Only by understanding and overcoming resistance would the individual truly be symptom-free. Two important therapeutic interventions used to achieve this goal were free association and interpretation, the former by allowing repressed material into consciousness and the latter by helping the client to assign different meanings to thoughts, feelings, and behaviors. Freud also developed his theory of unconscious processes and motivation and the developmental antecedents of human behavior, two revolutionary concepts that caused him considerable trouble with church and secular authorities of the time. While much of Freud's thought has been discarded in recent years, both because of cultural changes and more sophisticated concepts of human cognition, his basic ideas continue to influence psychotherapists and the popular culture.

While European psychotherapy has generally been psychodynamically and structurally oriented, American psychology and psychotherapy has been much more behaviorally oriented. This difference might be traced in part to the traditional American optimism and "can do" spirit. Beginning with John Watson and continuing with E. L. Thorndike and B. F. Skinner, the locus of study was the development and examination of the principles of behavior acquisition and change rather than introspection and the study of "mind." Indeed, mind itself was reduced to the status of an epiphenomenon, not because it was unimportant or nonexistent, but because it could not be observed by another person. In the process, psychotherapy lost its developmental focus, since the emphasis was on understanding the maintaining forces of current behavior and then changing them rather than understanding how and why that behavior developed. One needed only to understand the reinforcing contingencies maintaining the current behavior to foster change. Two fundamental principles of learning were *classical conditioning* (associational learning) and *operant conditioning* (consequential learning). West-

ern notions of linear causality and well as an optimistic belief in profound change pervade behaviorism.

Behavioral psychotherapy is still strong today. However, beginning
in the early 1960s, powerful forces for a reevaluation of much of behavioral thinking began to be felt. First were the data. While behavioral
strategies were demonstrably effective, research indicated that they were
no more effective in general than alternative interventions. In addition,
while behavioral strategies were effective much of the time, they were
not effective all of the time, contrary to predictions derived from laws
of learning. Second, reconceptualizations of behavioral psychotherapy
suggested that the effects might be due to something other than the laws
of learning (Murray and Jacobson 1971). For example, the effect of systematic desensitization did not seem to depend on the presentation of a
graded hierarchy of fear situations as had originally been thought. The
effectiveness of implosive therapy or "flooding" demonstrated that.

The first investigator to modify behavioral principles significantly
was Albert Bandura, who developed social learning theory. Bandura first
demonstrated that it was not reinforcement that altered behavior but
the *perception* of reinforcement. Second, he showed that, although the
environment influenced the person, people also influenced their environment—from which the principle of reciprocal conditioning arose.
Third, he demonstrated that reinforcement of a behavior was not necessary for that behavior to change; it was necessary only that individuals
observe *someone else* being reinforced for performing that behavior—
the modeling effect. These three findings indicated that what was happening in the Skinnerian "black box" was of great importance in understanding and fostering change. It also represented a move away from the
machine metaphor of Freudian/psychodynamic thinking and toward an
information-processing model.

In the early 1970s Donald Meichenbaum, originally trained in behavioral psychology, made an important discovery. Drawing on the work
of the Soviet psychologists Alexander Luria and Lev Vygotsky, he found
that children talked to themselves when faced with the performance of
a task, which served as an important regulator of their behavior. This
self-talk, Meichenbaum said, is initially overt, but as the child develops

it becomes increasingly covert to form the internal dialogue. Meichenbaum used these ideas to construct a training program for impulsive children who, he said, showed a deficit in their ability to regulate their behavior by self-instructions and it became the core of his cognitive behavior modification. The theory was later expanded to a theory of cognitive and behavioral change in clients. According to this theory, clients first become aware of their behavior and their internal dialogue about this behavior. They are then trained to emit incompatible behavior and an internal dialogue (i.e., talking to themselves differently), and finally are trained to exhibit this new behavior in the environment and to talk and think differently about it (Meichenbaum 1977). Not only is cognitive behavior modification essentially a behavioral theory, but it implicitly assumes that psychotherapeutic systems are largely conceptual systems for organizing and explaining cognitive and behavioral phenomena and not "true" in and of themselves. As Meichenbaum (1977) stated, "as a result of therapy a *translation* process takes place . . . The translation is from the internal dialogue the client engaged in prior to therapy to a new language system that emerges over the course of treatment" (p. 217). Thus the "truth" of a system lies in its utility to the client. In this regard Meichenbaum was a forerunner of what has come to be called *constructivism*.

Albert Ellis, a clinical psychologist, was originally trained as a psychoanalyst but became impatient with the slowness of classical psychoanalysis. He noticed consistent commonalities in the negative thinking content of his patients and developed rational therapy (RT) to help clients more quickly understand and overcome these thoughts. A major technique was the vigorous disputation of these negative beliefs. Later, RT was transmogrified into RET (rational-emotive therapy) and recently into REBT (rational-emotive-behavior therapy). Ellis (1962) developed the A-B-C method, where A (the activating event) leads to B (the irrational belief), and then to C (the consequence). Individuals, he said, commonly think that A causes C, whereas in truth B causes C. Thus one can change C by changing B, even if A does not change. For example, a young man rejected by his girlfriend may believe that A (the rejection) has caused C (his emotional distress) whereas it is B (his negative thoughts about the rejection) that has really caused C. Rational-emotive-behavior therapy is a highly active, ahistorical therapy and Ellis believes inquiring about past events, thoughts, or feelings is unnecessary. All that is necessary is to identify and dispute the current irrational beliefs and replace them with more rational beliefs. *Rational* beliefs are preferential beliefs that may allow individuals to get what they want; *irrational* beliefs are the dogmatic, fixed beliefs that one must have what one wants that often hinder individuals from fulfilling their goals. The A-B-C model is implicitly unidirectional.

Aaron T. Beck is a psychiatrist who, like Ellis, was originally trained in psychoanalysis. Unlike Ellis, however, who is primarily a clinician, Beck has been largely a theoretician and a researcher. He originally investigated depression from a psychoanalytic perspective and found that dreams of depressed individuals, far from being characterized by themes of inverted anger and hostility, were characterized by themes of loss and sadness (Weishaar 1993). From these beginnings he developed the cognitive theory of depression (later, anxiety and personality disorders) and identified two categories of cognitive errors (Beck et al. 1979). These are cognitive content distortions and cognitive processing distortions. *Content distortions* are negative automatic thoughts, or self-statements, such as: "In order to be happy, I have to be successful in whatever I undertake," "If I make a mistake, I'm incompetent," or "I can't live without love." Cognitive *processing errors* involve distorted thinking and include magnification, catastrophizing, dichotomous thinking, and overgeneralizing. A major technique in cognitive therapy is *collaborative empiricism*, in which the therapist and client jointly identify the latter's distorted self-statements and cognitive processing errors and together develop alternative, more adaptive ones. Especially in the treatment of depression, Beck also used a variety of behavioral techniques such as activity scheduling and pleasure and mastery experiences. While cognitive therapy was originally rather ahistorical and focused primarily on current cognitions, Beck's later work on personality disorders required inquiry into the past origins of cognitive distortions. Indeed, in its increasing growth and comprehensiveness, as well as its impressive research base, Beck's cognitive therapy has the potential to be the integrative theory of psychotherapy (Alford and Beck 1997, Alford and Norcross 1991), and Beck himself may rival Freud in the scope and breadth of his thought. Beck's work on cognitive themes in personality disorders led to schema-focused therapy (Young 1994), which developed clusters of cognitions organized around common themes. Thus the cognitive therapies began to take on a developmental flavor.

COGNITIVE-BEHAVIORAL MODEL

It can be seen from the previous discussion that the behavioral and the cognitive models represent two streams of influence leading to the cognitive-behavioral model. While behaviorism was gradually incorporating more cognitive (mentalistic) concepts and techniques, the cognitivism of psychodynamic therapy was becoming more conceptually parsimonious and incorporating behavioral techniques into its therapeutic armamentarium. These trends came together in the cognitive-behavioral model.

Behavioral psychology—from Ivan Pavlov to John Watson to B. F. Skinner—involved the application of principles of learning theory to the solution of human behavior problems. There are two fundamental learning theory approaches. Classical (or respondent) conditioning, first investigated by Ivan Pavlov, is based on the principle of learning by association. The basic paradigm is the pairing of an unconditioned stimulus (UCS) with a conditioned stimulus (CS). As a function of repeated pairing (association) of the UCS with the CS, the organism will eventually respond to the latter as it did to the former. Thus Pavlov's dog responded to the sound of a bell by salivation (as it did to food) because the bell was always paired with food. Eventually, the organism responds to the CS as it did to the UCS—without the UCS. Learning has now occurred.

Operant (or instrumental) conditioning is based on the principle of learning by consequence. Because the reinforcer follows the response, the probability of the organism's making that response in the future if reinforced is increased. Again, learning has occurred. The drawback to operant conditioning is that the conditioner must wait until the response is emitted before it can be reinforced. In classical conditioning, by contrast, the conditioner can immediately provide the conditions for learning. This problem can be overcome, at least to some extent, by shaping, in which the conditioner reinforces closer and closer approximations to the ultimately desired behavior.

Over the years, it became increasingly apparent that the learning resulting from the application of these two paradigms was not as invariant as the theory would predict. While the paradigms seemed to work well for nonhumans, the laws of learning often led to highly variable results for humans. For example, Bandura (1977) found that individuals did not have to be reinforced themselves for learning to occur (they needed only to see a model being reinforced) and that the perception of a reinforcing event was often more important for learning to occur than the presence of an actual reinforcer. Later he showed that individuals are not only "conditioned" by their environments, they also influence those environments. Research demonstrated that the graduated hierarchy thought to be necessary in systematic desensitization was in fact unnecessary. Learning could occur equally well whether one began at the bottom of the hierarchy, in the middle, or at the top! The latter led to the development of implosive learning or flooding. Murray and Jacobson (1971) argued that human learning occurs in the context of cognitive, personality, and social interaction variables and that all behavior has interpersonal meaning. Strictly behavioral explanations and interventions for human psychological and behavior change thus began to be supplemented by cognitive explanations and interventions. As Bandura (1977) stated, although behavioral interventions increasingly are invoked as causing change, cognitive principles are increasingly invoked to explain change.

The origin of cognitive therapy lies in psychoanalysis and its later psychodynamic offshoots. Both Beck and Ellis were trained in psychoanalysis and both abandoned it—the former for its lack of empirical justification and the latter for its slowness. Psychodynamic therapy itself has undergone significant modifications since the days of Freud, moving away from some of the more convoluted and problematical intrapsychic explanatory constructs and toward the more parsimonious and relationship-oriented explanations characteristic of, for example, object relations theory, which examines how individuals internalize representations of other people (objects). Psychodynamic therapists also became more therapeutically active, relying less on a passive fostering of the transference relationship and more on the active encouragement of insight and behavior change. Wachtel (1977), for example, developed an active-intervention psychodynamic approach that, while not ignoring the impact of early childhood experience, views personality development and change as a complex recursive process involving relations with other people.

While both Beck and Ellis relied heavily on the production of insight, in one form or another, the content of that insight differed significantly from psychodynamic approaches. Rather than insight about parental relations and childhood sexuality, insight into current negative automatic thoughts and dysfunctional cognitive processes was fostered—current functioning as opposed to past relationships. Beck and Ellis also used behavioral interventions more heavily than the psychodynamic therapists had. Beck's focus is more on the identification of client idiosyncratic cognitive distortions while Ellis tends to rely more on the identification of a few common maladaptive self-statements (e.g., "I should do everything perfectly," "Everyone should approve of me"). However, in an interesting circularity, cognitive therapists who practice schema-focused therapy (e.g., Young 1994) do investigate the cognitive schemas that are formed in childhood around relations with important caregivers. Thus the importance of early experiences, stressed by Freud, is once more in the ascendance.

The cognitive-behavioral model is therefore a combination of the behavioral interventions characteristic of behavior therapy with the cognitive interventions and explanatory constructs of cognitive therapy. In this model both behavioral and cognitive interventions are used, although behavioral changes resulting from the former are thought to be cognitively mediated. Behavioral interventions are often used first, especially for depression, to activate clients. In an early study Kelly and Dowd (1980) found that four weeks of behavioral interventions followed by four weeks of cognitive interventions resulted in a significantly greater decrease in depression than the reverse. Perhaps the best description of the cognitive-behavioral model was provided by Meichenbaum (1979), who said that clients "emit behaviors *in vivo* that lead to consequences that are incompatible with prior expectancies. Then one can have the client examine what gives rise to such expectancies, appraisals, attributions, etc." (p. 1). This is similar to Hobbs's (1962) notion that insight typically follows from behavior change rather than the reverse, as the client reflects on the meaning of the new behavior.

COGNITIVE-DEVELOPMENTAL MODEL

The cognitive-developmental model appears to derive from three sources. First, it is a direct outgrowth of the cognitive therapy for personality disorders (Beck et al. 1990) and schema-focused therapy (e.g., Young 1994), with its emphasis on the formation of early maladaptive schemas. The model is based on the assumption that many negative cognitions have their roots in past experiences. While straightforward ahistorical cognitive therapy seemed to work well for the acute Axis I disorders, such as depression and situational anxiety, it was not as effective, at least immediately, with personality disorders or comorbid syndromes. Not only was it necessary to identify and cognitively challenge the cognitive distortions characteristic of each personality disorder, it was also necessary to identify early experiences from which these distortions may have originated. Beck and his colleagues (1990) developed a comprehensive cognitive treatment approach for the personality disorders based on schema theory and devoted to an explanation of the cognitive content of each disorder and treatment strategies for each. Schemas are cognitive structures for screening, organizing, and evaluating the vast array of stimuli that impinge upon each organism and represent a necessary shorthand way of categorizing information. Essentially, they are organized systems of meaning around a specific topic. Some schemas are concerned with self- and other evaluation, others with self-identity, others with autonomy and control, and still others with personal relationships. Typically, the foundations of schemas are laid down in the early years of life and only modified thereafter.

Young (1994) has developed the concept of early maladaptive schemas, recurring systems of meaning that are dysfunctional in some way or other. They are the result of ongoing dysfunctional experiences with parents, peers, siblings, and other important people early in life. He has categorized them into five domains: disconnection and rejection, impaired autonomy and performance, impaired limits, overvigilance and inhibition, and other-directedness, with several schemas in each domain. Schema-focused therapy begins with an assessment of the client's particular early maladaptive schemas followed by interventions tailored to address them.

The second source is that of Guidano and Liotti (1983), in Italy, who developed a particular cognitive-developmental approach that combines cognitive therapy and attachment theory. Their early work identified the cognitive organization and core assumptions that were characteristic of several disorders, for example, depression, agoraphobia, obsessive-compulsive disorders, and eating disorders. Subsequent work in this area (e.g. Guidano 1987) stresses the developing cognitive organization around the concept of the "self" (or self-identity). Mahoney (1991) likewise organized his approach to human development and change around the notion of the "self." A recurrent theme in all of these theories is the importance of early attachment relations with important caregivers (especially parents). Dysfunctional cognitive organizations of attachment can lead to a variety of later psychological disorders.

Embedded in the cognitive-developmental approach are two concepts: tacit knowledge and the actively constructing mind. *Tacit knowledge* consists of deep, abstract, unverbalized rules that organize an individual's perception of self and the world, rules that were laid down at an early age by the tacit detection of covariation and thereafter elaborated and differentiated (Reber 1993). Tacit knowledge is evolutionarily older, automatic in nature, preverbal, acquired faster, and conceptually richer than explicit knowledge. (These concepts will be explained in more detail later.) *Active construction* refers to the processes by which the human mind creates its own reality by the ways in which it incorpo-rates and categorizes incoming stimuli. Mental categories act like tem-plates that selectively admit data that correspond to existing assump-tions and knowledge. These new data then confirm what the mind already "knows." Folk sayings such as "We see what we want to see" or "We find what we expect to find," and concepts such as the self-fulfilling prophecy and confirmatory bias express this idea well. The fundamen-tal guiding principle is that no one, neither therapist nor client, has a monopoly on truth (which is itself a socially constructed concept). Therapy thus becomes a collaborative search for new and co-created meaning structures for the client's life.

The third source of the cognitive developmental model is the ex-tensive writing of Michael J. Mahoney (Mahoney 1991, 1995). Over the years, Mahoney has moved gradually and seamlessly from a self-regula-tory behavioral model to a constructivistic cognitive model, integrating psychology, philosophy, and the physical sciences in the process. In constructivism, human cognitive activity is seen as active in nature rather than passive. That is, the mind is a constructing organ, creating its own reality by a recursive interaction with its environment, rather than an apprehending organ, which takes in information that is really "out there." Mahoney (1995) has argued that the early cognitive therapies were ra-tionalistic in nature in that they assumed that the therapist had the true view of reality and the therapeutic task was to get the client to adopt it. Constructivistic therapy, by contrast, assumes that neither possesses a "true" view of reality (indeed it denies that such a true view exists at all) and that the therapeutic task is to create together (co-create) a more beneficial and useful view. Constructivism is heavily phenomenal in nature and harks back to both George Kelly and Carl Rogers.

The cognitive-behavioral model assumed, although did not explic-itly state, that cognitions were accessible and that resistance was simply an annoying by-product of human cussedness, to be overcome by the proper techniques. The cognitive-developmental model, on the other hand, stresses the tacit, nonaccessible quality of much of human cogni-tion and the resistance to change of human cognitive structures. Self-knowledge, or the tacit knowledge of one's self as an independent person, is an especially important cognitive structure. Mahoney (1991), for example, sees resistance as fundamentally positive, protecting the human cognitive structure from a too-rapid assault on its basic integrity. In answer to the question "Can humans change?" he replies, "Yes . . . , but. . . ." They can change and do change, but there are significant constraints on how much and how fast. Core cognitive beliefs are seldom viewed as beliefs; they are generally experienced as "just the way things are!"

My colleagues and I have explored some of these same cognitive-developmental themes from a different vantage point. Dowd and Pace (1989) used earlier work on paradoxical interventions and client reactance in arguing that therapeutic models are essentially systems for the creation of meaning and that therapeutic change attempts often fail because they attack the problem (first-order change). If the therapeutic interventions do *not* change the problem, the only solution is to do more of the same. Second-order change, by contrast, can be fostered by attacking the solution that was originally devised to solve the problem and later, after repeated use, became the problem. Second-order change interventions thus change the meaning of the symptom from a problem to an aid. For example, an insomniac's repeated attempts to solve the problem by trying to fall asleep become the problem, since the attempts exacerbate the insomnia. The solution is not to try to fall asleep or even to try to stay awake. Dowd and Pace also suggested that client reactance (the potential for oppositional behavior) is an important client individual-difference variable, mediating outcome. These ideas should be familiar to Ericksonian hypnotherapists. Fleming and colleagues (1992), drawing on the implicit memory literature, argued that cognitive therapy involves the manipulation of the subjective experience of memory. Three variables influence the experience of memory: context, attention, and the number of times an event is recalled. *Context* includes aspects of the environment and one's internal states, and individuals have been shown to learn better and recall more in situations similar to those in which the learning took place. Focused *attention* enhances cognitive processing and encoding; divided attention reduces elaboration and awareness of the source of the memory. *The number of times an event is recalled* increases one's confidence in a memory but decreases its accuracy. Dowd and Courchaine (1996) investigated the experimental psychology literature on implicit learning and tacit knowledge. They found evidence that tacit knowledge is more comprehensive, more detailed, and richer than explicit knowledge, and that much important learning occurs implicitly. Early life experiences are especially likely to be implicitly learned and the identification of tacit cognitive themes is particularly important in the therapeutic process. It is also difficult to do, however, since these themes were developed early in life and are largely nonverbal. They are therefore difficult to access by verbal means. Indeed, if they can be easily accessed, they are probably not core themes.

Psychological reactance, or the potential to exhibit oppositional behavior (Brehm and Brehm 1981), has been shown to be an individual difference variable mediating both the process and outcome of psychotherapy (Dowd 1999). It is related to such personality variables as dominance, autonomy, nonaffiliation, and independence. Furthermore, reactance appears to be developmental in nature, since reactant people tend to have developmental difficulties in general, particularly around issues of trust and intimacy, and developmental successes around issues of autonomy and identity. While the literature has focused on the nature and effect of high reactance, it can be too low as well as too high; an intermediate level is probably optimal. Reactance may be fostered by strict and inconsistent parenting, reliance on physical punishment, and the use of coercive control techniques (Dowd and Seibel 1990).

Thus reactance may involve a core cognitive schema organized around the necessity and desirability of freedom and control. This schema may be especially potent in North American and Western European societies, in which self-awareness and introspection are highly valued attributes (Dowd 1999). Since this schema is likely to be deeply embedded in the self-concept, specifically tailored interventions may be necessary for resolving problems of excessively high or low reactance.

Cognitive therapy has progressed from a focus on relatively explicit and peripheral self-statements (both adaptive and maladaptive) to a focus on more tacit, schema-focused cognitions and to a consideration of developmental antecedents of these cognitive schemata (Dowd 1997a).

In the process, certain psychodynamic concepts, such as the unconscious, appear to have been resurrected, although often dressed up in different terminology (e.g., tacit knowledge). However, the development of cognitive therapy, recursive though it may appear to be, also represents real and substantial progress toward the understanding of human functioning. Concepts that recur, even though with different labels, probably have much to contribute toward the explanation of the human condition.

IMAGERY IN COGNITIVE THERAPY

A relatively recent development in cognitive therapy, but one that has particular relevance for cognitive hypnotherapy, is the use of imagery. Imaginal work in cognitive therapy has been especially well described by J. S. Beck (1995), who has illustrated several ways of using imagery, some of which resemble hypnotic techniques, as discussed below.

In *identifying images,* the therapist teaches the client to elicit a spontaneous image about a distressing situation. Often, however, clients do not recognize what images they might have or are reluctant to report them. Rather than using the standard cognitive therapy question, "What thoughts were going through your mind just then?" an imagery identification question might be, "What image (or picture) did (or do) you have in your mind about that event?" It may be necessary to elicit this image repeatedly, perhaps in a trance, before the client feels comfortable reporting it fully.

In *following images to completion,* the therapist encourages the client to imagine the remainder of a scenario rather than stopping at the distressing scene. For example, a client who imagines herself freezing up while beginning a speech may be asked to imagine herself getting through the next few minutes (because she is not likely to stand immobile indefinitely). Humor, carefully and sensitively used, may help clients to continue the image to completion.

In *coping in the image*, which may be seen as an extension of the previous technique, the therapist asks the client to imagine himself coping (better) with the image he has just envisioned. For example, a client who is unsure how to handle an angry boss may imagine himself standing tall and looking the boss in the eye. This coping image can gradually replace, through repetition, the previous image of cowering before his boss.

A further refinement of these techniques can be found in _changing the image_. Here the client is guided in changing the image she has about her problematic situation. For example, the therapist may ask her what she would rather have happen and then work with her in imagining that other scenario. This is a flexible technique that can be useful to modify painful memories (discussed later in this volume).

Jumping ahead in time is similar to hypnotic age progression and involves asking the client to imagine himself at a future point in time, perhaps at the completion of a long project (like this book!). It can be combined with the previous technique to help the client construct an alternative, less distressing scenario to the current painful situation.

Repeating the image is a new variation on an old theme—repetition of new behavior and cognitions is an effective way to cause change. It can be seen as a sort of systematic desensitization in that the client repeatedly evokes in an image the painful event so that it loses some of its power. It may even be seen eventually as humorous! Throughout this book you will see numerous examples of the principle of repetition.

The therapist may also train the client to _substitute_ one image (a less distressing one) for the current distressing one. The new image might be very different from the old one. For example, an image of lying on the beach may be substituted for an intrusive painful image. As mentioned above, it is important that the client do this repeatedly so that it becomes easier.

Distancing, either spatial or temporal, may also be useful. In spatial distancing the client is asked to imagine her problems moving farther and farther away, receding in the distance. In temporal distancing she is asked to imagine her problems becoming removed in time, or out of date as she grows up. Highly metaphorical images can often be used. The telescope technique, described later, is an example of distancing.

Albert Ellis and his colleagues have also used imagery in their work, *Rational-Emotive Imagery: RET Version* (Ellis 1993). Ellis suggests the following sequence of activities.

> 1. Imagine one of the worst things that might happen to you . . . Vividly imagine this unfortunate Activating event or Adversity (A) occurring . . . 2. Let yourself deeply feel the kind of inappropriate, self-defeating feeling that you often experience . . . Thus, let yourself strongly feel—at point C, your emotional consequence—very anxious, depressed, enraged, self-hating, or self-pitying . . . 3. Once you're feeling inappropriately upset (at C1) as you imagine this Adversity (A), hold this feeling for a minute or two . . . [then] *prescribe* an appropriate negative feeling (C2) . . . Thus, if you are enraged (C1) . . . you can prescribe changing your rage to an appropriate emotion of feeling very displeased with and sorry about their *acts*, instead of enraged at and damning *them* for these acts (C2). . . . [pp. II-8–II-9]

Ellis stresses that it is important not to change the image of the original Activating event, only the emotional Consequence (C), and that one should use coping imagery, not distraction, to change these inappropriate feelings. In essence, the client must stay with the disturbing image and then work at changing the feelings (emotional Consequence) in order to effect a real change. Ellis also emphasizes the use of repetition (as much as several times a day for thirty days for each inappropriate negative feeling!) to facilitate a permanent change. Characteristically, he encourages clients not to "damn themselves" if they do not complete this challenging assignment successfully at first but to continue their efforts until they are able to do better.

Imaginal work and a hypnotic trance are phenomena on the same continuum. It is possible to use imagery ideas within a hypnotic trance.

3

Models of Hypnotherapy

PSYCHODYNAMIC MODEL

Many of the more common hypnotherapeutic interventions have their roots in psychodynamic theory, so several important concepts in that theory will be discussed.

Two of Freud's primary concepts, unconscious processes and motivation and the developmental antecedents of behavior, were truly revolutionary and caused him considerable difficulties with the authorities of his time. Freud argued that much of human activity was not consciously directed but was the result of unconscious conflicts and motives that were often not understood or recognized by the individual or society. The significance of developmental constraints on human behavior was likewise important because it implied that childhood events had a powerful impact on subsequent attitudes and behavior—and that adult psychological change was therefore slow and uncertain (Dowd 1997a). In line with his emphasis on the sexual drive, Freud considered hypnosis to be erotic in nature (Eisen 1993).

Other important psychodynamic concepts are those of repression and resistance. Unacceptable impulses are thought to be repressed and therefore resistant to entering consciousness (Dowd 1997a). For Freud, there was one central therapeutic goal—to make the unconscious conscious by overcoming the resistance. Two important interventions to this end were free association and interpretation. The correct interpretation was especially important and fierce analytic battles were fought over this issue. Hypnotherapeutic interventions that stress the uncovering of repressed material, sometimes by age regression, derive from psychodynamic thinking. However, resistance may also be shown by the client's refusal to enter a trance. Like Ericksonian hypnotherapists, psychodynamic hypnotherapists argue that resistance should be worked with rather than attacked. Like newer forms of cognitive therapy (e.g., Mahoney 1991), psychodynamic hypnotherapy acknowledges that resistance can serve adaptive functions such as protecting the self from too rapid change.

The difference between primary and secondary process thinking is also important in psychodynamic theory (Eisen 1993). The former refers to preverbal imagery that is wishful, fluid, and undifferentiated, such as dreams. It does not operate according to logical thinking and does not follow linear causal relationships. The latter, by contrast, is logical and analytical and uses language rather than imagery. It also tends to be more reality-oriented. While primary process thinking is more characteristic of childhood and secondary process thinking is more characteristic of adulthood, elements of the former persist throughout adulthood, where it is expressed in dreams, play, and creativity. It is likely that forms of hypnotherapy that foster problem solving, personal growth, and playful activities make use of primary process thinking. There is also evidence that trance depth is related, although only generally, to mental activities characteristic of primary process thinking (Eisen 1993). Likewise, the "trance logic" (actually illogic) exhibited by many subjects, in which contradictory ideas can be simultaneously held without distress, is an example of primary process thinking.

The "double consciousness" between the participating ego and the observing ego is a creation of psychodynamic hypnotherapy. The participating ego (perhaps engaging in primary process thinking) ceases to engage in critical thinking and reality testing, and relinquishes control (although willingly) to the hypnotherapist. The observing ego (perhaps engaging in secondary process thinking) continues to engage in reality testing and self-control. Hypnotherapeutic interventions in which one client self (e.g., the image of the "helpless child") is talked to by another client self (e.g., the image of the grown-up, competent adult) make use of double consciousness. Other hypnotherapists (e.g., Eisen 1993) make use of nurturing images in trance, such as "the healer within," to promote personal integration. These are thought to reflect different ego states.

A client in hypnosis will sometimes show transference reactions toward the hypnotherapist (Eisen 1993). This often takes the form of excessive dependency on the therapist along with aggressive demanding, endowing the therapist with quasi-magical powers, much like a parent. Some therapists seem to thrive on such attention. A disappointed client, on the other hand, can then turn against the therapist equally unrealistically. Transference can also take an erotic, seductive form, especially in the context of the hypnotic trance, which can be implicitly sexual in nature. Thus the astute hypnotherapist recognizes the possibility of transference as well as countertransference problems and attempts to minimize them.

A later psychodynamic development is the notion of ego activity, passivity, receptivity, and inactivity (Eisen 1993). Ego activity is shown by the client's resistance or countertherapeutic suggestions. Ego passivity is shown when the client feels overwhelmed by the therapist or the hypnotic situation. In ego receptivity the client is receptive to the therapist's suggestions and experiences unconscious and preconscious material. Rational, analytical thought is minimal. In ego inactivity the client experiences nothing but comes out of the trance feeling relaxed and refreshed.

ERICKSONIAN MODEL

Milton Erickson (1901–1980) was a highly unusual therapist and a highly unusual hypnotherapist as well. During his first attack of polio (he was stricken twice) and because of his physical immobility, he greatly expanded his powers of observation, becoming able to detect very subtle cues and changes in human behavior. He developed a style of hypnosis that did not distinguish between induction and deepening techniques—indeed, that often did not rely on a formal induction at all. His method of hypnotherapy is sufficiently complex that a detailed explanation of it is beyond the scope of this book. Readers wishing training in this approach should contact the Erickson Foundation in Phoenix, Arizona, for a list of centers and workshops.

In many ways, Ericksonian approaches to hypnotherapy represent a real break from the traditional practice of hypnosis. Erickson's model of hypnotherapy developed slowly over the years and was set down systematically in written form only late in his life. There are several important differences between Ericksonian hypnotherapy and other forms of hypnotherapy, especially psychodynamic approaches.

The Unconscious Need Not Be Made Conscious

Unlike the psychodynamic approach, there is no attempt made to overcome early unconscious conflicts. Symptom relief rather than insight is the goal. Erickson considered the unconscious to be a vast storehouse of positive skills and tacit knowledge that could be useful to the client if harnessed. This tacit knowledge serves as a fundamental regulator of human behavior. Thus Erickson often spoke in trance directly to the unconscious mind, instructing it to use its resources to promote change. This conscious-unconscious split is characteristic of Ericksonian hypnotherapy. In talking to the unconscious mind, Erickson often made use of indirect communications and metaphors. Indeed, it often appears that the very concept of "unconscious mind" was, for Erickson, itself a metaphor or analogy.

Erickson believed that all people had more potential than they commonly thought or used and hypnosis was a method to help them to use it. Anecdotal stories about dramatic cures and major life changes after one session are probably overstated, however.

Mental phenomena are to be utilized rather than analyzed. No Ericksonian intervention is probably as famous as his "utilization technique," although often it is not well understood. Erickson believed in using whatever the client brought to therapy in service of change. For example, resistance was accepted and used. Some hypnotherapeutic suggestions were phrased in such a way that anything clients did was a sign they were going into a trance. Activities engaged in between sessions were interpreted (reframed) in such a way as to demonstrate client progress. Even negative symptoms were reframed in such a way as to suggest they were attempts to solve problems and many of Erickson's directives (hypnotic and nonhypnotic) were paradoxical in nature, often using symptom prescription (see Dowd and Trutt 1988).

Hypnotic Suggestions Are Indirect Rather Than Direct

Direct suggestions are requests for certain responses, whereas indirect suggestions permit a variety of responses or may request no specific response at all. Indirect suggestions are often made using metaphors, narratives, and paradoxes, and allow clients to find their own meanings in the suggestions (Matthews et al. 1993). Indirect suggestions can be made for change without the therapist's even knowing what the problem is. Suggestions can be so indirect that the therapeutic situation may not be defined as hypnotic at all—the therapist may introduce hypnotic-like suggestions in the course of ordinary therapy. For example, a direct suggestion for pain reduction might be, "Your pain will gradually disappear." An indirect suggestion (there are many possibilities) might be, "You may be able to find increasing comfort in the near future." Many of the hypnotic routines to be presented later in this volume have an indirect flavor about them.

All people can be hypnotized, at least to the extent needed for therapeutic work. Hypnosis researchers (see Bowers 1976) have generally found that hypnotic susceptibility (or trance capacity) shows substantial individual differences with long-term stability. They have stated that relatively few people can exhibit the hypnotic phenomena characteristic of a deep trance, such as positive and negative hallucinations, somnambulism, and glove anesthesia (in which the therapist suggests to the client that the client's hand is numb). Ericksonian hypnotherapists, on the other hand, have argued that individual differences, if they exist, are not relevant for therapeutic work since most people can do whatever they need to do in a light trance. They state that hypnotic skills training, in which people are trained to exhibit a variety of hypnotic skills, can increase hypnotic responsiveness. More recently, MacFarland and Morris (1998) have found that dysphoric individuals (those with mild depression) were more suggestible than nondysphoric individuals. Thus those people needing psychotherapy may be precisely the ones most capable of benefiting from hypnotherapy.

There are no formal stages of hypnosis. Traditional hypnotherapy has been divided into stages: preparation, induction, trance work, and termination. Ericksonian hypnotherapy, on the other hand, merges the first three stages and often eliminates the fourth. Hypnotic trance work tends to function as the induction, and occasionally hypnosis itself is not clearly differentiated from nonhypnotic therapy. Thus the therapist might adopt a hypnotic tone of voice and make indirect, embedded suggestions for change repeatedly within the context of an ordinary therapy session.

Some of these hallmarks of the Ericksonian approach have recently been challenged, however. In a comprehensive review of the experimental literature, Matthews and colleagues (1998) found little support for such Ericksonian assumptions as hypnosis as a special state of mind, the greater effectiveness of indirect than direct suggestion, and the ability of all people to be hypnotized. Rather, they argued, Erickson created a powerful expectancy for change and fostered a context in which the client could change his or her self-narrative. He did this by disrupting or distracting the limited conscious mind so that hypnosis became a special form of communication in which a more useful life narrative might emerge. The central role of expectancy in this formulation moves Ericksonian hypnotherapy closer to the cognitive-behavioral model.

Lynn and colleagues (1993a) surveyed the experimental literature and concluded that indirect suggestions did not decrease resistance to hypnotic suggestions when compared to direct suggestions, at least as measured by objective responding. Indirect suggestions were not found to have a consistent advantage for subjective measures either. However, the authors indicated that, because of methodological problems, these studies could not be taken as conclusive. For example, there has been no assessment of whether subjects have actually been able to distinguish between direct and indirect suggestions. Likewise, hypnotic suggestions are more or less direct or indirect, not one or the other. Suggestion style is a continuum, not a dichotomy.

COGNITIVE-BEHAVIORAL MODEL

Hypnosis has often been defined as an altered state of consciousness, qualitatively different from ordinary (or "waking") consciousness. This has been referred to as the "state" view of hypnosis. The state view stresses the discontinuity of the hypnotic state from the nonhypnotic state and sees the former as involving unique cognitive processes. It also sees hypnotic phenomena as fundamentally nonvolitional or involuntary. Indeed, this is the view of hypnosis held by the general public and may be responsible for the magical or occult properties attributed to it. However, there has always been a significant body of opinion that views hypnotic behavior as determined by the same motivational and expectancy variables that govern nonhypnotic behavior, which is known as the "nonstate" view. Nicholas Spanos (1996) has been one of the leading promulgators of this view and sees hypnotic situations as involving two components. First, the situation is explicitly defined as hypnotic by the use of a standard hypnotic induction procedure as well as nonvolitional suggestions usually associated with hypnosis. Second, suggestions are then made that the individual will experience specific behavioral or internal phenomena, again usually nonvolitionally. Spanos argues that these phenomena are experienced as hypnotic because the situation is explicitly defined as hypnosis. People experience hypnosis as they expect to experience it.

The cognitive-behavioral model is clearly nonstate in orientation (Kirsch 1993). Hypnotic phenomena are seen as products of social psychological variables, such as faith, hope, expectancy, and context. Hypnotic phenomena are thought to be more likely to be exhibited in situations that are defined as hypnosis, in which the client has positive views of hypnosis, and hopes and expects that it will help. Kirsch and Lynn (1997) argue that the experience of hypnosis is influenced by culturally based expectancies and response sets. They also argue that certain abilities, such as imaginative ability and fantasy-proneness, enhance the perception of hypnotic involuntariness by strengthening response expectancies and encouraging participants to identify their responses as hypnotic in nature. They are then more likely to attribute these responses as involuntary and as caused by the hypnotist's suggestions. However, there appears to be an implicit assumption in cognitive-behavioral hypnotherapy that hypnotic phenomena are largely volitional in nature even if that is not always obvious. The centrality of expectancy as an explanation of hypnotic phenomena is once again stressed.

The experience of hypnotic involuntariness, that is, hypnotic phenomena that are experienced by participants as outside of their conscious control, has been one of the cultural definitions of hypnosis. Kirsch and Lynn (1998) have presented three possible social-cognitive theories of this nonvolitional experience. The first theory argues that perceptions of non-volition are simply post hoc misattributions based on whether the exhibited behavior was consistent with the intended outcome. The second theory argues that hypnotic behavior is indeed triggered automatically because *all* behavior is automatically triggered. People expect to emit nonvolitional behaviors as part of the culturally defined role of hypnosis. The third model argues that previous altered experiences (such as a feeling of lightness in the arm) arouse expectancies of further hypnotic phenomena (such as the arm rising). Responding to suggestions, they state, requires using attentional resources, and responses to suggestions are reduced when participants engage in an additional and competing task. In these models, social-cognitive phenomena, such as expectancy, focus of attention, willingness to engage in the experience, and social definition and sanction, are important variables.

Cognitive-behavioral hypnotherapy assumes that most psychological disturbance is caused by a negative form of self-hypnosis in which negative thoughts are accepted uncritically and even without conscious awareness (Araoz 1985). For example, an individual may have repeated images or thoughts about failing at an important assignment at work or forgetting an important meeting, but be scarcely aware of their pervasive existence. The remedy for these thoughts is first to give clients an overt awareness of their presence and pervasiveness, and second to train them to make more positive, adaptive self-statements by hypnotic cognitive restructuring (Golden et al. 1987). The practice of cognitive-behavioral hypnotherapy is similar to the practice of cognitive behavior therapy in general. As Kirsch (1993) has pointed out, according to the cognitive-behavioral model, whatever can be done with hypnosis can be done without it, and vice versa. Hypnosis may be useful if the client's feelings about it are positive or if problems have been encountered in using nonhypnotic procedures, or with nonreflective clients (Kirsch 1993). Hypnosis skill training can also be given to clients so that they may be able to apply these skills to new situations. Cognitive-behavioral hypnotherapy has been found to have an effect size of .87 when compared to cognitive behavior therapy without hypnosis, meaning that the average client in the former treatment was better off than more than 80 percent of the clients in the latter treatment (Kirsch 1993). Kirsch and colleagues (1995), in a meta-analysis on eighteen studies comparing cognitive-behavioral therapy with and without hypnosis, found a 70 percent greater improvement by clients receiving CBT with hypnosis than by clients receiving CBT alone.

Cognitive-behavioral hypnotherapy involves several basic techniques that can be applied to a variety of problems. The first is relaxation. This can be taught as a coping skill useful in reducing stress and anxiety and can be prefaced by a hypnotic induction technique followed by suggestions for peace, tranquillity, and release of muscle tension. Second, guided imagery is often used, in which the individual is asked to imagine encountering a stressful or problematic situation and handling it by relaxing or using more adaptive coping strategies previously discussed in therapy. Often the therapist can talk clients through a stressful situation by instructing them to imagine themselves behaving or thinking in certain ways. Third, cognitive restructuring can be used, in which dysfunctional cognitions or self-statements are replaced by more functional self-statements while the individual is in a trance. Fourth, successive approximations can be used (Kirsch 1993), in which the time exposure to a stressful image is gradually increased or progressively more stressful situations are addressed. In this way clients may be encouraged and given hope by their increasing ability to cope rather than being expected to master their problems immediately. Fifth, hypnotic skills training can be conducted (Golden et al. 1987), in which the individual is trained to engage in trance behavior and respond better to hypnotic suggestions. This assumes that hypnosis is a learnable skill, which as previously noted is somewhat controversial. However, it appears that most people can improve their trance capacity at least to some extent or more fully use the trance capacity they have, as they become more comfortable with hypnosis and the hypnotherapist. Context is an important determinant of explicit hypnotic behavior. In addition, most hypnotic work can be done in a light trance, so that the use of a "deep" trance is not usually required. Relaxation and a light trance is often all that is necessary.

COGNITIVE-DEVELOPMENTAL MODEL

The cognitive-developmental hypnotherapeutic model is quite new on the therapeutic scene, having been presented explicitly as such in only two book chapters (Dowd 1993, 1997b). Its basic assumption is that hypnosis may be especially useful in directly accessing and modifying core cognitions revolving around personal identity, self-concept, and dysfunctional tacit rules, rather than by simply addressing more peripheral behaviors and attitudes. Because of its nonverbal nature, hypnotic imagery and related emotional processing may be useful in changing tacit knowledge, which is often preverbally and implicitly learned. The non-verbal nature of these hypnotic techniques may allow them to directly access the preverbal tacit cognitions. In addition, resistance may be reduced by the judicious application of hypnotic techniques. As discussed earlier, reactant individuals are more likely to be autonomous, independent, and dominant—and therefore more difficult to engage in therapy. Hypnotic interventions, especially of an indirect, permissive Ericksonian nature, may allow the client to remain in charge and in control, thus reducing the possibility of inducing reactance (Dowd 1993, 1997b).

There are two major tasks for the cognitive-developmental hypnotherapist: identifying core cognitive structures and changing these structures. One focus of this book is to describe methods for accomplishing both of these tasks.

We have seen that cognitive therapy has progressed from an emphasis on relatively accessible surface structure cognitions to a consideration of deep structure core beliefs and cognitive schemas (Dowd 1997a). Hypnosis has been used for a number of years as an important technique within a cognitive-behavioral framework and shows promise of being at least as important in accessing and modifying the core beliefs that are important in a cognitive-developmental model. It is time for hypnotherapy to progress as far as cognitive therapy has.

4

Hypnotic Induction

PREPARATION

Although it is important for the therapist to prepare the client carefully for hypnosis, it is surprising how often this is either not done or is done hurriedly. Most clients come to therapy with at least some impressions of hypnosis and it is important both to ascertain and to assess their validity. It is also important to determine the client's motivation for requesting or agreeing to the use of hypnosis, and to determine if the client has ever been hypnotized before and, if so, what the outcome was. In addition, it is important for the therapist to assess his or her own motivation for suggesting or agreeing to the use of hypnosis with this client (I am assuming that the therapist has already carefully considered his or her motivation for using hypnosis at all). Each of these issues is addressed in subsequent paragraphs.

Unfortunately, hypnosis has been associated over the years with magic and occult phenomena. Thus clients may be afraid of hypnosis and see it as controlling or demonic, or as seductive. The latter view is one that has been covertly discussed by hypnotherapists but rarely dealt with openly. It was reportedly one reason (perhaps the major reason) Freud abandoned it after a female patient threw her arms around him after a session. The association of hypnotic trance behavior and covert sexuality is also apparent as a theme in many vampire legends. While it is not generally appropriate to raise this issue directly in a first session, therapists dealing with a client of the opposite sex should always be aware of its potential as an intruding factor and be especially careful. If clients indicate in any way that they are concerned about sexuality in hypnosis, the therapist should discuss it immediately and perhaps refrain from using hypnosis. Alternatively, the therapist may wish to take other precautions, such as conducting the session by loudspeaker from another room, or arranging for a third party to be in the room or immediately available. I once had a client (who appeared to have borderline tendencies) express reservations about hypnosis because "You might take advantage of me." A former colleague of mine had a charge filed against him by a client who accused him of kissing her while she was in a trance.

Clients who are religious may view hypnosis as akin to demonic possession or see it as removing their free will, and therefore be reluctant to consider it. Indeed, the mere mention of it may in some instances rupture the therapeutic alliance. Thus, as a general rule, it may not be wise to discuss its use in the first session with a client unless the client brings it up.

Other impressions of hypnosis are not typically this lurid and are discussed later under myths of hypnosis. The guiding principle, however, is that the client's perception of hypnosis should be thoroughly discussed prior to its use and periodically thereafter.

Clients will often request hypnosis, sometimes immediately, and it is important for the therapist to assess the motivation. Hypnosis is sometimes viewed as a quasi-magical way to obtain results without effort, especially for entrenched habit disorders. For example, I have had several clients ask me to hypnotize them to lose five or ten pounds or to stop smoking. Probably everyone would like to lose five or ten pounds and most people would like to stop smoking—but not if it involves significant effort on their part. I have found that a good way to assess motivation is to ask the requesting individual, "Do you want to [stop smoking, lose weight] or do you *want to want to*?" Generally, they understand the distinction and sheepishly admit to the latter, providing an opening into a discussion of the realistic effectiveness of hypnosis. Clients may also request hypnosis because they know someone whom it has helped, which provides a way to discuss individual differences in hypnotic responsiveness. Each of these misconceptions, of course, may be present and influence client behavior even if the therapist suggests hypnosis. As a general principle, I recommend that the client's motivation be thoroughly explored if hypnosis is suggested either by the therapist or by the client, and that hypnosis be presented as useful with some problems, sometimes, with some clients.

It is helpful for the therapist to ascertain if the client has ever experienced hypnosis within or outside of therapy and what the results were. In this way the therapist can discover problems encountered before and perhaps avoid them. For example, certain clients may not like some inductions or may not wish to close their eyes while in trance. It is difficult to ask all relevant questions in advance, but asking about their prior experience with hypnosis may provide enough data to at least know what to avoid. Generally, I ask what they liked and didn't like about their prior experience with hypnosis and explore it in more detail if necessary.

Finally, it is important for therapists to assess their own motivation for using hypnosis, not only with specific clients but in general. Not all of our motives are necessarily noble ones and we may be more impressed with the apparent power and ritual quality (not to mention seductiveness) of hypnosis than with its ability to help our clients. Indeed, this is an occupational hazard of the helping professions in general—that we may be as much or more interested in enhancing our view of ourselves and our own self-esteem as in helping others. Because of the public image of hypnosis, it is especially likely to occur in hypnotherapy. Thus, in therapy as in life, the guiding principle is "know thyself." The human capacity for self-deception is great indeed.

DISPELLING THE MYTHS OF HYPNOSIS

Hypnosis has been associated for years in popular literature with power, control, and seduction. In addition to its connection with vampirism, as mentioned earlier, and Svengali, the stories of such authors as Edgar Allan Poe abound with tales of the extraordinary power of hypnosis (then called mesmerism) and the hypnotist. For example, Poe's story, "The Facts in the Case of M. Valdemar," describes the ability of hypnosis to keep a man's body intact for months after his death and the grotesque aftermath of his removal from the trance. The experiments of Mesmer in the eighteenth century originally may have been responsible for these exaggerated claims, which have been periodically reinforced by some of the less respectable purveyors of hypnotic cures. Some of the case reports of a giant like Milton Erickson seem to imply an unusual ability to overcome entrenched problems in a very short period of time, sometimes in one session. Even the views of the "state" theorists, which assert that the hypnotic state is qualitatively different from the "waking" or nonhypnotic state, have fostered this idea. The result has been a general public belief that hypnosis is somehow quasi-magical and that the hypnotist possesses powers not shared by mere mortals. For example, I was once asked, when I mentioned that I used hypnosis, "Oh, can you read my mind?" With a sense of humor I immediately responded, "Yes—and you ought to be ashamed!" Thus the central myth to dispel is the view of hypnosis as magical and the hypnotist as all-powerful—not always easy, since much of the general public would like to believe these myths.

With that as background, let me discuss some of the more common myths that are often believed by the public, and sometimes even by hypnotists.

1. *Hypnosis is caused and controlled by the hypnotist.* This has already been described and requires little additional discussion. However, this is a good time for the hypnotherapist to present the view that "all hypnosis is self-hypnosis." That is, it is the subject/client who is in charge of his or her own trance. Thus no one can become "stuck" in hypnosis and be unable to come out

of a trance if something were to happen to the hypnotist, as is sometimes thought. Nor does one become unduly dependent on the hypnotherapist, at least not to a greater extent than is found in other forms of therapy. The hypnotist merely guides and facilitates the trance. Indeed, training in self-hypnosis is often provided as part of the hypnotherapeutic work, sometimes aided by a tape recording of the therapist's trance induction to which the client can listen frequently.

2. *Hypnosis can make people do things against their will.* This myth is related to the first but is common enough so that it deserves to be treated separately. Published case studies seem to give a certain credence to this belief, since clients do appear to be controlled by a posthypnotic suggestion. Stage hypnotists also appear to control people when they do things they normally wouldn't, like barking like a dog or clucking like a chicken in public. Certainly the popular literature perpetuates this myth.

There is a certain truth behind this myth. In a situation defined as hypnosis, people may perform activities in which they normally would not engage. Hypnotherapists have often found certain individuals (those possessing good trance capacity) to be more susceptible to trance suggestions. However, while people may perform certain innocuous, unusual activities in a situation defined as hypnosis, they are not likely to engage in serious or criminal activities. For example, although someone may bark like a dog under stage hypnosis, he or she would probably not disrobe or murder someone. Although an adept hypnotist, under the proper circumstances and with the right client, may throw him or her into an internal conflict when suggesting a proscribed activity, it is highly probable that the individual would successfully resist the suggestion.

3. *Hypnosis is a form of sleep.* In a sense all of us contribute to this myth by the language we use. As mentioned earlier, the word comes from the Greek *hypnos*, which means sleep. Likewise, we say, "Go deeper into a trance" or "You will waken from the trance," and even ask people to close their eyes, which implies

sleep. Clients may show their belief in this myth when they say, "I wasn't really hypnotized. I was aware of everything you said."

The example I use to dispel this myth is that of highway hypnosis, a phenomenon in which drivers may be unaware of their surroundings on a boring stretch of road, yet be fully alert and active in piloting a car. Likewise, many people become so totally absorbed in an activity that they lose track of time, a form of time distortion. I inform clients that the experience of trance is highly individual. They may close their eyes or keep them open, they may be deeply relaxed or alert, they may have a spontaneous amnesia or they may remember many or all events. This discussion also allows clients to interpret whatever trance phenomena they experience as positive rather than judging every experience against an implied standard and then seeing themselves (or the hypnotherapist) as having failed. Hypnotherapists always want their clients to have a successful experience with trance.

4. *Hypnosis occurs only when a formal induction is used.* Many hypnotists believe this one! Certainly, according to the social psychological (nonstate) view, there is an additional suggestibility inherent in a defined hypnotic context. However, skilled therapists can create a quasi-hypnotic situation by the pacing and the tone of voice they use as well as by the repetition of certain words or phrases. The case reports of Milton Erickson contain numerous examples of hypnosis that were performed in situations not defined as such. The highway hypnosis referred to earlier is another example. There is a certain ethical dilemma concerning the lack of informed consent in deliberately using hypnosis in situations in which its use has not been discussed with the client, however, and hypnotherapists ought to proceed cautiously here.

5. *Hypnosis occurs only when one is relaxed.* Since hypnosis is generally associated with sleep, it is not surprising that it is also associated with relaxation. However, under a form of hypnosis

called alert hypnosis (to be discussed later) hypnotized individuals can walk, talk, and open their eyes. This is a common misconception. Many people are disappointed to find that they are not immediately deeply relaxed in a trance, and interpret that as a sign that "it isn't working."

6. *Hypnosis is a therapy.* This surprisingly widespread misconception is fostered by certain hypnosis centers that conduct hypnosis as their sole technique for solving many problems. Hypnosis is an adjunctive technique *only*, and should always be used within the context of a professional practice. For this reason most practitioners prefer the term *hypnotherapist* in clinical practice. Thus physicians may use hypnosis as one technique in treating, for example, warts or asthma; psychologists, as a tool for treating anxiety or depression; dentists, to treat pain from tooth extractions. Hypnosis should not be practiced outside the bounds of one's professional competency.

7. *Only some people can be hypnotized.* There is some truth in this, although it is one of the most controversial issues in hypnotherapy. Different theories of hypnosis have different opinions on this topic. There appear to be substantial differences in trance capacity (or hypnotic susceptibility) among people and these differences form a normal distribution. Some people may be extremely responsive (hypnotic virtuosos) and some may be almost unresponsive; the majority are in the middle. While training may increase an individual's hypnotic responsiveness to some extent, it is not likely to have a large impact (Bowers 1976). However, the context of the situation can influence greatly how an individual responds so that repeated assessment may be required to adequately determine a client's responsiveness. Hypnotic responsiveness does not appear to be correlated with much else, although there is some evidence that it is weakly associated (positively) with intelligence, ability to concentrate, and self-esteem (Yapko 1995) and (negatively) with age (Bowers 1976). It is correlated with treatment outcome only for such

bodily functions as pain, asthma, and warts, but not for such habit disorders as addictions (Bates 1993). Hypnotic responsiveness or trance capacity may also have a greater correlation with outcome when suggestions are tailored specifically to each client rather than when a standard protocol is used (Bates 1993). However, the bulk of hypnotic work can be done in a light trance, so that most people can benefit at least to some extent. (The interested reader should consult more specialized texts for details on forms of hypnosis that require a "deeper" trance.)

8. *Hypnosis can be used to help people accurately recall what has happened in the past.* This is a fairly recent and especially pernicious myth. Although hypnosis has been used for this purpose in some instances, without corroborating evidence one cannot be sure if the recalled information is accurate. The mind is a constructing organ as well as a recalling organ and tends to at least partially create memories (see Dowd and Courchaine 1996). This is an especially sensitive issue at present and will be dealt with in more detail later.

TRADITIONAL INDUCTION

In traditional hypnosis a formal induction is followed by a formal deepening technique designed to assist individuals in further involving themselves in the trance. Although the term *deepening* is used for procedures that help people experience phenomena that require a greater trance capacity, it is not really an accurate description and is similar to the perception of Heaven as "up." Both are metaphors. People experience more or fewer hypnotic phenomena but they do not go "deeper" into a trance. However, I will use the term because it has been used almost universally in the past and is the most parsimonious way of discussing the event. Formal tests of susceptibility or trance capacity, such as the Stanford, Harvard, or Barber scales, are often used to assess the ability of the individual to experience unusual hypnotic phenomena.

Induction

Wright and Wright (1987) have described five general conditions that, although not necessary, certainly facilitate trance induction: trust in the therapist, reduction of sensory input, fixation of attention, muscle relaxation, and heightened awareness of one's inner life. A wide variety of induction procedures are available in the literature and serious students of hypnotherapy should investigate them to determine which may be suitable to their own personal style.

One technique I particularly like, which meets all of the five conditions, is the eye fixation and closure induction. Although it has numerous variations, its basic structure is something like this (bold words are vocally stressed):

I'd like you to focus on a spot on the opposite wall. As you look at it, I'd like you to let your eyes focus behind the spot, into the distance, so that the spot becomes blurred and indistinct. As you gaze off into the distance, you may find your eyes becoming heavy. **When** your eyes feel heavy, you may **let them close.** [Pause if necessary.] As your eyes close, you may find your muscles becoming **more and more relaxed.** And the more you listen to my voice, the more your muscles can relax and the less you need to pay attention to any other sounds or sensations. You may hear [for example] the hum of the air conditioner, feel the pressure of your body in the chair, but as I continue to talk, you can **gradually allow** these sensations to fade from your mind—becoming **more and more relaxed, more and more comfortable.** And as you continue to feel more comfortable and relaxed, you can increasingly focus your attention on your inner sensations—becoming aware, for example, of your breathing, your muscular relaxation, even the blood flowing through your veins. And you can choose to notice whatever internal sensations are especially important to you right now. So, the more I continue to talk, the more comfortable and relaxed you can become.

This outline can be expanded as necessary and the therapist should watch postural signs and adjust the speed of the induction accordingly. Ask the client afterwards if the speed was correct so as to refine your future inductions.

Deepening

These techniques are designed to assist the individual in more fully experiencing whatever trance phenomena he or she is capable of. Generally, those who possess greater trance capacity are able to experience a greater number of phenomena or (metaphorically) go to a "deeper level" of hypnosis. Again, there are a wide variety of deepening techniques available in the literature. One I particularly like, both for its ease and low threat level, is the staircase technique. Although it can be varied greatly, its basic structure is something like this:

> I'd like you to see [or imagine] yourself at the top of a staircase. As I begin to count, you will walk down one step until I stop, when you will be at the bottom. One, **more and more relaxed**; two, **deeper and deeper**; three, **down and down**; four, five, **relaxing as you go** [etc.]. Now that you are at the bottom, I'd like you to sit back in the reclining chair, which you see off to your right, and **become even more relaxed**.

The hypnotherapist can go to five, ten, or more steps depending on the individual's response. However, it is important that the number of steps going down is the same as the number coming up. People with good trance capacity may be confused by discrepancies. Variations on this theme are an elevator (with the individual looking at the level indicator), an escalator (using an image of a gently flowing descent), and the diving technique (diving deeper into the sea). I learned by experience, however, to have the person don a breathing apparatus first if the last technique is used. As with inductions, it is important to watch the client's behavior and postural signs to ensure that the correct speed is used.

Suggestibility Tests

Some hypnotherapists may wish to perform one or more suggestibility tests prior to an induction to assess the individual's likely trance capacity. Many are available in the literature, but I like the arms rising, arms falling technique. In general, it is performed like this:

> I'd like you to place your arms and hands out in front of you like this with your palms down [demonstrate]. Now turn over your right hand so your palm is up. Then close your eyes. Now I'd like you to imagine that I've placed a heavy weight on the palm of your right hand and attached a helium balloon to your left hand. And your **right hand** becomes **heavier and heavier** and your **left hand** becomes **lighter and lighter**. And your **right hand** goes **down and down** while your **left hand** goes **up and up**. [Repeat this until you have obtained what you judge to be the maximum rising and lowering of the hands.] Now freeze your hands and arms and open your eyes.

Generally, the farther apart the right and left hands are, the greater is the trance capacity. This demonstration is especially impressive in a group format, as everyone can see the individual differences in the extent of arms rising and falling. However, it should be emphasized that any one test provides only an approximation of trance capacity, since other factors such as comfort with the hypnotist and the situation can influence responsivity. Repetition can often result in greater responsivity as the individual becomes more comfortable with hypnosis and the hypnotherapist.

ERICKSONIAN INDUCTION

Erickson's induction procedures were conversationally based and relied on the context of the situation as well. Thus Ericksonian hypnotherapists advocate creating a context that will allow hypnosis to occur (Matthews et al. 1993). This can be done by defining it explicitly as hypnosis and by accepting any client response as valid and a sign that he or she is going into a trance. Also important are the inner processes of the individual, including both the conscious and unconscious mind (Matthews et al. 1993). Erickson would structure a conversational induction, usually in an explicitly hypnotic context, that allowed and encouraged individuals to examine their implicit meanings and associations and perhaps create new meaning structures and different behaviors. Metaphors and analogies are often used within the induction. Client behavior is accepted and utilized, rather than opposed. Hypnotic suggestions are often phrased in such a way that anything one does is a sign that one is going into a trance. Although earlier in his life Erickson used direct suggestions, he increasingly relied on indirect suggestions and today the latter tend to be a hallmark of the Ericksonian approach (Matthews et al. 1993).

An example of a typical Ericksonian induction (though unusually short) might be the following:

> And one of the first things that a person does when he goes into a trance, he looks at some one spot. He doesn't need to move, he doesn't need to do anything except let his unconscious mind take over and do everything. And the conscious mind doesn't have to do anything. It's usually not even interested. And while I've been talking to you, you've altered your respiration, your heart rate is altered. I know from past experience that your blood pressure is changed, your pulse is changed, and your eyelid reflex is changed. And you really don't need to keep your eyes open, but you can close them now. That little flutter is learning to get acquainted with yourself at another level of being. [Lankton and Lankton 1983, pp. 158–159]

Although Ericksonian hypnotherapists often do not separate the induction phase from the hypnotic work, the following is an example of hypnotic metaphor trance work. The client in this example had adolescent enuresis and I used a metaphor of "catch and hold" to encourage urine retention. This routine was specifically constructed for a client who liked fishing with his father. Bold words were vocally stressed.

I'd like you to imagine that you are fishing with your father. You know, don't you, that you must first **catch** the fish, then **hold** the fish. Either one without the other is useless, isn't it! So, imagine yourself catching the fish and holding the fish, **catching and holding, catching and holding**, catching and holding. After a while, it becomes automatic, doesn't it! Catch and hold, **catch and hold**. And the more you think about it, the more you can apply that to other parts of your life, so that you can catch and hold other things as well. [Dowd 1996, p. 299]

Later the following hypnotic metaphor was used with the same client to encourage further development in different ways of relating to his parents.

As you are learning new ways of growing, new ways of being close in different ways, different but deeper feelings as you continue to grow and develop in different ways, feeling good about the changes you are making, wondering with interest and excitement where it all will lead. And feeling comfortable with your own internal growth processes, knowing that they will lead to new opportunities and new possibilities. So that you can relate to others not only differently, but better as well. [Dowd 1996, p. 299]

ALERT HYPNOSIS

This type of hypnosis can be used to energize instead of relax. It has been used in a number of situations, such as depression and athletic performance, when the goal is more activity. In alert hypnosis, both the induction and subsequent hypnotic suggestions are given in a lively rather than a lulling, soothing manner. It can also be helpful to gradually increase the tempo of your voice as you proceed. Although you may wish to begin the induction with the client's eyes closed, eventually it may be helpful to ask him or her to open them. Of course, prior preparation regarding the nature of hypnotic phenomena is necessary so that eye-opening is not resisted or interpreted as an indication of the lack of trance.

The following example of an alert induction uses arm levitation similar to the one presented earlier. However, any induction can be adapted to alert hypnosis.

> Close your eyes and let each hand rest gently on your legs. Imagine something that would make one of your hands light and buoyant, such as helium balloons attached to the fingers of one of your hands. . . . Be aware of whatever sensations develop in your hand. . . . Notice the difference between your hands. Notice how one hand is starting to feel lighter than the other. . . . Feel the lightness spreading . . . spreading throughout your hand . . . to your arm. . . . Spreading throughout your arm. . . . Your hand is getting lighter. . . . Getting lighter . . . so much lighter than your other hand and arm. . . . Soon it will feel so light that your hand will start to lift. . . . Feeling so light that it feels like lifting, like floating . . . [Repeat until the arm begins to lift]. As your hand lifts, you feel more and more energetic, alive, feeling pleasant sensations throughout your body. Comfortable but alert. You can feel positive and confident that you can control your feelings. Just as you can control simple sensations like lightness, you can control other feelings too. [Golden et al. 1987, pp. 35–36]

DIRECT AND INDIRECT SUGGESTION

Direct suggestions are what they imply: hypnotic suggestions that encourage the removal or reduction of certain sensations or behaviors or the request for a particular subject response. As such, they have been used since before Freud. In many instances direct suggestions are very effective, but the hypnotherapist is well advised not to make suggestions for immediate symptom removal, tempting though it may be. Even though research has not demonstrated conclusively that indirect suggestions are more effective than direct suggestions or arouse less resistance, direct suggestions may themselves arouse expectancies in the client that cannot be fulfilled. It is also important to stress again that suggestions are more or less direct or indirect, not one or the other. For example, an extreme direct suggestion such as "Your pain will disappear!" will rarely be effective. If successful, due perhaps to expectancy and placebo effects, it is likely to be temporary. If failure occurs, as it well might under those conditions, clients often blame the therapist for lack of effectiveness, to the detriment of therapeutic credibility, or blame themselves for not being good enough, and become discouraged. Either way, the therapeutic alliance may be damaged. It is better to suggest that the symptoms may become less noticeable or fewer in number. For example, a direct suggestion for pain control might be as follows:

> As you become more and more relaxed, you may begin to notice that the discomfort in your shoulder is less and less noticeable. You can imagine it becoming smaller and smaller, less and less noticeable . . . it's still there but almost feels now like a small pressure.

Note that the use of the term *pain* is avoided and that *pressure* is used instead to avoid reminding the client of his or her pain.

Likewise, a direct suggestion for anxiety reduction might be constructed as follows:

> As you become more and more relaxed, you can begin to feel less and less disturbed . . . as the relaxation spreads throughout your body, you can feel your mind becoming more relaxed as well . . . you can feel it slowing down as you feel increasing confidence in your ability to handle more and more events in your life as these events seem less and less dangerous. You begin to feel more and more at peace and more and more relaxed.

In this example, a reduction in anxiety is paired with physical relaxation and there is an implication of less danger from future events that is thought to be an indicator of anxiety (Beck and Emery 1985) as well as a greater sense of personal control. Again, the term *anxiety* is avoided and the less pejorative term *disturbed* is used.

Both examples are significantly shortened for demonstration purposes. In actual hypnotic trance work, certain phrases are repeated—sometimes several times—and the basic themes illustrated may be considerably elaborated and extended. As the reader may have guessed by now, a hallmark of hypnotherapy is therapist creativity.

Indirect suggestions were originally developed by the Ericksonian hypnotherapists and indeed are still largely identified with that group. However, a number of more traditional hypnotherapists now make use, at least on occasion, of indirect suggestion. In indirect suggestions the relationship between the therapist's suggestion and the client's response may only be inferred and may allow the latter a number of different response options. For example, an indirect suggestion for eye closure might be:

> As you develop the level of relaxation you desire right now and that will be most helpful to you, you may begin to notice changes in your eyes. They may close, close partially, or remain open. Whatever you choose, you may go deeper into a trance.

Another even more indirect suggestion for eye closure may be as follows:

> As you begin to find increasing comfort, you may begin to notice certain sensations in your eyes. Perhaps they will become heavier, perhaps they will become lighter, perhaps there may be other new sensations. It will be interesting, won't it, to observe these changes and what may happen next. And you can observe these changes and learn from them. . . .

Notice that in the second example eye closure is not mentioned at all. However, because the context of hypnosis for most people involves eye closure as a common response, it is very likely that the eyes will close. Since the individual will likely experience this as nonvolitional (since it hasn't been mentioned), he or she will interpret it, because of the context, as a sign of increasing trance. Even if the eyes do not close, however, the hypnotherapist retains credibility. There is also an implicit, embedded suggestion that there will in fact be changes; the only question is what ones. Embedded, implicitly constraining suggestions are an important part of indirect suggestions. Other examples of indirect suggestions were given previously and additional ones will appear through the remainder of this book.

TRANCE TERMINATION

Although people do not remain "stuck" in hypnosis if there is no official termination, it is important to provide some sort of closure to the hypnotic state. Termination provides contextual indication that the trance should end and thus acts as a signal. Some individuals, especially those possessing high trance capacity, may be confused and discombobulated without a formal termination procedure. In particular, their reflexes may be slower at first and they should not operate motor vehicles in that condition. In addition, some people do not immediately emerge from a trance (though they will eventually) and may need to be assisted in "coming out of it." I have seen individuals who at first appeared to be completely out of a trance, but who soon indicated by certain signs that they were still partially hypnotized. These signs may include slower motor functioning and response time as well as difficulty in focusing on tasks or on other people.

For the sake of symmetry, if nothing else, I recommend that the termination procedure parallel the induction procedure in reverse. For example, if the induction included a staircase deepening technique of ten steps, the termination should include ten steps counted backwards. A common termination procedure might be this:

> And now it is time to come out of the trance. As I count backwards
> from five to one [or ten to one], you will [or can] feel progressively
> more alert and awake so that when I reach one you will open your

eyes and come out of the trance [or "wake up"] feeling alert and re-freshed. Five, more alert—four, beginning to come out of the trance—three, more and more alert—two, feeling more awake—one.

Another method that gives even more control to the client is the following:

> Now you will begin, at your own pace, to return to the fully alert, wide-awake state. Feel free to take your time. Go at a pace that is com-fortable for you. Take it slowly. Start to move a little, very slowly and at your pace, starting to open your eyes, returning to an alert state, feeling relaxed, refreshed, and wide awake. [Golden et al. 1987, p. 29]

The advantage of this termination procedure is that it allows the client to make the transition from the trance to the nontrance state at his or her own pace and validates the dictum that "all hypnosis is self-hypnosis." Even though clients may require a more therapist-directed termination at first, after repeated hypnotic work they are likely to prefer and be able to use a more client-centered termination procedure.

Even though "awake" or "wake up" are metaphors, they are often used by hynotherapists for lack of better terms and because most people tend to think of hypnosis that way. However, in the preparation stage the hypnotherapist should emphasize that those terms and others that are similar are only metaphors and do not reflect actual hypnotic reality.

BASIC HYPNOTHERAPEUTIC TECHNIQUES

Hypnotherapy is an extremely creative endeavor. Nonetheless, a few basic interventions recur and can be used to organize a wide variety of spe-cific techniques. I will describe some that have particular relevance for cognitive hypnotherapy.

Hypnotic Relaxation

If there is one hypnotic technique that is universal, it is this. Virtually every induction and deepening exercise, as well as most hypnotic routines, makes implicit or explicit use of relaxation. Only alert hypnosis does not involve relaxation. Indeed, systematic desensitization has a strong hypnotic quality. In disorders such as anxiety and phobias, hypnotic relaxation may be a major component of effectiveness; in other disorders it is certainly an important one. Hypnotic relaxation uses a well-known idea—that it is difficult to be anxious while relaxed and that the cognitive system incorporates new data more easily in a state of relaxation.

Age Regression

This technique essentially takes clients back to an earlier time in life. Because of certain highly dubious and controversial claims for it, such as regression before birth, past lives regression, or recovered memories of sexual abuse, it is sometimes considered to be somewhat less than respectable. However, age regression is simply the assisted recall of previous events in an individual's life. It is quite possible that memories of these events are at least partially constructed and not necessarily true in all details, but in psychotherapy it is the memories that are important, not necessarily the literal accuracy of them. People are affected by events as they remember and interpret them, not the events themselves. In forensic (legal) matters, however, it is quite different.

Hypnotically assisted recall of memories may be experienced with startling reality, as if they were being reexperienced. Or they may be recalled only as memories, with little of the emotional intensity once felt. Likewise, the degree of newness may vary. Sometimes an entirely new memory may surface, or a previously incomplete or fragmentary memory may be filled in with more detail. However, the recall of previous memories and images can provide a rich source of data for a review of past memories and subsequent cognitive restructuring (Dowd 1997b). In one form or another, age regression is a commonly used technique. J. S. Beck's (1995) imagery techniques of identifying images, following images to completion, and coping in the image have age regression characteristics.

Age Progression

As its name implies, age progression involves a move forward into the future. Of course, there are no real memories to recover in the future, but it is quite possible for individuals to create images of how they would like an event to be or how they would like to remember a situation. Thus a speech-anxious client may be asked to imagine himself one month from now (when he will give his speech) feeling comfortable and giving his speech well. Indeed, an entire imaginary scenario can be constructed for some future time that is better than what occurred in the past. J. S. Beck's (1995) imagery techniques of jumping ahead in time and following images to completion have age progression characteristics. Dowd (1997b) has described a similar technique under the heading of replacement and coping imagery. Of course, in both age regression and age progression repetition is very important.

Suggested Amnesia

This is an example of a layperson's conception of hypnosis—that nothing is remembered that occurred in a trance. There are, however, two aspects of hypnotic amnesia: amnesia for past events or amnesia for events in the trance (Teitelbaum 1969). The latter often occurs spontaneously, but the former almost never occurs without the intervention of the hypnotherapist. Yet it is the former that may be useful in therapy.

It is an important aspect of the human cognitive system that negative, rather than positive, events tend to be forgotten over time. Indeed, this tendency helps all of us maintain our optimism and sense of well-being; we would feel worse if we remembered all of our failures and problems well. Many distressing events are remembered by clients, however, as extremely painful and the memories are often intrusive and ruminative. It is precisely in these areas that suggested amnesia, even if partial, can be useful. Of course, the therapist should be careful not to suggest too much amnesia. Suggestions such as, "You may gradually begin to forget, or forget to remember, many of these incidents" may be best. There is also evidence that suggested amnesia works best with those with great trance capacity or hypnotic susceptibility (Teitelbaum 1969).

Memory Substitution

There is increasing evidence that memories are not encoded permanently in the brain but are at least partially constructed over time (Loftus and Pickrell 1995, Zaragoza and Mitchell 1996). Fleming and colleagues (1992) present evidence indicating that three variables manipulate the subjective experience of memory: context, attention, and number of times an episode is recalled. Contextual features include aspects of the environment (such as defining the situation as hypnosis), internal features such as mood or drugs, and the semantic context (types of language used). Attention refers to the amount of deliberate attention directed to the task. For example, Milton Erickson commonly used divided attention wherein the client's overt attention was diverted from the hypnotic message. The number of times an incident is recalled also influences the memory of that incident. Events repeatedly recalled are remembered with more confidence but less accuracy, often in a self-serving or externally suggested direction. Thus it appears that memories can be shaped, for good or bad, in significant ways. The process of memory shaping can be natural or deliberately fostered. Teitelbaum (1969) goes so far as to say that entirely new memories can be substituted, as demonstrated by wartime examples of brainwashing, a point also made by Loftus (1993). This is a highly controversial topic at present, given the interest in repressed memories of sexual abuse. Regardless of whether traumatic early memories can be completely repressed or entirely constructed, it does appear that there are significant memory shifts about many events over time. Certain memory shifts may be therapeutically beneficial and an astute hypnotherapist can foster them.

Cognitive Rehearsal

Dowd (1997b) has described the use of this technique in cognitive hypnotherapy. It is possible for the client, while in a trance, to imagine himself behaving in new ways in problematic situations. Furthermore, the client can be asked to observe and identify the feelings that accompany this new behavior and to compare them to usual feelings in similar situations. The hypnotic trance allows the client to imagine these new behaviors and the subsequent cognitions and feelings with an intensity not normally encountered in imaginary situations.

Creating Imaginary Dialogues

There are occasions where it is no longer possible to talk directly with another person (e.g., when the other person is dead) or when it is too distressing (e.g., when the other person is an intimidating figure). In such situations the use of an imaginary dialogue while in a trance can be useful (Dowd 1997b). In some ways this resembles the Gestalt therapy two-chair technique. Clients can play either themselves or the significant person in their life, or alternate between the two, or the therapist might role-play one or the other. This is a very flexible technique in cognitive hypnotherapy.

Part II

Treatment of Psychological Disorders

5

Introduction

There is probably no past or current psychological or physical problem that someone, somewhere, somehow, has not attempted to cure using hypnosis. Furthermore, hypnosis has been used or has been claimed to have been used with a variety of occult and controversial phenomena, such as satanic rituals and abuse, past lives regression, and the investigation of multiple personalities. Hypnosis is still associated sufficiently in the public mind with magic and the occult that such claims have a certain plausibility. While this turf is generally the province of questionable practitioners, some more traditional practitioners of hypnosis have occasionally slipped into an attitude of acceptance of, rather than an appropriate scientific skepticism toward, such phenomena. Such an unthinking and credulous attitude hurts the ultimate acceptance of hypnosis as a reputable psychological therapeutic technique.

Some practitioners of hypnosis also treat it, implicitly or explicitly, as sufficient in itself for therapeutic gain. That is, hypnosis becomes the whole therapy rather than an adjunctive technique used within the context of a comprehensive therapeutic regimen. For example, some "hypnosis centers" advertise that clients can lose significant amounts of weight or stop smoking permanently with one or two hypnosis sessions as the sole treatment. Such blandishments feed the age-old human yearning for a quick (and of course cheap) fix that requires little effort in overcoming entrenched problems. Despite anecdotal evidence in the literature attesting to substantial gains in one or two sessions, entrenched human problems typically do not yield easily to short interventions. The inevitable disillusionment that results from failure also hurts the credibility of hypnosis as a reliable and valid technique. Occasionally mainstream practitioners appear to subscribe to this view of hypnosis.

This section describes and illustrates the use of hypnosis in helping to overcome a variety of psychological problems that clinicians typically encounter. The overall orientation is that hypnosis is a cognitive technique that under the right conditions can modify cognitive content, cognitive processes, and cognitive structures. First, however, we must describe the various types of cognitive phenomena that hypnosis can address.

Meichenbaum and Gilmore (1984) described three aspects of human cognitive functioning that form the conceptual basis for the interventions and examples described in this book. They distinguish among cognitive events, cognitive processes, and cognitive structures. Cognitive events are conscious, easily accessible thoughts, self-statements, and images. For example, a client's immediate thoughts, such as, "I'm stupid to have made such a dumb mistake!" or "I'll never succeed at this task!" are cognitive events. Likewise, one's image of becoming highly anxious while giving a speech, sweating heavily, and forgetting what to say is a cognitive (imagery) event. Cognitive events are relatively easily identified and accessed with help and are considered to be surface cognitions. Standard questions for accessing cognitive events are, "What was going through your mind just now?" or "What were you thinking when 'X' occurred?" or "Describe how you see yourself performing."

Cognitive processes can best be described as ways of thinking. For example, the cognitive errors identified by Beck and colleagues (1979) such as overgeneralizing, catastrophizing, and dichotomous ("black-and-white") thinking, are examples of dysfunctional cognitive processes. Likewise, the irrational beliefs identified by Ellis and Dryden (1997) are examples of cognitive processing errors. Such beliefs include "awfulizing" (assuming something is awful when it is merely inconvenient), "musturbation" (assuming something must or must not happen when it is merely preferential), and assumptions of personal worthlessness from ordinary mistakes. Other common examples include minimization of good events or actions and magnification of bad events. In essence, dysfunctional cognitive processes involve a selective attention to negative information and a filtering out of positive information. Cognitive errors can also occur in a positive direction, although they are less commonly implicated in psychological distress. In this case individuals may interpret events in an overly positive light, leading to a Pollyannish attitude that can also be problematical. Our own cognitive processes are typically not immediately accessible to us, although we are generally much better at identifying cognitive processing errors in others. We can learn to identify our own thinking errors, however, with the help of a skilled therapist, which is one aspect of cognitive psychotherapy.

J. S. Beck (1995) has provided a useful summary of the major cognitive distortions. They include:

1. *All-or-nothing thinking*: Viewing situations as either-or, rather than as continuous.
2. *Catastrophizing*: Predicting the future entirely negatively.
3. *Discounting the positive*: Not counting positive experiences.
4. *Emotional reasoning*: Thinking something is true because you "feel" it to be true while discounting contrary evidence.
5. *Labeling*: Attaching a fixed and global label to yourself or others.
6. *Magnification/minimization*: Magnifying the negative and minimizing the positive.
7. *Mental filter*: Paying more attention to negative information than to positive.

8. *Mind reading*: Believing you know what others are thinking without evidence.
9. *Overgeneralization*: Making a sweeping negative conclusion based on limited evidence.
10. *Personalization*: Unreasonably believing yourself the cause of others' behavior.
11. *Using imperative statements*: Having a fixed and unreasonable idea of how you and others must behave, reflected in many "should" and "must" statements.
12. *Tunnel vision*: Seeing only the negative aspects of a situation.

Cognitive structures have also been called cognitive schemas (or schemata) and can be thought of as tacit networks of rules and assumptions that organize prior experience. They are predispositions to think, interpret, and respond in certain ways and are outside of conscious awareness. While cognitive structures can be very adaptive in that they enable people to process information rapidly (Beck and Emery 1985), the same rapid processing can result in entrenched maladaptive structures. Because they are laid down at an early age and are part of the implicit knowledge structure (Dowd and Courchaine 1996), it is difficult for an individual to access them or accept them if they are accessed by others. Schemas are typically experienced by people as "just the way things are!" and attempts to help them see things differently are usually met with considerable resistance. They can be functional or dysfunctional and are core cognitive constructs in what is typically referred to as *personality style*. Dysfunctional schemas are strongly implicated in personality disorders. For example, someone may have a schema of personal incompetence, from which his or her actions are consistently interpreted as "not good enough." Someone else may have a schema of mistrust, from which all interpersonal overtures by others are rejected as suspicious. A third person may have a schema of dependence, from which he or she may feel unable to function alone and without outside help. A fourth may have a schema of defectiveness, so that he or she feels perpetually unloved. Once established, these schemas act like templates that filter in consistent data and filter out discrepant data and therefore tend to be self-perpetuating in nature. Given the early origin and strength of these long-standing schemas, it's a wonder that people change at all!

Young (1994) has provided a comprehensive taxonomy of early maladaptive schemas (EMS) organized into four domains. EMSs are stable and enduring cognitive themes that develop during childhood and are only elaborated upon thereafter rather than significantly changed. They form our view of ourselves, the world, and our place within the world. They are unconditional beliefs, self-perpetuating; are activated by environmental events; are associated with high levels of affect; and are the result of early dysfunctional experiences with caregivers and peers. Young has identified the following EMSs as of January 1994, organized into five themes:

DISCONNECTION AND REJECTION

1. *Abandonment/Instability*: the belief that others will not be available to continue providing support and protection.
2. *Mistrust/Abuse*: the expectation that others will hurt or take advantage of one.
3. *Emotional Deprivation*: the belief that one will not obtain a normal degree of emotional support from others, divided into deprivation of nurturance, deprivation of empathy, and deprivation of protection.
4. *Defectiveness/Shame*: the belief that one is defective, bad, or inferior in important respects. The flaws may be internal or external.
5. *Social Isolation/Alienation*: the belief that one is isolated from the rest of the world or different from others.

IMPAIRED AUTONOMY AND PERFORMANCE

6. *Dependence/Incompetence*: the belief that one is not able to handle one's responsibilities competently without help from others.

7. *Vulnerability to Danger*: an exaggerated fear that catastrophe could strike at any time and cannot be prevented.
8. *Enmeshment/Undeveloped Self*: an excessive emotional involvement with significant others, at the expense of becoming fully individual.
9. *Failure*: the belief that one has failed, will fail, or is fundamentally inadequate compared to others.

IMPAIRED LIMITS

10. *Entitlement/Domination*: the belief that one should have whatever one wants, whenever one wants it, regardless of the cost to others. "I want what I want when I want it!"
11. *Insufficient Self-Control/Self-discipline*: difficulty in or refusal to exercise self-control, low frustration tolerance. Individual excessively avoids discomfort.

OTHER-DIRECTEDNESS

12. *Subjugation*: an excessive surrender of control over one's behavior and feelings to avoid retaliation, anger, or abandonment by others.
13. *Self-Sacrifice*: an excessive focus on meeting the needs of others at the expense of one's own gratifications.
14. *Approval-Seeking*: an excessive emphasis on gaining approval and recognition from others at the expense of one's own ideas. May involve an overemphasis on status, money, achievement.

OVERVIGILANCE AND INHIBITION

15. *Vulnerability/Negativity*: an exaggerated expectation that things will go wrong at any moment, an inordinate fear of making mis-

takes that could lead in that direction. "That which can go wrong, will!"

16. *Overcontrol*: an excessive inhibition of spontaneity to avoid making mistakes, alienating others, or losing control.

17. *Unrelenting Standards*: a belief that one must always strive to meet very high internalized standards, usually to avoid criticism.

18. *Punitiveness*: a belief that one must be angry and punitive with those people (including oneself) who do not meet one's (high) expectations or standards.

Young states that people typically have two or three of these schemas and has developed the Schema Questionnaire to assess them (Young 1994). Obviously, many, perhaps most, of these schemas are facilitative in moderation. It is only when they become excessive that they can become maladaptive. Individuals who have a powerful EMS in an area have great difficulty understanding why it may be maladaptive. To them, it is obvious: "That's the way things should be!"

These, then, are the basic cognitive phenomena that are addressed in cognitive psychotherapy. In many instances hypnosis can aid the clinician substantially in helping clients to overcome cognitive errors and distortions at all three levels of cognition and replace them with more adaptive cognitions. The use of hypnosis to modify dysfunctional cognitions for a variety of psychological problems is described in the following chapters.

1. Events = surface ⊖ beliefs   ⋁ — Surface
2. Processes = "errors"
3. Structures = ∤ ems — Maint   Deep
                        Comper   (Tacit)
                        Avoid

6

Anxiety and Phobias

At the outset, it is important to distinguish between the terms *anxiety*, *fear*, and *phobia*. Beck and Emery (1985) have argued that fear is a cognitive process, whereas anxiety is an emotional reaction. According to this line of thinking, fear is a cognitive appraisal of a threatening future situation. Beck and Emery have in fact stated that the perception of a future danger is the hallmark of anxiety. Phobias are especially intense and unrealistic fears characterized by an avoidance of the feared object. Emotional arousal is implicated in all of these states, however, so that many of the same interventions can be used for both anxiety and phobias.

ANXIETY

The twentieth century has been called the "Age of Anxiety," and indeed it was. Rarely has the perception of a future danger been as pervasive or as long-standing. In past ages, anxiety generally resulted from the perception of physical danger. Today, however, the danger is primarily social and interpersonal.

Social dangers are all around us. The loosening of social ties that formerly bound individuals to their communities and community members to each other has resulted in deep feelings of aloneness and atomization. While these loosening social strictures often result in an exhilarating feeling of freedom at first, this selfsame freedom can eventually generate anxiety. As one newly emancipated young adult said, "The upside is that I can do what I want; the downside is that no one cares what I do." Freedom allows us to experiment with new ways of thinking, acting, and feeling, but it also leaves us responsible for the results. Thus it is not surprising that some people try to escape from freedom as shown by the paradoxical nostalgia by some Russians for the former Soviet Union. Freedom has its price.

Humans are highly social animals and the loosening of family and community ties resulting from the new freedom and mobility has meant that we must form new social relationships rather than inheriting them. The increased divorce rate is both a cause and an effect of this trend. Thus we must constantly create new relationships and therefore risk rejection and social isolation in a way that would have been unthinkable even a hundred years ago. Occupations and careers must likewise be chosen rather than inherited, with anxiety resulting from the possibility of a poor choice. When boys did what their fathers had done and girls did what their mothers had done, choice was not an option and anxiety was therefore reduced.

There are also biological and temperamental individual differences in anxiety. Some people just seem to be more anxious and high-strung than others, a fact known since ancient times. Perhaps some of these individual differences can be traced to biochemical factors and variations in overall activity level. However, psychological interventions designed to reduce anxiety can have a significant effect even for chronically anxious people, though perhaps not to the degree they would like. In addition, appropriate medications designed to lower arousal level may be useful at times.

In some ways, hypnosis is tailor-made for the treatment of anxiety. The emotional arousal characteristic of all anxieties and phobias can be reduced, if not eliminated, by the relaxation that accompanies many forms of hypnosis. There is evidence from clinical studies that therapeutic outcome is consistently related to hypnotizability (Wadden and Anderton 1982), so that an assessment of this individual difference variable should be undertaken before treatment by hypnosis. The remainder of this chapter illustrates the use of hypnosis in addressing the cognitive content, processes, and structure in anxiety.

COGNITIVE CONTENT

Jim came into therapy because of persistent ruminative, anxious thoughts about his job performance. These were primarily of the "What if . . . ?" variety: "What if I do a poor job on this project?" and "What if I lose my job?" The more Jim engaged in these statements, the more extreme they became, indicating that he was catastrophizing. Once begun, this rumination was difficult to terminate and he felt himself becoming more and more tense.

Therapy for Jim began with teaching him hypnotic relaxation. The therapist used a relaxation induction technique to help Jim relax his muscles and to learn where he was especially tense:

> And now, Jim, I'd like you to sit back in the chair and close your eyes. Although you may not feel very relaxed at the moment, just allow yourself to be as relaxed as you can. It is important to allow yourself to feel comfortable with your ability to do whatever you can right now—without worrying about what you can't do. As you sit there, I'm going to mention each of the muscle groups in turn and ask you to note how tense they are and then relax them. During this time, pay particular attention to the sound of my voice. Note first the muscles in your head: behind your ears, around your eyes, your jaw, and your tongue. Note especially any tension in your tongue, since

that's often one of the tension points in the body. That's good . . . now let these muscles slowly relax. [The therapist can obtain some information about progress by observing bodily changes such as the slackening of the jaw.] Now pay attention to the muscles in your neck and shoulders, relaxing them as you do—and feeling your shoulders sag. [In a good hypnotic subject the head may begin to roll slightly, which should cause the therapist no concern.] Now pay attention to the muscles in your arms and hands, relaxing them as you do. Now pay attention to the muscles in your stomach and your thighs—feeling yourself sink deeper into the chair as you do.

The therapist then proceeded to move down Jim's body with different muscle groups, observing and mentioning bodily changes and interpreting them as progress in going into a trance, and adjusting the speed of the relaxation accordingly. Alternatively, the therapist might have instructed Jim to feel the tension draining down through his body as he relaxed more and more.

The second set of interventions addressed Jim's catastrophic "What if . . . ?" ruminations. Since Jim was not always aware of the content of his ruminations, the therapist used two methods to uncover them. Jim was asked to keep a log of the thoughts that ran through his mind when he was feeling anxious. Although he had difficulty with this assignment at first, with the therapist's prompting and support, he was gradually able to be more precise in reporting these thoughts. While in a trance, Jim was taught to imagine himself in a problematic situation (identified beforehand) and to report what thoughts were going through his mind. As part of the prehypnotic preparation, Jim had been told that it was common for hypnotized people to talk while in trance. The therapist wrote these statements down. The following hypnotic routine was used:

Therapist: Jim, I'd like you to imagine that you have been called into your boss's office for your six-month evaluation. As you focus on that scene, allow yourself to feel the typical anxiety. Now feel yourself relaxing your body as we practiced before and feel your anxiety diminish somewhat. Now tell me what you are thinking.

Jim: I'm thinking, "What if he doesn't like my work?" "What if I get fired?" If I lose my job, I'll be a total failure!

During the next session, the therapist helped Jim to construct positive self-statements to counteract each negative thought. The two-column method (Table 6–1) was used in this manner:

Table 6–1. Negative and Positive Content for Jim

Negative Thoughts	Positive Self-Statements
1. What if he doesn't like my work?	1. He's always liked it before and I have no reason to think he won't now.
2. What if I get fired?	2. There's no evidence I will be fired and I've always been able to find another job before.
3. If I lose my job, I'll be a total failure.	3. Even if I were to fail at this job, it doesn't mean I'd fail at everything else.

The therapist then, while Jim was in a trance, asked him to think first of the negative thought, then say the positive statement to himself. Similar to J. S. Beck's (1995) coping in the image, he was also ask to imagine his boss before him while doing so.

> Now that you're feeling comfortably relaxed, Jim, I'd like you to say out loud one of the negative things to say to yourself. That's good! Now relax your body as we've practiced! That's good! Now say out loud the positive statement you learned. Now practice to yourself first saying the negative, then the positive statement, continuing to relax. Now let those thoughts fade from your mind; count from five to one, and gradually come out of the trance.

The replacement of the negative statements with positive statements should be repeated within a single hypnotic session as well as across sessions. Strongly entrenched cognitions, of whatever variety, do not easily yield to alternative ones and repetition is important. Despite anecdotes in the literature describing one-session hypnotic cures, in almost all instances hypnotic repetition is necessary for new learning to take place. Repetition of the relaxation process is also helpful and many therapists make audiotapes of this technique that clients can play periodically between sessions. In this way clients can begin to relax more easily and more quickly so that it starts to become an automatic activity. Eventually they may begin to relax the moment they walk into the therapist's office.

COGNITIVE PROCESSES

Beck and Emery (1985) have described some of the thinking distortions common in anxiety disorders, such as hypervigilance (always on alert), catastrophizing (expecting the worst), selective abstraction (noticing only the bad aspects of a situation), loss of perspective (not realizing what is statistically likely to happen), and dichotomous thinking (if things are not perfect, they are terrible). For an example of the modification of cognitive processes, consider the case of Jane. Jane came to therapy because of a strong fear of public speaking. Unfortunately, her new job required that she speak before audiences periodically and she was terrified at the prospect. She imagined herself speaking in a high-pitched, quavering voice, hands shaking, and the object of ridicule by her audience. As is common in anxiety disorders, Jane's limited exposure to public speaking did not habituate her to the experience; rather, it simply validated her worst fears. What she feared did indeed happen: her voice was high-pitched, she spoke rapidly, and her hands shook.

Jane exhibited many of the cognitive processing distortions of anxiety. She catastrophized and expected the worst to happen. She expected herself to be a perfect speaker, with no distress at all and with flawless diction, thus demonstrating dichotomous thinking ("If I'm not perfect,

I'm no good!"). When speaking, even in small groups, she constantly scanned her environment, looking for signs her listeners were displeased with her, thus demonstrating hypervigilance. This had the added drawback of diverting her attention from what she was saying and causing her to stumble vocally and mispronounce words. Naturally, these instances were all she remembered later (selective abstraction), and she was unable to recall examples of a relatively successful verbal presentation. The failures came to dominate her thinking about herself as a public speaker, thus demonstrating loss of perspective.

After initially teaching Jane relaxation techniques as described earlier, the therapist decided to use age progression, or, as described by J. S. Beck (1995), jumping ahead in time. In age progression, which orientates the client toward the future, the therapist asks the client to imagine herself in a future problematic situation with all the fears associated with that situation and then to imagine herself coping with the anxiety in new ways. In preparation for this hypnotic session, the therapist asked Jane to describe how she would act in a public speaking situation if she weren't anxious. Jane provided the following description:

> I'd speak in a deep, clear, and slow voice. I'd feel confident about what I was saying. My hands wouldn't shake and I wouldn't feel a sinking feeling in my stomach. I wouldn't keep looking at the audience all the time, trying to figure out what they were thinking about my presentation. I would feel that I really had something worthwhile to say, rather than simply wasting their time.

The therapist also discussed with Jane when her next speech would be, the audience to be addressed, its size, and other relevant data.

After hypnotizing Jane via a relaxation method and using the deepening staircase technique ending in a reclining chair, the therapist used the following hypnotic routine:

> You have told me that you will give your speech one week from today, on a Wednesday. As I count off the days, we will go forward in time to the day of your speech. This is Wednesday (*pause*)—Thurs-

day (*pause*)—Friday (*pause*)—Saturday (*pause*)—Sunday (*pause*)—
Monday (*pause*)—Tuesday (*pause*)—Wednesday. It's Wednesday
next week, 2:00 P.M. and it's time for your speech. Now I'd like you to
imagine [or see] yourself preparing to give your speech. As you walk
onto the stage, you see people in the audience looking at you ex-
pectantly. You feel a momentary anxiety but you relax yourself as
we've practiced (pause), that's right. You walk slowly out onto the
stage feeling more relaxed and comfortable. You notice the audience
and say to yourself, "Isn't it great that they have come to hear me!"
You remind yourself that you know the material and you feel excited
about the chance to share it with them. Just continue to relax and
feel good about your opportunity to share what you know—that's
right (*pause*). Now imagine [or see] yourself beginning the speech.
You deliberately slow down and lower your voice—knowing that it
will seem much lower and slower than it does to them . . . lower and
slower, lower and slower—feeling better and better about your speech
as you speak lower and slower, lower and slower. That's right! And
you can also feel even more relaxed and confident as you feel yourself speaking lower and slower, lower and slower. You notice the
audience looking intently at you and you say to yourself, "They are
really interested in what I'm saying—and I'm saying it well! I can feel
myself saying it well and I feel enthusiastic about giving this speech."
Now continue to imagine [or see yourself] giving your speech, relaxing as you go, and feeling more and more confident—speaking
lower and slower, lower and slower . . . and the more you speak lower
and slower, the more confident and energetic you feel . . . and the
more confident and energetic you feel, the lower and slower you
speak.

This routine, with variations, was continued for several more minutes with periodic pauses to allow Jane to absorb the material and to
both imagine (see) and feel herself in the situation. The word *see* can
have a more immediate quality to it than the word *imagine*; hypnotherapists may wish to use the latter term if the client does not appear
to be in a deep trance, or if a high level of anxiety is aroused, and the

former term if the client is in a lighter trance or has less anxiety. If desired, the therapist can gradually substitute "see" for "imagine."

COGNITIVE STRUCTURES

As discussed previously, these are enduring tacit predispositions to think and respond in certain ways. Beck and Emery (1985) have referred to (tacit) cognitive rules that are often part of anxious cognitive structures. Examples include: "Any strange situation should be regarded as dangerous," "It is always best to assume the worst," "In unfamiliar situations, I must be wary and keep my mouth shut" (p. 63). Behind all these rules is a guiding assumption of personal danger, which Beck and Emery argue is the central cognitive construct in anxiety. Leahy (1996) suggests that the cognitive themes behind anxiety are threat, imminent loss and failure, and loss of control. Thus anxiety has an anticipatory, future-oriented locus.

Several of Young's (1994) early maladaptive schemas, described in the previous chapter, have a strong anxious cognitive component as part of their structure, including dependence/incompetence, vulnerability to danger, approval-seeking, vulnerability/negativity, defectiveness/shame, mistrust/abuse, and unrelenting standards. Indeed, most of Young's EMSs appear to have an anxious component, at least in part. Anxiety is truly the malady of the age!

Because these cognitive structural schemas are experienced by people as simply "the way things are," it can be difficult to address them directly. Therapist attempts to challenge these tacit schemata openly are often met with considerable resistance because clients may feel they are being asked to give up a central aspect of their identity. As Mahoney (1991) has observed, challenges to people's sense of personal identity are deeply unsettling and are appropriately met with considerable resistance. Therefore, indirect methods for addressing these core cognitive structures are often more likely to be successful. However, a skilled therapist can often use more direct methods for addressing tacit core beliefs. Therefore, both types will be discussed.

Direct Methods

Jay initially presented with anxiety regarding his performance both at work and in his relations with women. At work he was haunted by a fear that he would not perform to the expectations of his supervisor. While he felt he had thus far duped his boss into thinking he was competent, he was constantly afraid he would be found out and exposed as a fraud. He described himself as constantly scanning his environment for signs that his boss was displeased with his work and checking it for minute errors.

With women he found himself constantly checking (verbally and nonverbally) for signs they approved of his behavior and liked him. His manner therefore tended to be ingratiating and, needless to say, his behavior exasperated and alienated most women. This only reinforced his feeling of interpersonal anxiety, resulting in a redoubling of his ingratiating efforts and checking behaviors, leading in turn to more failure and more anxiety. Jay was caught in a vicious circle.

During the initial sessions, the therapist identified two major tacit (core) beliefs that appeared to be behind Jay's distress. In his work situation Jay seemed to exhibit unrelenting standards, which is part of Young's (1994) overvigilance and inhibition early maladaptive schema. This is similar to Ellis's (Ellis and Dryden 1997) irrational beliefs of phonyism and perfectionism, as well as one of the helpless core beliefs ("I am incompetent") described by J. S. Beck (1995). Likewise, Jay's relationship problems with women seemed to stem from an early maladaptive schema of defectiveness/shame and perhaps, to some extent, emotional deprivation (deprivation of nurturance). These are similar to several of J. S. Beck's negative core beliefs, such as "I am unlovable," "I am bound to be rejected," and "I am unworthy."

Dowd (1997b) has described several methods for modifying core cognitive schemata. For modifying Jay's work-related EMS, the therapist chose replacement and coping imagery. This is similar to J. S. Beck's (1995) following images to completion and coping in the image. After entering a hypnotic trance, Jay was asked to imagine himself being scolded by his boss for inadequate work and coping with the situation.

The hypnotic routine went as follows (vocally stressed words are in bold type):

> I'd like you, Jay, to see yourself facing your boss. He has found a problem with one of your recent jobs and is asking you about it. As you listen to him, you can feel your anxiety rising. But you also see yourself straightening up and looking directly at him [Jay tended to look at the floor when anxious]. As you continue to look at him and stand tall, you can feel your anxiety diminish. As your anxiety starts to diminish, you begin to feel more **competent**, less of a **phony**, more **in charge**. You even feel **less perfect**, but you know that's okay— because no one can be perfect and that's okay too. You can see yourself being **competent** too; **competent** and **in charge**—as you stand tall and face your boss. Now you see yourself answering him, **clearly**, **calmly**, and **without fear**. That's right! And the more you see yourself answering him **clearly**, **calmly**, **without fear**, the less anxiety you feel—and the less anxiety you feel, the more you see yourself answering him **clearly**, **calmly**, **without fear**. It's really interesting, isn't it, how you can feel **more relaxed** by feeling **less perfect**—almost like a relief, isn't it? And you can have this feeling of relief anytime you want, by relaxing your perfection away and using this feeling of relief to help you relax even more. Now I'd like you to let that scene fade from your mind while continuing to feel more and more comfortable, more and more relaxed.

After Jay came out of the trance, the therapist discussed with him his reactions to the coping imagery and what he had learned from it.

For Jay's problem with women, the therapist chose hypnotic cognitive rehearsal (Dowd 1997b) along with hypnotic relaxation. The hypnotic routine went like this:

> See yourself walking up to _____, standing up straight and looking her in the eye. You wonder if she likes [loves] you but you decide not to ask her. You really don't need to, do you? She's with you right now and that's really all the information you need, isn't it? If she didn't

like [love] you, she wouldn't be with you, would she? Isn't it relaxing to know that **you're really a likable [lovable] guy?** Isn't it relaxing to know that **you're really a desirable guy?** See yourself just talking with her, being yourself, not checking her behavior, **feeling comfortable and relaxed** just being with her, knowing she is with you because she wants to be with you, feeling comfortable in that knowledge, not needing to do anything more. Feeling again the tremendous power of doing nothing or doing less. [This is a technique discussed earlier with Jay.] Now spend a few moments seeing yourself interacting with _____ in that way and then let that scene slowly fade from your mind.

After Jay came out of the trance, the therapist discussed the scene with him—how realistic it had seemed, how he had felt, and what he had learned from it. In doing hypnotic cognitive rehearsal, it is important to ascertain the client's response to and comfort with the cognitive imagery in order to modify it in future sessions.

Indirect Methods

Because Jay was unusually open and nondefensive, the therapist chose direct methods of working on his problems. However, had he been more resistant, the therapist might have chosen indirect methods. Following is an example of the use of indirect hypnotherapy applied to Jay's hypothesized core cognitive schemas.

Ericksonian hypnotherapists generally (though not always) rely on indirect inductions and routines (e.g., Erickson and Rossi 1979). Because these can be highly complex and convoluted, the reader is advised to obtain further training before attempting to use them. They are neither as simple nor as easy to implement as they often appear. In general, they rely on implanting suggestions via metaphor and allusion rather than by direct suggestions. These suggestions are often embedded in a natural flow of conversational communication so there is no clear break between the induction and the hypnotic routine. They can also make use of divided consciousness, wherein the client's attention is diverted from important aspects of the communication as a way of gradually shaping memory (Fleming et al. 1992). Occasionally, Ericksonian hypno-therapists appear not to even address the problem behavior or situation at all. A truncated example of a more indirect hypnotic routine for Jay's work-related problem might look like this. Stressed words are in bold type:

> Jay, I'd like you to listen as I talk—paying attention to my words but gradually letting your mind drift off into other things. You really don't need to pay close conscious attention to what I say . . . your **unconscious mind** will hear what it needs to hear—what it wants to hear. **You can enter into a trance** any way you choose—either by closing your eyes or keeping them open, whichever you choose. As I continue to talk, you can allow yourself to go as deeply into a trance as you wish—that's right—feeling good about whatever you do (*pause*). When you were very young, Jay, you probably wondered if you were good enough—good enough to do all the things you wanted to do— all the things others wanted you to do. As you got older, you discovered that you could do many things well—more and more things well. You began to feel good about your ability. Yet perhaps there was still that childhood voice—wondering if you were **good enough**—wondering if you were **going to make it**. As the years went by, **you did make it**—but the childhood voice still remained—wondering and asking if you were good enough, if you would make it. Perhaps the childhood voice is still there—still asking if you are good enough, if you will make it. But that childhood voice can now be replaced by an adult voice, saying, "**I** *have* **made it; I** *am* **good enough!**" And, as I continue to talk to you, you can hear these two voices—and gradually let the adult voice dominate. So, the more you think, "**I** *have* **made it!**," the more you can begin to feel confident and comfortable, **confident and comfortable**—knowing that you can continue to find comfort in your ability—knowing you, Jay, **don't have to be perfect**, just good enough. And you can find comfort and relaxation in not being perfect, in being good enough—knowing that the more comfort you

find, the better you will feel about your abilities and the better you feel about your abilities, the more comfort you will find. It's comfortable, isn't it, to **feel not perfect—good enough**.

An indirect hypnotic routine for Jay's problem with women might look like this:

> As you become more and more comfortable, you can, if you wish, begin to experience trance in any way that you wish—knowing that your unconscious mind will learn what it needs to learn—what it wants to learn. As you become more comfortable, your unconscious mind can begin to look at your concern—focusing on all the ways it influences your relations with women. And your unconscious mind can **begin to look at new ways of thinking—new ways of acting**. Your unconscious mind can begin to see **new and desirable** possibilities, not only what you desire but also what **others desire in you— how others desire you**. And you can begin to think of all the **desirable parts of you—all the ways others desire you**. And the more you think of that, the more comfort you can feel—**desiring even more comfort**, and seeing **yourself as desirable**. All these new ways of looking at yourself are exciting, aren't they? Opening up new and **desirable** possibilities for you . . .

In both of these examples, the early maladaptive schemas are addressed, though in different ways. In Ericksonian hypnotherapy, creativity is very important and each hypnotherapist learns how to adapt the general guidelines to his or her own personal style.

PHOBIAS

Phobias can be thought of as especially strong unrealistic fears that are also characterized by avoidance of one or more objects or situations (Golden et al. 1987). They generally persist over time and can become worse or generalize to other situations. Crawford and Barabasz (1993) discuss evidence indicating that the effectiveness of hypnosis with phobics may be due to their unusually high hypnotic capacity and their ability both to visualize and construct vivid images and to focus their attention. In fact, traditional systematic desensitization may be more effective when used in a hypnotic context with highly susceptible individuals. Although a relationship between higher levels of hypnotizability and therapeutic outcome has been shown in several studies (Crawford and Barabasz 1993), it is still necessary to screen individual clients for hypnotic capacity because high hypnotizability is not found in all phobic individuals.

Because phobias are organized around one or more specific objects or situations, I will illustrate the cognitive hypnotherapy of phobias by addressing the cognitive content only. The cognitive processes and cognitive structures implicated in phobias can be addressed as with anxiety disorders.

As an example of the hypnotherapeutic treatment of cognitive content, consider the case of Mary. Mary had been referred for therapy by her husband because she had become progressively more afraid of traveling so that now she could leave her house only in the presence of her husband, and even then for only short periods of time. Mary was afflicted with the disorder commonly known as agoraphobia, or the progressive restriction of movement due to the fear of open spaces.

A cognitive assessment indicated that Mary had catastrophic expectations of fainting or having a heart attack while in a public space. She feared that no one would be able, or want, to help her. When away from home she experienced a variety of somatic symptoms, such as heart racing, muscle weakness, and perspiring, which she interpreted as "proof" she was going to faint or have a heart attack. These symptoms had begun several years before after she had tripped and fallen at a shopping mall. Although not hurt, she had been embarrassed by the attention she had received and thereafter avoided that mall. Gradually she became anxious whenever she went to *any* mall, and then to any public place where she might embarrass herself. Eventually she felt comfortable only at home.

An initial assessment of her trance capacity showed that Mary had the potential to be a good hypnotic subject. Accordingly, after discussion with her, the therapist chose to use a hypnotic routine for phobia treatment. Following the cognitive model, the therapist conducted cognitive restructuring (Beck and Emery 1985) in an attempt to change Mary's beliefs that her somatic symptoms were indications that she would faint or have a heart attack.

The therapist's first task was to reeducate Mary concerning the meaning of her symptoms by providing basic information about the symptoms of anxiety and panic and how they can be easily mistaken for heart problems. Mary had never actually fainted and the therapist was able to show her that the likelihood of her doing so was small. The second task was to teach her basic muscle relaxation techniques that she could later use in a trance. After three sessions of looking at the evidence for her symptoms as being heart-related and examining other ways of interpreting her symptoms, as well as practicing relaxation, Mary felt ready to proceed to the hypnotherapeutic stage.

Because Mary was able to visualize very well (she in fact constantly visualized having a heart attack or fainting), the therapist chose a modification of imagery approach (Beck and Emery 1985), using hypnosis to recall the image and modify it. Many of Beck and Emery's imagery-modification techniques have a strong hypnotic quality. After a standard induction, the therapist used the following hypnotic routine to modify the image by repeatedly substituting a coping image for it:

> Now, Mary I'd like you to imagine [or see] yourself in the shopping mall. You're walking around looking at things, and as you do you begin to notice a little anxiety; your heart starts to beat faster and your palms begin to sweat. But you now realize that these are signs of anxiety, not heart problems, and you let yourself relax as we've discussed, letting your muscles relax and letting your mind relax—that's right. As you do so, you can feel your heart slow down a bit—feel yourself feel more comfortable. You notice people around you—but you realize they really aren't looking at you and they aren't even interested in you—they're too busy with their own lives, just like you are. And you can find comfort and relaxation in knowing that—they really don't notice you very much, and even if one did, how would that hurt

you? It really doesn't matter, does it—and as you realize that, you can relax even more. And as you look around the store, you can feel yourself more comfortable—relaxing, relaxing. Now you begin to walk around the store, looking at different things . . . and if you begin to feel anxious or weak, you can relax your muscles and your mind—feeling yourself **let go** of your anxieties, your tension, **let go** of your fears . . . knowing that what you have feared really won't happen.

This routine was repeatedly practiced, with variations as appropriate, several times over the course of several sessions until Mary could easily relax her anxiety away (repeating the image; J. S. Beck 1995). At first, when she was unable to relax sufficiently, the therapist instructed her while in the trance to "let that scene fade from your mind and let your mind go blank." Eventually, with patient coaching, Mary was able to begin venturing from her house (though not immediately to the mall) by using the relaxation and imagery coping strategies she had been taught.

SUMMARY

Anxiety is an extremely common psychological disorder, indeed perhaps "the" disorder of the twentieth century. Occasionally it can become extreme and focused enough to be classified as a phobia. Fortunately, it is a very treatable condition. Hypnosis, in conjunction with relaxation and imagery techniques, is well suited to treat the cognitive manifestations of anxiety at all levels. Clients typically can learn a variety of coping strategies that they can use in other anxiety-arousing situations.

7

Stress-Related Disorders

In many ways, stress disorders are similar to anxiety disorders; indeed Golden and colleagues (1987) include them as part of a chapter on the hypnotic treatment of anxiety and phobia. However, they are different enough, especially as manifested in posttraumatic stress disorders, that a separate treatment is warranted. Accordingly, this chapter describes the use of hypnosis in treating PTSD as a class of stress disorders.

Stress has been defined by Selye (1956) as the nonspecific result of any demand upon the body. This definition is response-based and nonspecific. Other theorists, however, have argued that stress occurs because of a complex interaction between environmental demands, one's perceptions of these demands, and one's perceived ability to meet or alter them. For example, Lazarus and Folkman (1984) stated that stress is defined by the appraisal of the environmental stressor and an individual's perceived ability (or lack of it) to cope with the demands presented by the stressor. In this conceptualization, stress is seen in terms of environmental or internal demands that tax or exceed the adaptive resources of the individual. Thus both the nature of the demand, or stressor, and the quantity and quality of the resources available to the individual should determine the experience of "stress."

Stressful life events have been consistently shown to be associated with a variety of psychological and physical disorders. Even positive events may result in some stress; negative events result in even more stress. Positive events include marriage, childbirth, and purchasing one's first house. Negative events include death of a loved one, divorce, rape/sexual abuse, and rarer events such as natural disasters and wartime experiences. Many of these negative events, if sufficiently severe, can result in what is commonly known today as posttraumatic stress disorder. Earlier terms for this disorder under wartime conditions were "shell shock" and "battle fatigue." Thus the newer concept of PTSD encompasses but is not limited to trauma due to war.

Two different theories have been used to account for war-related PTSD (Donovan et al. 1996), reflecting the interaction between person and event. Residual stress theory (RST) focuses on the aversive and toxic nature of the war experience in accounting for PTSD. In other words, combat itself is the cause. However, stress evaporation theory (SET) proposes that premilitary variables play a primary role in PTSD. In other words, individual differences are the key. Donovan and colleagues found combat exposure to be the strongest single predictor of PTSD. However, they also found childhood physical punishment to be a significant predictor. They suggested that PTSD may be fostered or increased by a history of childhood abuse, since abused individuals may be more vulnerable than others.

There are three major types of symptoms in PTSD (Spiegel 1996): intrusive symptoms (flashbacks, preoccupation with the traumatic event), emotional numbing (a loss of pleasure), and hyperarousal (exaggerated responses to trauma-relevant stimuli). Hypnosis may be especially useful in treating PTSD because there is an analogy between these types of symptoms and three major components of hypnosis: absorption, dissociation, and suggestibility (Spiegel 1996). Consequently, it may be especially important to assess clients for trance capacity before using hypnosis in treating PTSD. It is possible that highly hypnotizable individuals may be more likely to experience PTSD symptoms as a response to trauma. They may also be more likely to become absorbed in the symptoms without conscious reflection. Likewise, the emotional numbing suggests a hypnotic dissociation and the hyperarousal state resembles heightened hypnotic responsiveness to cues (Spiegel 1996). These abilities may all be used in the hypnotic treatment of PTSD.

According to Spiegel (1993), the use of hypnosis in the treatment of PTSD fundamentally involves providing a controlled access to the traumatic memories and helping clients to control the strong emotions and physiological responses that can result. In addition, hypnosis can help clients in distancing and decentering from the immediacy of their traumatic experience and assist them in putting it in a larger perspective. Suggestions for resolution of the traumatic experience can be given in a hypnotic trance. Finally, the actual memory of the traumatic event can sometimes be modified as well.

COGNITIVE CONTENT

The cognitive content of many PTSD disorders consist of intrusive and uncontrollable flashbacks to the traumatic event itself along with a strong emotional arousal. What is important in treating these cases is providing clients with a way of reducing the arousal and controlling the intrusive symptoms. For an example of how this might be done, let us look at the case of George.

George was a Vietnam veteran who had gone through the Tet Offensive in 1968. He had been in the middle of some especially savage fighting and had seen many of his men killed. Because he was the platoon leader, he felt a special responsibility for these deaths and blamed himself for not having led his men out of danger. His flashbacks consisted primarily of gruesome visions of dead men along with visions of himself moving very slowly and ineffectually in battle. An analysis of his automatic thoughts during the flashbacks provided the following as examples: "I never should have led my men into that situation!" "I'm a terrible leader, responsible for all those deaths!" "I should have done more; it's all my fault." These flashbacks and automatic thoughts were immediately followed by strong emotional arousal, including shaking, sweating, and inability to concentrate.

In actual fact, according to his superiors, George had behaved in an exemplary fashion and was responsible for saving many of his men. He had been led into a trap by the Vietcong and had held off a superior force until reinforcements arrived, at which time the Vietcong had been routed. Nevertheless, he held himself responsible and would not believe those who told him otherwise.

George proved to be a moderately hypnotizable client and was quite interested in using hypnosis. It is important that the client be comfortable with hypnosis as a treatment method because some PTSD clients are afraid they will be overwhelmed with uncontrollable memories while in trance. The therapist initially chose to focus on George's automatic thoughts during flashbacks and to help him distance from the immediacy of these flashbacks (distancing; J. S. Beck 1995). After an induction, the hypnotic routine was as follows:

> Now, George, I'd like you to imagine yourself once more in one of your flashbacks—but this time looking at yourself from a distance [a distancing technique]. See the fighting, yourself in the fighting, but it seems a long ways away—almost like it's happening to someone else. You feel curiously detached, almost like you aren't entirely there. And your feelings about the image are reduced too—like they're there but not as strong. It's an interesting feeling, isn't it? Now, as you hear yourself saying, "I'm not doing enough, I never should have led my platoon here," immediately say the following words instead: "I'm not responsible for being here, I'm doing the best I can in a bad situation." Keep repeating those thoughts [therapist repeats alternative statements over and over]—that's right. And as you repeat these thoughts, you can begin to feel yourself calming down, becoming less aroused. It feels good, doesn't it?

After practicing these alternative self-statements with George for several sessions, the therapist then taught George a coping strategy for controlling the flashbacks—the telescope technique. The hypnotic routine was structured like this:

> I'd like you once again to bring the flashback image into your mind—but this time look at it through the wrong end of a telescope [a distancing technique]. As you see the smaller image, you can make it even smaller by extending the telescope even longer—and make it bigger by shortening the telescope. Shorter and longer—bigger and smaller, you can control the size of the image. And you notice that every time you make the image smaller, you feel less arousal. Bigger, more arousal—smaller, less arousal. That's right, very good. And you can feel more and more comfortable about your ability to raise and lower your arousal. So when you experience the flashbacks, you can immediately look at them through the wrong end of the telescope and make them smaller and less powerful, smaller and less powerful, smaller and less powerful . . .

The telescope technique was used to help George reduce, through distancing, his immediate absorption in the traumatic flashback and enable him to more rationally assess the reality of his thoughts and feelings. The coping self-statements were used to assist him in this process of reality testing and reconstructing. George reported that the flashbacks had begun to diminish both in frequency and intensity.

COGNITIVE PROCESSES

George also exhibited at least two of the cognitive distortions identified by J. S. Beck (1995) and discussed in Chapter 2, disqualifying or discounting the positive and labeling. George discounted the heroic efforts he had made in extricating several of his men from a bad situation and concentrated only on the ones he had been unable to save. There were also echoes of magnification/minimization because George magnified his failures and minimized his successes. Consequently, he labeled himself as a "terrible" leader. In addition to the interventions directed at the cognitive contents described previously, the therapist also used the following hypnotic routine directed at these cognitive processes.

> It's very easy, isn't it, George [The use of "isn't it?" is designed to encourage a set of acquiescence in the client.] to look only at negative interpretations of a situation? It's easy for all of us and part of the human condition [normalizes his cognitions]. But as I'm sure you know [another use of the acquiescence set], it's important for all of us to look at both positive and negative interpretations of a situation. Reality isn't complete without it. And, if we look at only one interpretation, we begin to label ourselves accordingly. So if we look at only the negative, we label ourselves negatively . . . (pause) . . . if we look only at the positive, we label ourselves positively. So while it's important to look at all aspects of a situation, it's important as well to look at as many positive aspects as we can. Let me suggest about a 60–40 split in general; 60 percent positive, 40 percent negative* (pause). So now, George, I'd like you to imagine all the men in your unit whom you managed to save. Focus on their faces, remember their names, see them as they were, feel their expressions of gratitude toward you for your help and leadership. Let the index finger of your right hand rise when you have that image [ideomotor signaling]. That's right! Very good! Now keep that image in your mind and slowly let it unfold, seeing the men you saved, seeing and hearing their expressions of gratitude for your leadership . . . savoring the unfolding image [pause for several seconds, even up to a minute or longer]. And as you focus on this unfolding and continuing image, you can begin to see yourself in a more positive light, as an effective leader who did his best and whose best was very good indeed. You don't have to be perfect, do you, to be effective? And you now have a new coping tool, don't you? So whenever you feel bad about your behavior in combat, you can think about all the men who valued and appreciated your help and leadership.

---

*Research by Schwartz and Garomoni (1989) on "states of mind" (SOM) indicates that a positive-negative automatic thoughts ratio for optimal mental health is 62.

This routine was used, extended and with variations, for additional sessions. As mentioned on several occasions, repetition is crucial in changing cognitive distortions to more adaptive ones.

COGNITIVE STRUCTURES

For an example of the use of hypnosis in the treatment of another form of PTSD, let's examine the case of Nancy. Whereas George's symptom cluster revolved around intrusive cognitions and hyperarousal, Nancy's symptoms were more complex. They consisted primarily of emotional numbing with some intrusive cognitions. A close male family member had sexually molested her over a period of several years, which she was able to remember. Eventually she told her mother, who responded by not allowing that family member to have further contact with Nancy. She thought she had "put the whole incident behind me" but reported that she had occasional flashbacks to a molestation incident. In addition, she did not enjoy sex with her husband and tried in general to avoid physical intimacy as much as she could. She said she deliberately "turned off" emotionally at moments of closeness and tried not to feel anything. Often she was able to do so by thinking of other things or by seeing herself from a distance.

Tests of hypnotic susceptibility indicated that Nancy had good trance capacity and she was interested in using hypnosis. Preliminary conversations revealed that she understood that, as a child, she was not responsible for the molestation. However, she still had some ruminative thoughts that she was at least partly responsible for it because she liked his company and "I enjoyed it." Although she could not describe it as such, the therapist thought that Nancy felt she was somehow "soiled" and did not deserve to have an enjoyable intimate relationship with her husband. In Young's (1994) schema terms (see Chapter 5), there appeared to be elements of punitiveness. A hypnotic intervention was therefore structured first around changing her cognitions of self-blame (the cognitive content) and second around increasing her sense of pleasure from physical intimacy and decreasing her emotional numbing (the cognitive structures). After a hypnotic induction placed Nancy in a trance, the therapist used an indirect hypnotic routine designed to reduce Nancy's feelings of self-blame for the abuse. This routine can thus be seen as a memory change, if not a substitution, because the therapist used divided attention to inculcate the message that Nancy was not at fault. The routine went somewhat like this (vocally stressed words are in bold type):

> Nancy, I'd like you to gradually relax and let your mind float free—thinking about whatever it wants to think about. And you can **feel confident** that you will hear what you need to hear, what you want to hear—**right here, right now**. That's right, just let your mind float, relaxing itself, feeling free, **listening but not really listening** . . . (*pause*). Nancy, you are aware, I am sure, that children and adults think differently about events, don't they? Children often feel responsible for everything—while adults know that they often are not responsible for what happens. It's a relief, isn't it, to know, as an adult, that you are not responsible for everything, perhaps for less than you think. As an adult, you can instruct the child you once were about responsibility. You can, **Nancy, realize you were not responsible**, learn about responsibility in new and different ways, as you, **Nancy, grow and develop**. . . . Constant change, new ways of looking at things, new sense of power but at the same time sense of your limits—**limits on your responsibility**. And it feels comfortable and relaxing, doesn't it, to realize, to **know** for the first time, that **you weren't responsible**—finding increased comfort in knowing that.

This routine was repeated with variations over several sessions. It is important in this type of hypnotic work to check progress with the client to ensure that the images generated are not causing further distress. Nancy reported that her ruminative thoughts of self-blame had begun to diminish.

Removal of distressing symptoms is a positive outcome but Nancy still had an emotionally impoverished life. The therapist therefore decided to address her emotional numbing and lack of comfort with physical intimacy. She first discussed with Nancy her (Nancy's) interest in actually achieving more intimacy with her husband, especially in the sexual area. Nancy assured her that she indeed did want more intimacy and therefore the therapist chose a combination of hypnotic relaxation and cognitive rehearsal. The hypnotic routine went as follows after a standard induction:

> Nancy, I'd like you to become more and more relaxed, feeling comfortable and full of pleasant feelings. You know that you can become as deeply relaxed as you want right now, at whatever level of trance you feel comfortable with. [It is important to pace yourself in these sensitive areas so as not to push the client too fast.] Now take a moment to find that level of trance, comfort, and relaxation that's just right for you . . . (*pause*). When you have that level, raise the index finger of your right hand [ideomotor signal]. . . . Good! Now I'd like you to see [or imagine] yourself being approached by your husband. As you see [or imagine] him approach, you see [or imagine] yourself reach out to him. It's a new behavior, isn't it—and you can feel comfortable knowing you can always say "No"—but right now, at this moment, you don't really want to. You reach out and hold him as he holds you—just feeling the warmth of his closeness, feeling good about wanting him, feeling happy and relaxed. Now hold that image for a few moments, for as long as you're comfortable with it. If you begin to feel uncomfortable, back away—knowing you can come closer again whenever you want. [It's important to give the client ultimate control.] That's right! (*Pause.*) Now see [or imagine] yourself approaching him once again, this time at your initiation. Feel the happy feelings from wanting to do this. Hold him for as long as you feel comfortable . . . (*pause*). Now let that image fade from your mind as you continue to feel relaxed and comfortable.

Especially in sensitive areas like physical intimacy and sexuality, it is important to move slowly. In this example the intimate images and positive feelings were at first modest in nature. If Nancy is able to approach her husband comfortably in this manner, future sessions can explore greater levels of intimacy and heightened feeling. If not, this level of intimacy should be practiced repeatedly until Nancy becomes comfortable with it. The ultimate level and degree of cognitive hypnotic rehearsal is dictated only by the client (and therapist!) level of comfort with explicit detail. It is best, in situations like this, that the therapist and client be of the same sex to avoid potential embarrassment or other problems.

SUMMARY

Stress-related disorders are quite common in today's world. Whereas anxiety disorders often have no readily identifiable cause, stress disorders do. The stressor may arise from any area of an individual's life and is sometimes severe enough to disrupt functioning on a large scale. If the stressor is severe enough, the resulting disorder may be classified as a posttraumatic stress disorder. Whereas PTSD was once confined to wartime experiences, today it has broadened to include a variety of severe stressors in many aspects of life.

8

Depression

Depression is one of the most common psychological ailments and has been called the common cold of mental health. Everyone feels depressed or at least "down" periodically and generally the feeling is self-limiting. In some instances, however, it is serious and long-lasting enough to require treatment.

There are two types of depression. In unipolar depression, the individual experiences only depression, although it may vary from severe to near normal. In bipolar depression (formerly called manic-depression), however, the individual swings from depression to mania and back again, in cycles of varying length. Because bipolar depression is now considered to be primarily a medical disorder, this chapter focuses on unipolar depression and the less severe dysphoria.

The best developed and researched treatment program for depression is the cognitive therapy of depression as developed by Beck and his colleagues (Beck et al. 1979). They found that depression is characterized by a negative view of the self, the world, and the future. Whether or not these negative cognitions actually *cause* depression, there is ample evidence that cognitive and cognitive-behavioral strategies are effective in *treating* depression, especially of the unipolar variety (Golden et al. 1987). In addition, some individuals experience dysphoria, or mild depression, a condition that, while not severe enough to be classified as clinical depression, is sufficiently debilitating at times to warrant treatment.

Depression may be considered as reactive, in which case it occurs in response to a situational loss or disappointment, or it may be chronic. Individuals with chronic depression or dysphoria are generally seen by others as typically "down" or somewhat sad. Biochemical factors may be implicated in chronic depression; indeed, it has been known for centuries that there are individual differences in depressive style. The ancient Greeks, for example, identified the melancholic as one of the Four Temperaments. Nevertheless, psychological causes may also be present, and psychological interventions may be useful in treatment even with chronically depressed individuals, though their depression may not lift as much as they would like. Appropriate medications may be useful, especially in the initial stages of treatment. However, research has generally shown cognitive therapy to be at least as effective as pharmacotherapy in treating depression and in protecting individuals somewhat against relapse (Evans et al. 1992, Hollon et al. 1992). In reactive depression or dysphoria that is not appropriate and time-limited, cognitive events and cognitive processes are generally the preferred targets for intervention. For more chronic depression or dysphoria, cognitive structures are likely to be implicated in addition to cognitive events and cognitive processes.

Depression has many manifestations (Golden et al. 1987), including emotional symptoms (e.g., crying spells), cognitive symptoms (e.g., excessive self-criticism), behavioral symptoms (e.g., low energy), and physical symptoms (e.g., sleep disturbance). Although one might intervene with any of these classes of symptoms, interventions with the behavioral and cognitive classes of symptoms have shown the most promise. In addition, it has been shown that behavioral activation followed by cognitive interventions can produce the best results (Beck et al. 1979, Kelly and Dowd 1980). Therefore, depressed clients might initially benefit from alert hypnosis (Golden et al. 1987).

Historically, hypnosis has been thought to be contraindicated for depression because it is characterized by a low level of arousal, and traditional hypnotic techniques reduce this arousal even further (Yapko 1993). In addition, some therapists were concerned about symptom substitution should hypnosis succeed in eliminating the depression. However, the use of alert hypnosis should reduce these concerns because it actually activates the client.

ALERT HYPNOSIS

The popular view of hypnosis is that it is a relaxed, almost drowsy state— sleeplike in its attributes. Indeed, hypnotherapists themselves foster this image when they use relaxation as an induction technique and use metaphors of sleep and depth (e.g., "You are going deeper into a trance, you are becoming more and more sleepy"). However, hypnosis can be used to create an energetic and alert state, fostering activation in the process.

Recall that the cognitive view of hypnosis is based on a social influence model. It follows, therefore, that clients will take their cues from the hypnotherapist about what kinds of phenomena are appropriate while in trance. It is thus important to tell clients that they can experience trance as an energizing, rather than a torporous, state and that different people experience trance in different ways. Using "highway hypnosis" or absorption in an activity as examples may help make the point, as well as repeating the definition of hypnosis as focused attention rather than somnolence. In addition, when using alert hypnosis it is important for the therapist to speak in a lively fashion, rather than the soft, soothing tone of voice generally used, and to gradually increase the tempo during the induction. A generic example of alert hypnosis, useful in a variety of situations, is as follows:

> Close your eyes and let your hands rest gently on your legs. Feel yourself as relaxed yet alert, fully in charge, sitting up straight yet not too straight. Now imagine that I have attached a helium balloon to one of your hands—and how that hand begins to feel lighter than the

other. . . . Notice the difference in feeling between the two hands. Feel the lightness in one hand spread to your entire arm, lighter and lighter. . . . Your entire arm is getting lighter and lighter. As it becomes lighter and lighter, you can feel it begin to lift off your leg . . . gradually floating upwards, becoming lighter and lighter . . . up and up . . . higher and higher. As your hand and arm lift, you feel more energetic and alive, full of energy . . . so the higher your arm rises, the more energetic you feel . . . as if the sensation were coursing through your body, filling you with energy and confidence. When your arm rises to the level of your head, it will stop . . . as you continue to feel more energetic and confident.

Now, I'd like you to imagine that you are walking in the woods on a pleasant autumn day. The sky is clear and the air is crisp. . . . You can smell the forest scents and feel the breeze on your cheek. . . . You can hear the crunch of the fallen leaves beneath your feet, the scurrying of little animals in the brush, and the chirping of the birds. . . . On your left you can hear the sound of a busy stream, running over stones. . . . [It is important to engage as many of the senses as possible.] You can feel the energy in the woods as all the creatures gather in food for the winter, busy about their tasks, energetic in their activity. As you see, hear, smell, and feel all the aspects of nature, the cool air and the busy activities encourage you to walk faster and faster . . . and as you walk faster, you can feel yourself becoming more confident and more energetic . . . more energetic and more confident. It feels good! Your whole body feels more energetic! Every time you inhale you can feel yourself becoming more energetic and confident . . . as you exhale you can feel yourself renewing yourself [attaching energy and confidence to a common human activity]. . . . You can feel your heart beating, full of vitality and energy. You can feel the flush on your cheeks and the blood coursing through your veins. . . . And you can recover this feeling whenever you want . . . simply by recalling this invigorating walk; the things you saw, heard, felt, smelled; and the energy and confidence you felt.

It is important to discuss the energizing scene in broad outline with the client before hypnosis is begun. Not everyone likes walking in the woods; what one individual finds energizing another may find boring. Since depressed individuals find few activities to be currently interesting or enjoyable, the hypnotherapist might ask the client what he or she once found enjoyable and use that to construct a pleasant experience. Codevelopment of hypnotic routines with the client is an example of collaborative empiricism (J. S. Beck 1995). Of course, it will not be possible to develop collaboratively all routines, but I recommend that as many as possible be developed together.

COGNITIVE CONTENT

The cognitive self-statements of depressed individuals are characterized by themes of loss and sadness. As Beck and colleagues (1979) stated, clients think they are no good (negative view of the self) and never will be any good or have a good future (negative view of the future) and believe that the world itself is not a good place (negative view of the world). Beck and colleagues (1979) have listed some general assumptions that may predispose an individual to depression, such as:

> In order to be happy, I have to be successful in whatever I undertake.
> To be happy, I must be accepted by all people at all times.
> If I make a mistake, it means I'm inept.
> If somebody disagrees with me, it means he doesn't like me.
> My value as a person depends on what others think of me. [p. 246]

Examples of more specific depressed self-statements include "I'll never be a success, I can't do anything right! I'll never finish this book! The world is an evil place." These self-statements often occur in an obsessive, ruminative fashion and it is difficult to intervene effectively to change them. In addition, clients may be more likely to spontaneously remember past sad events and to negatively interpret current ambiguous stimuli when they are depressed. Or, as Schacter (1996) put it, people seem to remember events through the filter of their later emotional state. This is known as the *mood congruence effect* and is explained in greater detail by Dowd and Courchaine (1996). Thus ruminative depressive self-statements tend to reinforce themselves in a circular fashion, making intervention difficult. Some attempts have been made to deliberately facilitate recall by matching one's current mood to one's mood at the time of the original experience, but this phenomenon has been unreliable (Dowd and Courchaine 1996).

Because of the circular, self-reinforcing quality of depressive self-statements, I recommend that an alert hypnosis routine be conducted first, especially with more depressed clients. It can provide a pleasant introduction to hypnosis in general, as well as an energizing experience, and can encourage the client to continue. Alert hypnosis can in fact merge seamlessly into a form of age progression known as *time projection* (Golden et al. 1987).

In time projection the client is first asked to construct a list of activities that used to be or are currently enjoyable (in case the client still finds some events enjoyable). These events can, and perhaps should, be relatively simple activities such as walking, bicycling, listening to music, or reading. The client is then asked to imagine him- or herself engaging in these activities in the future. Audiotapes can be made of these sessions so the client can listen to them at home. Throughout the session the therapist makes suggestions about how much the client is enjoying these activities. Since these events are safely in the future, it is easier to imagine them providing pleasure than it would be now. But for all of us the future eventually arrives.

For an example of time projection, let's consider the case of Jan, who came to therapy because of depression after being laid off from work. Although she "knew" she had been laid off because of a general reduction in the workforce, she had obsessive ruminative thoughts about her inadequacies as an employee. These perceived inadequacies had begun to generalize to other areas of her life so that she was now beginning to criticize her activities as a wife and mother as well. The therapist, in collaboration with Jan, determined that she had once enjoyed taking long bicycle rides and found this activity to be both relaxing and energizing. Once Jan was in a trance, the following routine was used:

Jan, you know that bicycling was once a very enjoyable activity for you. And you know people change, don't they [an example of a truism designed to foster agreement] . . . and "what was once so yet may be." You do remember, don't you, how you once enjoyed it? So now I'd like you to go with me to the future, where perhaps it may again be enjoyable. It's now November, and as I count off the weeks and months you will be able to imagine yourself traveling into the future. . . . December, first week, second week, third week, fourth week; . . . January, first week, second week, third week, fourth week; . . . February, first week, second week, third week, fourth week; . . . March, first week, second week, third week, fourth week; . . . April, first week, second week, third week, fourth week; . . . May, first week, second week, third week, fourth week; . . . June, first week, second week. . . . It's now the second week in June and a beautiful day! Imagine yourself taking your bike off its hooks and adjusting the mechanism. You hop on and begin to ride . . . as you do so, you begin to feel the old sense of excitement and energy as your legs go up and down . . . up and down . . . you feel the wind in your hair, on your face . . . feeling the sun on your skin, warming you all over. And as you continue to ride, you can feel your heart beating faster—not racing—but a steady, solid, energetic beat. You can feel the blood throbbing through your veins—a good feeling, energizing. It feels very pleasant, doesn't it, to have this much energy in your body! And as you continue to ride, you can feel this energy and aliveness pervade your entire body—moving through it, suffusing your body with warmth and energy. Now continue to ride for a few more moments, savoring and relishing these feelings, these exciting feelings . . . (pause). Now gradually slow down so you are riding slower and slower, gradually slowing down . . . but continuing to feel energy in your body, a slower form of energy, until you stop (pause). Now I'm going to count backwards from the second week in June, the first week; fourth, third, second, first week in

May; fourth, third, second, first week in April; fourth, third, second, first week in March; fourth, third, second, first week in February; fourth, third, second, first week in January; fourth, third, second, first week in December; and back to November. It's November again and you can relax but still feel alive, energetic, and excited about your activity.

When she came out of the trance, Jan reported that she had not felt as energetic since she was laid off.

Energizing a depressed client, whether by alert hypnosis or time projection, is analogous to behavioral activation in cognitive therapy; it provides a first and necessary step. By itself, however, it may not be sufficient to maintain progress or prevent relapse. The modification of self-statements (cognitive contents) may prove useful as well.

Jan's therapist helped her to identify the negative self-statements she was generating about her job loss and those that were beginning in other areas of her life. The following were identified and written down:

> "I'll never get another job—at least not as good as that one!'
> "It's really my fault I was laid off; they were just trying to be kind in telling me it was a general reduction."
> "I don't interview well for jobs so I won't be successful."
> "I'm not as good at home as I thought I was; my family will find out what a fraud I am!"

The therapist then helped Jan to generate some more positive, or adaptive self-statements to counter these negative statements. Jan was somewhat resistant to this task, claiming she "really didn't believe them," that is, the positive statements. This is not an uncommon client reaction. All of us typically feel more comfortable doing what we have always done and often respond to a request for new behavior with, "But that's just not me!" The therapist persisted, however, suggesting that it was important to say the new statements even if she didn't believe them immediately, and pointed out that she had had a lot of practice with the negative statements. Therefore, practice would be required for the positive statements. The therapist "primed the pump" by offering some positive statements to Jan, suggested modifications to her as appropriate, and wrote them down. Since Jan had a positive experience with hypnosis earlier, the therapist used the two-column technique (Table 8–1) as follows:

Table 8–1. Negative and Positive Cognitive Content for Jan

Negative Self-Statements	Positive Self-Statements
1. I'll never get another job—at least not as good as that one!	1. I've gotten good jobs before and I can do it again! Every new job I've gotten has been better.
2. It was my fault I was laid off; they were just trying to be kind in telling me it was a general reduction.	2. It really was a general reduction. Several of my friends were laid off as well. And I know they're good!
3. I don't interview well for jobs so I won't be successful.	3. If I didn't interview well, I would never have gotten the jobs I have! And I can improve.
4. I'm not as good at home as I thought I was; my family will find out what a fraud I am.	4. My family has been very supportive of me and no one has ever said I was at fault. There is no evidence I'm not doing what I should.

While Jan was in a trance, the therapist asked her to say the negative statement, then the positive. This was done repeatedly for each negative statement. Jan began by saying the negative statement firmly and the positive statement weakly; after several minutes of practice, however, she was saying the positive statements more definitively. The therapist stressed once again that she had had substantial covert practice with the negative statements and should not expect to believe the positive statements quickly and readily. It is worth repeating that these hypnotic interventions are not magic and should be repeated until the client has made progress. Then they can be phased out.

COGNITIVE PROCESSES

Beck and colleaues (1979) have identified the major cognitive errors associated with depression: overgeneralizing (something true in one case is true in every case), selective abstraction (noticing only failures), assuming excessive responsibility for outcomes (I am responsible for everything), predicting without sufficient evidence (if it has been true in the past, it will be true in the future), catastrophizing (always expecting the worst), and dichotomous thinking (everything is all good or all bad; if it isn't perfect, it's terrible). These are similar to some of Ellis's (Ellis and Dryden 1997) cognitive distortions, such as all-or-nothing thinking, focusing on the negative, disqualifying the positive, allness and neverness, and minimization. Notice the similarity of these cognitive errors to those associated with other disorders. Ellis (Ellis and Dryden 1997) also makes a particular point of helping clients separate their intrinsic worth from their behavior; if they do one or two bad things, that does not make them bad people. Conversely, doing one or two good things doesn't make them good people.

The therapist's second task (establishing a collaborative relationship is the first) is to help the client to identify the cognitive errors he or she is using. Because it is difficult for depressed individuals to examine alternative ways of looking at reality, this may not be easy. Initial behavioral activation, whether by behavioral means or by appropriate medication, is often a necessary first step to beginning the analysis of cognitive errors. Only then may clients be willing or able to examine collaboratively cognitive errors they may be employing without realizing it.

For an example of the use of hypnosis in modifying cognitive processes, let's go back to Jan. After she started to engage in more activities and to feel more alive, the therapist began to assist her in examining the cognitive errors she was using. Jan was rather resistant at first to this activity because she thought she was assessing her situation accurately. The therapist helped her to normalize her thinking patterns by pointing out that all people tend to interpret situations predominantly or entirely from one perspective—the only question is how much. The therapist had suspected by this time that Jan had an early maladaptive schema of defectiveness/shame (Young 1994) and that a normalization process would free her up to examine other ways of looking at things without the implication that she was defective for having to do so. Eventually, after collaboratively examining the evidence, they agreed that Jan was overgeneralizing and using selective abstraction (or mental filter; J. S. Beck 1995). The therapist also suspected that Jan was assuming excessive responsibility for events outside her control, but Jan was more resistant to this possibility. Note that the latter cognitive error is similar in some ways to the EMS of self-sacrifice. Accordingly, the therapist used the following hypnotic routine to help Jan overcome the cognitive errors of overgeneralization and selective abstraction. These errors can be seen as mirror images of each other in that overgeneralization expands the perceptual field and selective abstraction narrows it. After an induction, the following hypnotic routine was used:

> And now that you're comfortably relaxed, I'd like you to think of how people interpret things. All of us interpret the meaning of events— we have to in order to think [normalizing the process]. The only differences are, are the interpretations we make similar to those others make, and are we seeing everything so we can make the best interpretation? None of us can pay attention to everything, can we? [normalization]. But it's important, isn't it, to pay attention to the important things, and, even more so, to a variety of ways of interpreting things? All of us tend, if we're not careful, to look at only one side of an issue, don't we? But it's important that we look at several sides, isn't it? We can make better interpretations if we do . . . (*pause*). Many of us make two related errors. Either we look at everything as similar or look at only one side of an issue. For example, we may assume if we make one mistake, we're going to make another. But why should

we? All of us make mistakes sometimes and do things correctly the next. It makes no more sense, does it, to assume that we will always make mistakes than to assume we never will? And of course you already know, don't you, that you will never not make any mistakes? It's no more logical, when you really think about it, to assume that you will always make mistakes! As you think about that, you can begin to understand its meaning at a deeper level—just like you can never avoid mistakes, you can sometimes avoid them . . . it's like part of the same thing; sometimes we make mistakes, sometimes we don't. But one doesn't mean the other, does it? Now I'd like you to spend a few moments thinking about that idea, letting it play around in your mind . . . (pause). Now I'd like you to think of another idea—what should you pay attention to? All of us can only pay attention to a few things at a time. So we tend to notice things that confirm what we already believe. Most people do that; perhaps you do too. But it's important, isn't it, to deliberately look for ideas that are different from what we already believe, to deliberately look for disconfirming evidence? For example, you may notice when you do something wrong but not notice when you do something right. It's only human nature, isn't it? But I'd like to suggest, right now, that you think of one recent thing you did correctly. Spend a few moments thinking and when you have it firmly in your mind, raise the index finger of your right hand [ideomotor signaling]. That's right! Now think about that image, let it play around in your mind and notice how good you feel as a result. And you can have this good feeling anytime you want by relaxing and thinking of a time and situation when you did something well.

In this illustration notice how the therapist used the "yes set" (Erickson and Rossi 1976), in which questions that presuppose a "yes" answer are asked repeatedly. This is an excellent way of helping the client to overcome negative conscious attitudes and introduce a more positive attitude toward change. The therapist also used "truisms" (Erickson and Rossi 1976), which are statements so obviously correct (e.g., "None of us can pay attention to everything") that the client has no choice but to agree. The normalization statements were used to reassure Jan that she was not different, strange, or crazy. All of these techniques were designed to help foster positive, change-producing attitudes and an openness to new experiences in Jan.

COGNITIVE STRUCTURES

The cognitive themes underlying depression revolve around loss, failure, and emptiness (Leahy 1996), which are generally laid down relatively early in life. Because of these early experiences, individuals differ in their cognitive vulnerability to depression. While people who possess these underlying depressive schemas may function reasonably well most of the time, these schemas may be activated in times of stress—a phenomenon known as the *cognitive diathesis-stress model.*

People may also become depressed in different domains of their lives. Beck (1987) has discussed two broad areas of vulnerability. Those with a *sociotropy* vulnerability tend to become depressed when their needs and desires for interpersonal acceptance and closeness are lost or threatened with loss. They are depressed by rejection. Those with an *autonomy* vulnerability tend to become depressed when their needs and desires for independent functioning and achievement are lost or threatened with loss. They are depressed by failure. These domains are not mutually exclusive, however; it is possible to be vulnerable in both. Historically, women have tended to be more vulnerable in the sociotropic domain while men have tended to be more vulnerable in the autonomous domain. With the gradual reduction of gender-specific social and familial roles, however, it is likely that men and women will increasingly share domain vulnerabilities.

Several of Young's (1994) early maladaptive schemas have depressive implications: emotional deprivation, abandonment/instability, social isolation/alienation, defectiveness/shame, dependence/incompetence, failure, and self-sacrifice. Most of these lie in the disconnection and rejection area. Note that several are implicated in the anxiety disorders as well, thus indicating the overlap between depression and anxiety.

As in anxiety, either direct or indirect hypnotherapeutic methods may be used to modify cognitive structures. For an example, we will return to the case of Jan. However, because Jan appeared to be especially resistant to examining her core cognitive structures, the therapist chose an indirect method.

Jan, it will be recalled, appeared to possess an EMS of defectiveness/shame. In addition, failure and self-sacrifice appeared to be present as well. Multiple EMSs are not uncommon and Young (1994) states that clients typically have two, three, or even more. Jan's EMSs are similar to some of J. S. Beck's (1995) helpless core beliefs ("I am inadequate/ineffective, I am incompetent, I am a failure, I am not good enough [in terms of achievement]" and increasingly some unlovable core beliefs as well ("I am not good enough [to be loved by others], I am defective, I am unlovable"). It appeared that her perceived inadequacies had begun to generalize from achievement to home activities through the core beliefs these domains have in common.

AN INDIRECT HYPNOTIC ROUTINE

Because of her earlier positive experiences with hypnosis and in the hope it could help her, Jan agreed to participate in an indirect hypnotic approach. The therapist did not present it as an intervention designed to modify her core cognitive structures, but simply asked Jan if she were willing to participate in an exercise that might help her. Both her prior positive experiences and the therapist's structure offered the hope and the expectation that further hypnosis might be beneficial. Recall that, from a cognitive perspective, positive expectations are a major reason hypnosis is successful. This is why it is so important that therapists structure initial hypnotic experiences so the client sees them as success experiences. After initial induction and deepening techniques, Jan's therapist used the following routine:

> You've experienced many things in trance already, haven't you? And
> they've been valuable and interesting, haven't they? [setting a posi-

tive and expectant tone]. Now you have the chance to learn more things about yourself, things that may not be obvious right away . . . but you can learn and reflect upon them at your leisure. It isn't even necessary to listen to me at a conscious level—your unconscious mind will hear what it wants to hear, what it needs to hear. So you can let your mind lay flat, let it relax, think of whatever it wants or even nothing at all [the latter is a logical impossibility, but in hypnosis one's critical functions are often suspended and this suspension tends to encourage a trance]. But as you listen to me, you will be able to learn many things about yourself and the way you think about yourself and relate to others. Now just allow your mind to lay flat (*long pause*).
. . . I want to talk to you about learning . . . learning and growing. As we grow up, we learn many things, don't we? We learn to do new things, to act in new ways. Sometimes these are exciting; sometimes they are scary. Will we ever learn to do things correctly? How do we even know what "correct" means? But eventually we do learn, don't we? We learn how to do new things . . . sometimes quickly, sometimes slowly; sometimes by succeeding quickly, sometimes by not succeeding right away but then succeeding later . . . sometimes not at all. But we can use this lack of success, can't we, to learn more about how to succeed next time? We feel different things as we learn, don't we? We sometimes feel excited, sometimes ashamed, sometimes happy, sometimes sad. Just like we sometimes succeed right away . . . sometimes not until later . . . sometimes not at all. But we learn in the end that we learn what we need to learn . . . and that life isn't a straight line . . . it's a very crooked line, with many detours and back-tracks [learning by metaphor]. But the detours and back-tracks are important because they help us to learn and grow even more . . . without them we wouldn't learn as much about what we really need to know. We really need to know how to learn about how to learn . . . and the detours and back-tracks help us to learn how to learn. For in the end, learning how to learn is really more important than learning—so rather than feel ashamed of our detours and back-tracks, we should feel proud of them [a reframing]. All of them are helping us to learn better how to learn—even helping us to learn better how

to learn better how to . . . but you get the idea, don't you? . . . in your unconscious mind, where it can really make a difference, where most learning really takes place anyway [a reference to implicit learning]. So think about the detours and back-tracks in your life, Jan . . . and understand them as learning how to learn, how to grow and continue growing, how to . . . Jan—be your own person [embedded suggestion]. And as you continue to think about this, you can begin to feel yourself more and more as a strong and independent person—being **with other people but not for other people.** Becoming more alive and self-confident, more engaged **with** others but not engaged **for** others, seeing the detours and back-tracks in life as opportunities for learning how to learn and opportunities for even further growth. . . . Now as you let those ideas sink deeply into your mind, I'm going to count backwards from ten to one; as I do, I'd like you to become more aware of your surroundings so that when I reach one you'll come out of the trance, feeling refreshed and alive—knowing you've learned something important even if you don't know right now exactly what. . . .

In this illustration notice that the word "failure" was never used, but was replaced by "not succeeding immediately or perhaps not at all." In addition, failure was reframed as a metaphorical detour and back-track that was in the service of further learning. We can often learn better from metaphors because resistance may not be aroused. The meta-learning process (learning how to learn) was connected to failure through the metaphors of detours and back-tracks. This routine was actually a little direct because the core cognitive themes in her life were addressed, even if mostly metaphorically. As Milton Erickson and his followers have shown, it is possible to construct an indirect routine such that the themes are not directly mentioned at all.

This routine helped Jan begin the process of addressing the core cognitive schemas in her life, to see herself as someone who had had both successes and failures—and who had learned from her failures. Of course, a routine like this conducted once would not be immediately successful. It was repeated, with variations, on several occasions and interspersed with nonhypnotic sessions in which her core schemas were examined collaboratively.

SUMMARY

Depression is a multifaceted disorder, with biochemical, psychological, and behavioral components. Since depressed individuals are often motivationally and behaviorally inert, it is important to activate them initially before other work can be begun. This can often be accomplished by a combination of appropriate medication and alert hypnosis. Once the client is more energized, cognitive hypnotherapy can be helpful in addressing both depressogenic assumptions and core cognitive themes of loss and sadness.

9

Habit Disorders

Self-initiated, voluntary disorders present a particularly difficult situation for treatment. Unlike other disorders, the client knows exactly what to do to overcome the problem; for example, not putting food or cigarettes in his or her mouth. An important issue in treatment is short-term versus long-term gain and loss and consequently motivation for change. Anyone familiar with the basics of operant conditioning knows that short-term reinforcement is more powerful than long-term reinforcement. In part because of low motivation, people often turn to hypnosis as an ostensibly magical cure that will remove the desire for problematical substances without effort on their part.

Habit disorders tend to be characterized by short-term hedonic gain and long-term loss. For example, smokers now know full well that cigarettes are detrimental to their health (even if they and the cigarette companies officially deny it), but the short-term reinforcing power of nicotine outweighs the knowledge of the long-term loss. To further complicate the situation, the short-term reinforcers are both physical and social. Nicotine is a powerful chemically addicting substance and both cigarettes and food are strong social reinforcers because they are associated with pleasant social activities.

Not only are the reinforcers for maintaining the current behavior strong, the motivation for change is often conflicting and ambiguous at best. People are sometimes strongly motivated to modify entrenched habits but usually only as a result of some immediate problem with their behavior. For example, they may have had a recent illness traceable to smoking, or their spouse may have told them to lose weight or stop drinking to save the marriage. When the immediate problem disappears, the motivation to change often does too. Hypnosis is sometimes sought out as a treatment intervention precisely because of its popular image as a magical, effortless technique. People in general look for the "magic bullet" that will remove their problems and general dissatisfaction with their lives, hopefully without much effort on their part. In order to address this issue with potential clients, especially those who explicitly request hypnosis, I ask them if they "want to change or want to want to change." If it's the latter, motivational issues may need to be addressed first.

Because of these issues, modification of entrenched habit disorders is problematical at best—whether by hypnosis or other treatment strategies. Therefore, hypnotherapists should be alert to client motivation in seeking hypnotherapy for these problems and quickly address any delusions they may have about its efficacy. Nevertheless, hypnosis has been shown to be effective in treating obesity (Bolocofsky et al. 1985, Levitt 1993) and in smoking cessation (Golden and Friedberg 1986, Lynn et al. 1993b), although there is a wide variation in the number of clients who actually reduce or eliminate their problematical habits. While early reports (e.g., Wadden and Anderton 1982) indicated that hypnotic susceptibility was not related to treatment outcome, more recent studies have suggested that highly hypnotizable clients may do better at both weight loss (Levitt 1993) and smoking cessation (Lynn et al. 1993b). Lynn and colleagues have developed a two-session smoking cessation program that has shown good results. However, Spanos and colleagues (1995) found hypnotic treatment methods to be no more effective than nonhypnotic treatment in reducing smoking.

Thus it can be concluded that hypnosis may be at least as helpful as other treatment strategies in changing habit disorders, although the results may be highly variable. Clients should be told that, while hypnosis might be of some value, it should not be used as the sole treatment. Hypnotic interventions are generally supplemented with education about the effects of their behavior and behavioral, self-regulatory strategies in overcoming their problem as well (Levitt 1993, Lynn et al. 1993b). Furthermore, it appears that at least some of the variation in treatment outcome may be due to individual differences in hypnotic susceptibility. Issues of client motivation should also be addressed before treatment has begun. The remainder of this chapter describes and illustrates the use of hypnosis in treating smoking and substance abuse, respectively. While other habit disorders exist, these two are widely considered to be common and significant health problems.

SMOKING CESSATION

Cigarette smoking is an especially difficult habit to overcome because nicotine is both physically and psychologically addicting. The immediate consequence of smoking (the physical addiction) is experienced as a "rush" and is highly reinforcing. Smoking is therefore quite stimulating in the short run. This aspect of the addiction might be addressed by such techniques as the nicotine patch. The psychological addiction can be addressed by a combination of behavioral and cognitive hypnotherapeutic strategies. Because smoking is typically associated with a wide variety of pleasurable social activities, it is important that the client keep a log for several days of the time, place, activity, and thoughts experienced while smoking. Clients may have only a vague idea of the simple details of their addiction, such as the number of cigarettes smoked per day or when heavier smoking may take place. As they begin to focus more on the details of their smoking behavior, important information may become available that the therapist can use. Thus the therapist can come to understand the environmentally maintaining reinforcers of smoking and construct an individually tailored hypnotic intervention. Because smokers tend to have friends who also smoke, it might be best for clients initially to stay away from situations in which cigarettes are commonly used and available; for example, in association with alcoholic beverages. Unfortunately, this means that clients may be better off constructing a new social network, a situation also faced by recovering substance abusers. Especially at first, it is difficult to refrain from smoking when all your friends smoke. Once the environmental triggers that provide cues for smoking have been addressed, hypnotic interventions can begin.

COGNITIVE CONTENT

Steve came to therapy for help in quitting cigarette smoking. He was 32 years old and had been smoking since he was 16. Although he had attempted several times over the years to quit, he had little real motivation to do so and his periods of abstinence had typically been two to three weeks at most. Lately, however, his wife (who did not smoke) had been complaining about the obnoxious smell in the house (and on him). In addition, Steve and his wife had recently had their first child and he was concerned about the effect of secondhand smoke on his new daughter. The therapist determined that Steve now had both intrinsic and extrinsic motivation to change.

Initially, the therapist and Steve worked together to pinpoint the situations that acted as triggers for cigarette smoking and the negative thoughts or self-suggestions that led to actual smoking behavior. Although the physiological addiction resulted in his smoking about a pack and a half of cigarettes per day, Steve found smoking urges to be particularly powerful when he was drinking with his friends and just after meals. A further assessment indicated Steve did not have a drinking problem. When these urges were especially powerful, Steve found himself overwhelmed with negative and hopeless cognitions about smoking.

Steve was interested in trying hypnosis, partly (it appeared) for its novelty effect. But after the therapist explained the nature of hypnosis, Steve readily agreed to work at using it diligently and repeatedly rather than viewing it as a magical intervention that would remove the need for effort on his part. Steve was an energetic businessman who worked hard at everything he undertook and the therapist believed he would work hard at this too.

Steve agreed, although somewhat reluctantly, to reduce the social contacts with his friends (all of whom smoked) to once or twice a week. In addition, he agreed not to smoke in his house. Steve's discussions with the therapist revealed several negative self-statements, and together they created alternative self-statements. Steve was a reasonably good hypnotic subject and was able to achieve a light-medium trance. After an initial induction, the therapist used the two-column technique illustrated in Table 9–1. Steve was able to say the negative self-statements first and

Table 9–1. Negative and Positive Cognitive Content for Steve

Negative Self-Statements	Positive Self-Statements
1. What difference does it make if I smoke or not?	1. Of course it makes a difference! I have the health of my daughter and wife to think of.
2. I can smoke all I want now; I'll just smoke less later.	2. I know perfectly well, from past experience, that if I smoke more now, I'll smoke more later!
3. I'll never succeed in stopping smoking. It's hopeless.	3. Of course I can succeed—even though it will be difficult. I've succeeded at many difficult things in the past.
4. Smoking isn't really bad for me.	4. Smoking is terrible for me; I have a cough and feel out of breath all the time.

then the alternative positive self-statements while in a trance, and he practiced them repeatedly in several sessions. He was also instructed, with therapist modeling, to say the positive self-statements with increasing confidence. The therapist made an audiotape of a typical session that Steve could listen to at home at regularly scheduled times. Hypnotic sessions were followed by discussions about their effect (Steve kept a log of cigarettes smoked each day) and modifications in self-statements or in the hypnotic trance were made as appropriate.

After in-session and home practice of these positive self-statements, Steve reported that the number of cigarettes he smoked each day had diminished and he had begun to feel more confident about quitting entirely. He also had begun creating a new social network of nonsmokers through the church he and his wife attended.

COGNITIVE PROCESSES

An examination of Steve's cognitive distortions suggested they lay primarily in the area of relapse. Like many smokers, Steve was not convinced, based on his past behavior and his physiological craving, that he could ever really stop smoking. In essence, he had tacitly defined himself as a smoker (to be discussed in more detail later). The therapist discussed with Steve his cognitive processing distortions. Eventually Steve agreed that he engaged in catastrophizing and hopeless thinking (believing he would never be able to stop), dichotomous thinking (believing if he didn't stop completely he had failed), and using "should" and "must" statements (believing he should be able to stop immediately and, if he didn't, he was "no good"). Although nicotine has a dose effect (the less one smokes, the better it is), Steve was not able to see reduced smoking as a desirable goal or even a possible goal. Given his hard-driving "can do" attitude (which had actually served him well in the past), it was difficult for him to accept the inevitable setbacks and frustrations that are associated with efforts to change entrenched habits. These failures, however temporary they might be, resulted in his feeling bad about himself and his ability to change.

After an initial induction, the therapist constructed the following hypnotic routine around themes of slow and steady progress, upward movement, and increased self-respect.

As you look back over your life, you know that you've done many good things, don't you, Steve? Many things—some large, some small . . . but all accomplishments to be proud of. You may recall, for example, when you first learned to ride a bicycle [an almost universal experience for children]. You might be able to remember how it seemed like you'd never learn how to make those two wheels go in the same direction . . . and make that machine stay upright. Perhaps you thought you'd never be able to learn. But you now know you did learn, didn't you? And, as you **gradually learned** how to ride, you **felt better and better** about yourself, didn't you? Just the act of **gradually learning** led to **better and better feelings**, didn't it? Perhaps you can focus on that scene right now, seeing yourself riding and slipping . . . riding and slipping . . . but always getting better and better . . . see yourself not just failing but getting better and better, learning from your mistakes [following the image to completion]. See yourself learning to ride . . . getting better and better and, as you do, **feeling better and better**. Those two go together, don't they? . . . doing better and feeling better; feeling better and doing better . . . [suggesting an adaptive spiral]. And the better you do, the better you feel . . . the better you feel, the better you do. But it all takes time, doesn't it? And perhaps you don't even have to do it perfectly to feel good—it's enough to do better today than you did yesterday . . . knowing you will do even better tomorrow, but maybe not yet perfectly, but that's all right, isn't it? (*Pause.*) Now I'd like you to focus your mind on your first job [a prior discussion with Steve had indicated that the tasks on this job had been especially difficult to learn]. See yourself beginning the job. When you have that scene firmly in your mind, raise the index finger of your right hand . . . that's good! [ideomotor signaling]. Now I'd like you to see yourself doing the job . . . feeling the frustration you felt, not being able to get it exactly right the first time . . . seeing yourself coping, going right on . . . as you did; not perfectly but good; feeling good about not being perfect [coping in the image]. Seeing yourself getting better and better the more you try, doing better and better the more you do, feeling better and better the more you try and do . . . understanding in a new way how doing and feeling are connected. So the more you do, the better you feel . . . and the better you feel, the more you do . . . but seeing these as gradual activities, like learning to ride a bicycle, learning to play the piano [something the client had done as a child with moderate success], learning to do so many things, learning gradually, gradually learning to feel good about yourself, gradually learning the connection between doing good . . . and feeling good, feeling good . . . and doing good. Gradually learning how to gradually learn . . . gradually . . .

Notice in the latter part of this example the repeated embedded suggestions of "gradually learning" and those stressing the connection between "doing good and feeling good." These repetitions and embedded suggestions are important in modifying cognitive processes. It is also helpful to use common activities that almost all people have done at some time in their lives, like learning to ride a bicycle, as staging images for further work.

COGNITIVE STRUCTURES

It is more difficult to find cognitive structures that are directly implicated in habit disorders than in depression, anxiety, or other more internal psychological problems. In part this is because habit disorders tend to be maintained by externally reinforcing activities, either by a physiologically addicting substance like nicotine or a pleasurable event such as eating. There is also some evidence that certain addictions, such as substance abuse, may be partly genetically based. There is some evidence that genetic structure may be implicated in individual differences in alcohol metabolism, and body structure likewise has a genetic basis. In addition, habit disorders may not be considered a part of the self in the way other psychological problems are. They may be seen as "things one does" rather than "things one is." Problematical habits, unlike personality styles, may arise later in life or gradually become worse over time.

However, it is also possible that some habits may be experienced as a part of one's core self and identity. Individuals who have smoked or used addicting substances for many years may become defined, to themselves and to others, as a "smoker," a "drunkard," an "addict," or even a "loser." Defining themselves in this manner may create a sense of hopelessness about ever really changing; indeed, it may even remove any willingness or desire for change. The individual may simply think, "That's just the way I am," and not be able to even consider a different identity.

Furthermore, certain core cognitive structures may contribute to the maintenance of habit disorders and counteract change-inducing efforts (see Chapter 5). For example, punitiveness (Young 1994), the tendency to be harshly critical and impatient with those who do not meet one's expectations, can hinder the often-gradual change that is typical of the modification of entrenched habits. Clients with an early maladaptive schema of punitiveness are often harder on themselves than on others and are extremely critical of their "slow" progress, expecting quick changes. Similarly, clients with an EMS of unrelenting standards often expect to attain impossible goals quickly. Others may turn to addicting substances for comfort and solace when an EMS of abandonment/instability or emotional deprivation is triggered by events. And certainly an EMS of insufficient self-control/self-discipline is directly implicated in the failure of efforts to modify habits, since habit disorders can be seen as disorders of impulse.

It appeared to the therapist that Steve had tacitly defined himself as a smoker and, as a result, didn't really believe he could change. Only recently, with the birth of his daughter, had the motivation to change become even partly internal. Previously, smoking was just something he did as an expression of who he was; if others didn't like it, that was their problem. Heavy substance abusers often think the same way. Thus the problematic behavior is ego syntonic (i.e., consonant with the client's self-image).

As a result of the schema questionnaire (Young 1994) and the interview assessment data, the therapist determined that Steve had primary EMSs of unrelenting standards and punitiveness, with a secondary EMS of overcontrol. Note that all three fall within Young's area of overvigilance and inhibition, indicating that Steve had an excessive emphasis on control and rigid expectations. Often there is a covert feeling of anxiety and pessimism in these individuals, as if things could deteriorate quickly if one is not careful. Young states that the typical family of origin of individuals who have these schemas stressed performance, duty, perfectionism, following rigid rules, and avoiding mistakes. These take precedence over pleasure, joy, and relaxation. It should be noted that such a profile is quite common in high-achieving people and often can be very useful if kept within limits. Apart from the physiological addiction, Steve appeared to use cigarettes to calm himself and reduce anxiety.

To address these EMSs, the therapist developed the following hypnotic routine. After a standard induction, it proceeded as follows.

And now that you're comfortably in a trance, I'd like to talk to you, Steve. You can listen to me any way that you want; with your entire mind or only part of your mind; it doesn't really matter [seeding an important suggestion for change] because your unconscious mind will hear what it wants to hear and make use of it. . . . So your conscious mind, which you use to pay attention, can take a vacation, can step aside and let your unconscious mind take over. And you can do this comfortably, knowing that your conscious mind can come back from its vacation any time it wants . . . but it doesn't want to right now, doesn't need to . . . it really doesn't matter (long pause). Over the course of our lives, all of us learn many things [normalizing the process of what is to follow]. Sometimes we learn to achieve, sometimes we learn to relax . . . sometimes we learn to do our duty, sometimes we learn to relate better to others. . . . Sometimes we learn rules, sometimes we learn when rules can or should be broken [juxtaposition of EMS themes with more adaptive themes]. Likewise, in your life, Steve, you have learned many things. Perhaps you learned to follow rules, to work hard, to always try to do better, to be in control, to do your duty. Perhaps you learned to judge yourself . . . perhaps others judged you too and you learned to judge yourself before others judged you. When we learn things early, it's sometimes difficult to know anything else, isn't it? We don't know what we don't know, do we? We think that the way we think is the only way to think, don't we? But there are many ways to think, aren't there? More than we ever knew. And you can begin to learn new ways of thinking . . . new ways of knowing . . . new ways of relating to others [introduction of new alternative idea to EMS] . . . and you can begin to allow this to happen [alternative to the EMS concept of "do"] by allowing yourself to relax, let your mind lay flat, and begin to allow new ideas to enter your unconscious mind. That's right . . . as you allow yourself to let your mind relax, you can feel it open itself to new ideas, exciting ideas . . . some scary, because change is always scary [acknowledgment of ambivalence], but even the scary part can be exciting as you open yourself to new growth, new possibilities, new ways of thinking and acting. And perhaps it's sometimes difficult to even tell the difference between scary and exciting because they can feel the same . . . so perhaps if it feels scary, it's really exciting. It's all in the way we think about it sometimes. Now as you begin to allow your mind to open itself to new possibilities, new ways of thinking, you can begin to relax in other ways too. You can begin to feel more at ease in setting new and more flexible standards for yourself, feeling more at ease in judging yourself, feeling more kindly about your efforts, increasingly knowing that competency is not perfection, that perfection is not necessary, not even possible—and you can allow yourself to relax from very high standards and still be competent. You can learn to give up some control, knowing that only someone who is really in control can afford to give some of it up; knowing that you can take control back any time you want to. You can allow yourself to relax in many ways; your body, your mind, your standards, your feelings . . . and as you do, you can continue to learn new things about yourself. . . .

In the latter section of this routine, notice that the therapist used positive phrasing (e.g., "more at ease . . .") rather than negative phrasing (e.g., "reduce your punitive feelings about yourself"). Such positive phrases orient the client toward a future goal rather than past feelings. In addition, positive phrases function as encouragers rather than punishers, encouraging the client to continue his or her change efforts and to plant seeds for present and future optimistic attitudes, rather than pessimistic ones.

SUBSTANCE ABUSE TREATMENT

At the outset, it should be emphasized that hypnosis cannot and should not be a complete treatment for substance abuse problems. Addicting substances have powerful physiological and psychological maintaining factors and are difficult to treat by any means. Certainly, the physiological aspects of substance abuse should be treated by appropriate physiological interventions. Even psychological aspects of substance abuse may best be treated in a multifaceted way (Dowd and Rugle 1999) and different types of substances may require different methods for treatment. Nevertheless, hypnosis may be a valuable adjunct intervention as part of a comprehensive treatment program for certain common elements behind substance abuse.

Very little has been written on the use of hypnosis in the treatment of substance abuse—and much of it consists of anecdotal case studies, highly general descriptions, or vague, unsupported opinions. Rarely are detailed descriptions given of specific hypnotic interventions. There are similarities between smoking and chemical substance abuse, and many of the concepts and hypnotic routines previously described for smoking cessation may be used with substance abusers as well. Indeed, according to one case report in the literature (Page and Handley 1993), a cocaine addict was able to first break her addiction to cigarettes and then to cocaine by listening to a commercial weight-control tape three times a day and mentally substituting the word "smoking" or "coke." No face-to-face therapy of any kind was used. While success stories of this kind are intriguing, they are highly atypical and it is likely that hypnosis functioned as an expectancy-increasing placebo. However, there are important differences between smoking and substance abuse because smoking is legal for adults and most drugs are illegal. Also, there are its psychological and physiological maintaining factors, so that a separate treatment is warranted. Nevertheless, concepts and techniques described for the hypnotic treatment of smoking could be used for substance abusers as well.

There is evidence that chemically dependent individuals use substances to reduce tension, relax, and improve their mood. This is unlike nicotine, which tends to be used for its stimulating properties. Like nicotine, however, chemical substances have variable physically addicting properties, though nicotine is considered to be among the most physically addicting of all substances. Substance abusers may also use chemicals to obtain an altered state of consciousness. Cognitive hypnotherapeutic techniques that achieve the same results could thus be important interventions (Resnick and Resnick 1986). Accordingly, the remainder of this chapter is organized into three parts: the use of hypnosis to help substance abusers relax, to improve mood and increase self-esteem, and to achieve an altered state of consciousness.

USING HYPNOSIS TO ASSIST RELAXATION

Vandamme (1986) presents an example of the use of meditation and relaxation with a heroin addict in which he describes a 20-year-old female who had become a heroin addict during her senior year in high school. At the time of treatment, she was injecting herself once every other day, and pursuing her career was an increasing problem. She found it difficult to separate from her mother and identified with her maladjusted father. The therapist began treatment with the assumption that opiate addiction is an attempt to deal with chronic stress. After initial rapport-building and a contract to stay off drugs for at least two weeks, the therapist used the following meditation:

> Sit back comfortably but remain erect with your head well supported
> and your hands resting in your lap or on your thighs. Keep your legs
> in a relaxed position and close your eyes. Breathe gently and exhale
> slowly and say quietly alpha alpha alpha [after the rhythm has been
> checked]. Now continue to say alpha but not aloud, in your mind
> instead. If you see images do not become involved with them; merely
> watch them and continue to say in your mind alpha alpha. I will leave
> you alone for 20 minutes. When I return I shall knock on the door
> but will not come in immediately. When you hear me knock you
> slowly open your eyes and sit quietly for a few moments. [Vandamme
> 1986, p. 44]

The relaxation component of this mantra is apparent. What may
be less apparent is the mind-emptying aspect of it. When people repeat
the same word or phrase over and over, it becomes difficult, if not impossible, to think of anything else. The word *alpha* itself becomes mean-
ingless after a while, so that it is essentially a nonsense syllable that is
being repeated. This type of exercise is much easier to do than the instruction not to think of anything, which is similar to the instruction
not to think of a pink elephant; paradoxically, it becomes difficult to do
anything else. Meditation using a mantra is a hallmark of Eastern forms
of spirituality and personal growth. From a cognitive perspective, one
can think of this technique as a generalized cognitive content that dis-
places, by means of the mind-emptying referred to earlier, negative cognitive content statements.

The therapist then used a hypnotic relaxation exercise with the
client, avoiding the use of the word "hypnosis" in order to reduce her
anxiety. Following eye-fixation suggestions (e.g., "focus on a spot on
the wall . . ."), the therapist used the following routine:

> Think of your legs, your legs, you can feel the muscles in your legs
> relax; let go! The muscles of your legs let go. As they let go you just
> feel the weight of your legs, the weight of your legs weighing down
> on the chair. Heavy, heavy relaxation, your legs are heavy with it. The

heavy relaxation comes all through you. Eyelids are heavy with it. Heavy drowsy relaxation. . . .

Notice how easy and effortless your breathing has become, every time you breathe out you become more relaxed. Relax your arms, feel how relaxed they have become. Relax your neck muscles, let your head sink back. Take a deep breath—breathe out, feel how relaxed you are. . . .

You have now become so deeply relaxed, so deeply relaxed that during this deep relaxation you are going to feel physically stronger and fitter in every way. Every day your nerves will become stronger and steadier, your mind calmer and clearer, more composed, more placid, more tranquil. You will become less easily worried, less easily agitated, less easily fearful and apprehensive, much less easily upset. You will be able to think more clearly, you will be able to give your whole undivided attention to whatever you are doing. . . .

You have now become so deeply relaxed, so deeply relaxed that everything that has happened to you will continue to influence your thoughts, your feelings and your actions just as surely, just as strongly when you are back home as when you are here with me. . . . [Vandamme 1986, pp. 44–45]

I have quoted this routine because it illustrates, in addition to hypnotic relaxation, some rather direct suggestions for enhanced functioning or what is called in another literature "ego strengthening." These statements are similar to that which Emile Coué instructed his patients to say: "Every day in every way, I am getting better and better!" Such statements can be seen as implicit cognitive contents, in which the therapist infers what dysfunctional thoughts the client might have. Direct suggestions can occasionally result in significant client change, though the effects are often transitory. While it is tempting to use such direct forms of suggestion, with the hope of rapid improvement, I would caution beginning hypnotherapists not to use them regularly. First, the client may not improve as rapidly as expected and, with such direct suggestions, the therapist may lose credibility as a result. Hypnotherapists should strive to make or define every hypnotic experience as successful for the client. Second, such direct suggestions may arouse resistance in certain types of clients. Third, direct suggestions may give clients (and the general public) the idea that hypnosis is a form of magic wherein changes can occur quickly without much effort on the client's part. There is a part of all of us that wants to believe this and constantly searches for the "magic bullet," but human change is difficult and requires effort. I advocate using more tentative suggestions for change, such as, "You may be able to allow yourself to become less worried" or "You can find yourself gradually becoming stronger and more self-assured every day, as you continue to repeat these instructions." Suggestions like these set up more realistic expectancies for change.

USING HYPNOSIS TO IMPROVE MOOD AND INCREASE SELF-ESTEEM

Substance abusers often have a negative mood and low self-esteem. It is difficult to untangle the direction of causality—that is, do they have negative mood and low self-esteem because they use drugs or do they use drugs because they have negative mood and low self-esteem? Nevertheless, any intervention that affects mood and self-esteem may have an impact on substance abuse. Therefore, I will describe and illustrate a hypnotic intervention designed to enhance mood and self-esteem by using general positive self-statements.

Channon-Little (1994) has described a variant of Spiegel and Spiegel's (1978) hypnotic smoking treatment approach. She stresses a positive approach toward respecting the body, the basic message being, "My body gives me pleasure. I not only respect it, I enjoy it. I will give it a gift in return" (p. 161). Channon-Little suggests building this routine around things the client enjoys, drawing attention to various pleasurable physical sensations.

For an example of how to use this technique, let us look at the following case. Jack was a marijuana abuser who had gradually increased his use over the years to the point that it was interfering with everything in his life and he had little motivation for anything. His schoolwork, which hitherto had been good, began to suffer and he received several F's because he did not complete assignments. Consequently he was dysphoric and his self-esteem was low.

The therapist constructed the following hypnotic routine around respecting his body and suggesting a better mood. Because Jack was a weight lifter, imagery around that activity was used to enhance his mood.

> Jack, I'd like you to think of your body as a pleasure machine—ready to give you pleasure if you treat it right. The body is a unit with the mind—if the body feels good, the mind feels good; if the mind feels good, the body feels good. So you can influence one by the other. I'd like to go with you through a simple exercise. . . . I'd like you to imagine preparing for a weight-lifting session—carefully stretching each muscle group in turn as you prepare for the session. That's right, spend some time doing that and notice how good it feels, how supple your body feels, how your muscles ripple. Notice how you begin to feel stronger as you stretch and relax, relax and stretch. You don't really need or want anything to come between you and these pleasurable sensations, do you? Now see yourself approaching your first weight machine, sitting down on the stool and taking several deep breaths. Notice how relaxing the breathing feels, how it mentally and physically prepares you for the task to come. You can feel yourself concentrate on the lift as you grab the handles and pull down, breathing rhythmically and deeply as you go—up . . . and down . . . in . . . and out, up . . . and down . . . in . . . and out. That's right, you can feel your muscles become stronger with each pull, feeling the pleasurable sensations move through your body, feeling an increasingly more positive attitude and mood as you continue to lift; up . . . down . . . in . . . out [repeat as many times as seems necessary and at an appropriate speed], over and over. Feel the increased pleasure spread throughout your body, into your mind . . . feel the increased good feeling spread throughout your mind, into your body. You don't really need anything else that's not part of your body and your mind, do you? Anything else would just get in the way, wouldn't it? You

can get all the pleasure you need and want right from your body, what it does, and the connection between your body and your mind. So the more you lift, the better you can feel about yourself and the better you feel about yourself, the better your lifting will be (*pause*). So continue to lift a few more times until you comfortably feel you have done enough, then slowly relax as you take several deep breaths and gradually cool down . . . relaxing as you do. Notice how good your body feels, how strong, how powerful, how connected in its parts and with your mind. And you don't really need anything else in your body from the outside to feel this good. . . .

This routine can be repeated as often as needed and a tape of it can be made for the client to use between sessions. The type of routine used will depend on the type of activities the client finds pleasurable. For example, a client who likes music can be taken through a favorite composition, noticing all the pleasurable sounds and their associated bodily sensations. If Jack had been a fan of Beethoven's music, the routine might have gone as follows:

Hear in your mind the opening of Beethoven's Seventh Symphony. As the music progresses, you can feel it thrilling your mind—and your body. Feel in your mind the sheer exuberance of the orchestration, the dancing of the strings [Beethoven's Seventh Symphony is known informally as his "Dance Symphony"], the brass—and feel it percolate into your body, feeling shivers of pure joy. You can feel the music in your body as you hear it in your mind. And you know that you need nothing else from outside to enhance this pleasure, nothing at all! All the pleasure your body and your mind need is right here, right now!

It might even be helpful to play a recording of the symphony in the background so the therapist can pace the routine to the music, drawing attention to actual passages and describing its effect on the client. Of course, a music-loving and -knowledgeable therapist would be a decided asset!

USING HYPNOSIS TO ACHIEVE AN ALTERED STATE
OF CONSCIOUSNESS

There is increasing evidence that addicts use chemical substances to obtain an altered state of consciousness and that the "high" addicts experience when using drugs is similar to what they experience from hypnosis (Krupnick-McClure 1994). The state view of hypnosis discussed in Chapter 3 essentially defines hypnosis itself as an altered state of consciousness. This point of view sees the hypnotic state as qualitatively different from ordinary forms of consciousness on the basis of the radically different phenomena exhibited by people while in trance. Certainly, people do not normally hold their arms aloft (arm levitation), experience numbness in their bodies (glove anesthesia), or see things that aren't really there (positive hallucinations). But attempts to differentiate the hypnotic state from the nonhypnotic state on the basis of chemical and electrical levels in people's bodies have not been successful (Yapko 1995). Nor have other differentiating markers been found. A cognitive-behavioral explanation of trance behavior would see these events as resulting from situational expectations for change occurring in a context in which such phenomena were allowed and fostered. Indeed, Matthews and colleagues (1998) seem to argue for a cognitive-behavioral view of Ericksonian hypnosis when they state that Erickson himself created powerful expectancies for change in a hypnotic context. The question is, therefore, can an altered state of consciousness be fostered within a cognitive hypnotherapy explanatory framework? I think it can, and I will attempt to do so. However, I should note that Krupnick-McClure (1994) found hypnosis was more effective than relaxation when hypnotic susceptibility was taken into account, so there may be individual differences in the extent to which clients may be able to make use of these techniques.

Recall from Chapter 2 that schemas are the cognitive structures we use to screen and classify the information we receive from the environment on a constant basis. These schemas become the filters or templates that enable us to form concepts and to see and interpret events in certain ways. Indeed, schemas influence not only how we interpret information, they even influence the information we notice. These schemas are part of the implicit memory structure of every human. We all have them, good and bad, helpful and unhelpful. Indeed, they are necessary if we are to think at all—otherwise we would have to approach every situation as a completely fresh experience and we would be unable to draw on past experience to help us understand new events and phenomena.

Existing schemas, however, interfere with our ability to enter unusual or altered states of consciousness (Walters and Havens 1993). Because schemas organize new experiences on the basis of past constructs, they are deeply conservative and act to prevent us from seeing things in new ways, getting past our biases, or experiencing new phenomena. They constrain the future in terms of the past.

Traditional cognitive therapy, even of the more recent schema-focused and developmental type, helps clients to identify and challenge core cognitive schemas. There is also an assumption in many instances that eliminating negative schemas will automatically result in positive schemas (Peterson and Bassio 1991). Achieving an altered state of consciousness, however, may demand something different. It may demand that schemas be at least temporarily suspended or altered in a more positive direction. Ericksonian hypnotherapists stress the utilization of "unconscious" mental resources by removing blocks to these resources. They argue that the task of the hypnotherapist is to let these natural processes occur by allowing and giving permission to clients to experience what it is their "unconscious" mind wishes to experience. Rather than the word *unconscious*, which is loaded with irrelevant and archaic conceptual baggage, I would suggest using the word *tacit*. Both refer to cognitive material outside of immediate awareness, though the accessibility of this material may vary.

The first task of a client who wants to experience an altered state of consciousness is to learn to create a stable and focused attention. Walters and Havens (1993) have described the benefits that follow from a focused and concentrated attention (what Mihaly Csikszentmihalyi has called *flow*), including intense absorption in activities, a heightened sense of creativity, increased happiness and pleasure, better performance, and a feeling of mystical transcendence. This phenomenon has been known historically by other names, such as meditation and yoga, during which people claim to have discovered important revelations or communed with gods.

Herbert Benson (1975) used a simple technique to help people focus and stabilize attention. He had them spend twenty minutes twice a day focusing on and repeating silently the word "one." Any time their attention wandered, they were to redirect it back to that one word (pun intended). He called this focused relaxed state *the relaxation response* and reported that his participants felt happier, more relaxed, and more competent after engaging in this exercise. Such effects have also been noted for religious meditation and yoga over the centuries. By contrast, people suffering from attention deficit disorder, which involves an inability to focus and concentrate, often describe themselves (and are described by others) as being unhappy and dissatisfied with themselves and their lives.

For an example of the use of hypnosis to achieve an altered state of consciousness in substance abuse treatment, consider the case of Bev, a middle-class married woman who had been a recreational cocaine abuser for some time and used it to obtain a peak experience or high. Her use had begun to seriously interfere with her marriage and family life, and her husband had told her to kick the habit or he would file for divorce and custody of their two young children. In a panic, Bev sought treatment. As part of a multifaceted treatment program, the therapist decided, in consultation with Bev, to use hypnosis to help her achieve the peak experiences she desired. Initially, the therapist used Benson's (1975) relaxation response to enable Bev to concentrate and focus her attention, a task that proved more difficult than imagined. The therapist first monitored Bev's use of this technique within the session, redirecting her back to meditation as necessary. After Bev had become somewhat proficient in using it, she was asked to practice it at home twice a day and report the results to the therapist.

When Bev had become comfortable in using the relaxation response, the therapist then used a hypnotic routine to allow her to begin to change her negative schemas. A previous assessment following Young's (1994) schema-focused cognitive therapy (Chapter 5) had uncovered the following early maladaptive schemas, presented in order of prominence:

1. *Insufficient self-control/self-discipline.* This refers to a difficulty or refusal to exercise sufficient self-control and tolerance of frustration to achieve one's goals or to restrain immediate expression of one's impulses. Bev could not stand temporary discomfort or boredom. When she felt uncomfortable or bored, she immediately used cocaine to avoid the feelings.

2. *Entitlement/domination.* This refers to an insistence that one is entitled to whatever one wants, whenever one wants it, without a need to consider others' wishes. Bev felt she was entitled to get high even when it interfered with her family and its welfare. Only when she was presented with an ultimatum from her husband did she seek help.

3. *Defectiveness/shame.* This refers to feelings that one is flawed, bad, unwanted, or inferior and often underlies feelings of entitlement. People with this schema tend to be unusually sensitive to criticism and rejection and feel personally insecure. Bev regarded herself as not as worthwhile as others and used cocaine to deny or avoid these feelings. She was especially likely to use it after a real or perceived slight, which to her demonstrated her inferiority.

To increase the probability that Bev would experience an altered state of consciousness (or peak experience) during a trance as well as to address these underlying EMSs, the therapist used the following hypnotic routine:

> Bev, you have already been able to experience the wonderful feeling that comes from simple meditation—and you have learned, haven't you, that you are good at it? Really good, in many ways, deep down inside [addresses schema of defectiveness]. You've learned also, haven't you, that you have the ability, in many ways, deep down, to

work at something and to succeed—even when you don't want to [addresses schema of insufficient self-control]? You feel good about your ability to do these things, don't you [addresses both schemas]? Now you can begin to learn even more about your ability to use your own potentials in ways you never thought of, opening up yourself to new possibilities. It's all within you . . . everything you need, everything you want. All you have to do is empty your mind of all existing preconceptions, all existing ideas that get in your way, get in the way of intense enjoyment, the ability to see new things, new possibilities, old things in new ways. So let your mind lay flat . . . feel your mind emptying itself, opening itself, like a flower, as you concentrate on nothing, on no-thing, thinking only of no-thing, hearing my voice . . . but thinking of no-thing [the inherent paradox of thinking and not thinking simultaneously acts as a confusion technique]. Now you can begin to feel yourself expand in many directions, feeling the rush, the intense pleasure from this expansion, feeling yourself opening up inside, opening to new possibilities, new directions, feeling the intense pleasure from the realization that you are already beginning to open to new possibilities—feeling stronger, better about yourself— better able to direct yourself in ways you want to go [suggests alterations in schemas 1 and 3], feeling the intense pleasure that comes from knowing that you are in charge of yourself, can deep down make changes you want. And you can feel good, very good, this way—any time you want, without hurting those around you, those you love. You can take care of yourself while taking care of them too [suggests alteration in schema 2]. So continue to feel yourself expanding, growing, feeling intense and increasing pleasure in growing, seeing yourself expanding, growing, opening up to new possibilities, yet unknown and unrealized but exciting. And you know that you can have this intense feeling anytime you want, simply by going through this exercise, allowing yourself to think of no-thing and expand your range of thinking and being . . . being and thinking. Now I'd like you to allow these ideas to settle deep down in your mind, into the deepest layers, where they can continue to influence you as you come out of the trance.

This exercise was repeated with variations, repetitions, and expansions several times during the therapeutic sessions. Eventually, the therapist made a tape that Bev could play in her own home during her agreed-upon "meditative times." Notice the juxtaposition of suggestions leading to an altered, intense state of consciousness with suggestions for changes in early maladaptive schemas. However, I want to emphasis once again that repetition is very important in changing these deeply entrenched schemas and one or two iterations of any hypnotic routine will not result in lasting change. But repeated practice of these types of hypnotic suggestions in a therapeutic context can be very beneficial. Creativity in making and modifying hypnotic routines is also important.

SUMMARY

Habit disorders are especially difficult to treat by any modality because of both their physically addicting aspects and the short-term psychologically reinforcing aspects. In addition, habit disorders differ among themselves in a variety of ways so that the same treatment strategies may not be appropriate for all. Core cognitive schemas may be implicated in many habit disorders. This chapter has described the use of hypnosis as a partial strategy in treating smoking and substance abuse. Other habit disorders may be treated by a modification of these techniques.

Cognitive Hypnotherapy
and the Reconstruction of Memory

Memory is a slippery phenomenon. Although we think we know what it is, recent research has shown that memories are at least as much constructed as they are recalled. This chapter describes and illustrates the use of hypnosis in modifying dysfunctional memories. While at first glance that may appear to be an impossible or at least undesirable activity, there is evidence that it can be helpful in certain circumstances.

THE NATURE OF MEMORY

Most of us, when asked what memory is, might reply that it is the recall or remembrance of past events. Implicit in that definition is an assumption that memory is always accurate. We know, of course, that we cannot always recall everything that has happened or that we wish to recall, but when we can we assume it is accurate. The only task is to learn to remember more. The analogy of the mind we often use is that of the tape recorder or, more recently, the computer. Everything is encoded and stored in our memory banks; the only problem is accessing it. We know that people may deliberately lie or misrepresent the truth, but we think they know what the truth really is. Hence, we have little patience with or understanding of those individuals who appear to have distorted the truth or remembered incorrectly what we "know" to be the truth. This assumption is inherent in Freud's concept of repression, which postulated that painful events are repressed from conscious awareness. The task of the psychoanalyst, in that system of therapy, is to lift the veil of repression so that the patient may recall these events; in other words, to make the covert overt.

But what if memory could not be assumed to be accurate? What if it were subject to constant changes over the years in response to people's ongoing experiences and changing life circumstances? What if memory were partly or perhaps largely constructed in response to people's fears, wishes, and hopes? In that case we could not and should not assume that people who remember events differently from others, especially us, are necessarily lying. Perhaps they are but perhaps they aren't, at least not completely. Or perhaps they or we have engaged in reconstructive memory. Recent research has indicated that this indeed appears to be the case.

ASSESSING MEMORY

Traditionally, there have been three procedures for assessing retention or memory: recall, recognition, and relearning (Bugelski 1984). Of these, recognition demonstrates the most substantial retention. In this procedure the individual is presented with material, some of which was originally learned, and asked to identify the previously learned material. Depending on the nature of the nonlearned material (distractors), people can usually recognize a substantial amount of previously learned material. For example, if the distractors were quite similar to the previously learned material, people can recall less of it than if the distractors were less similar. Thus, recognition memory can be deliberately manipulated by the inclusion of variously similar distractors.

In recall, individuals are asked to recall previously learned material without prompts. Typically, less retention is demonstrated by this method than by recognition, the amount recalled depending on the number of exposures to the material, the length of the material, and the motivation to recall. Sometimes subsequent recall is more complete than the first recall, in what is called *reminiscence*. Often, individuals can be guided or "cued" to recall more by the presentation of associated material. For example, if the word dog was on the list of previously learned material, an experimenter cue might be to ask if any animals were on the list. So recall memory can also be manipulated by the presentation of cues.

It has been demonstrated repeatedly that material previously learned and partially or completely forgotten can be relearned in a much shorter period of time. For example, individuals who previously learned German can relearn it quickly in the proper context, perhaps on a trip to Germany. Thus context and rehearsal can manipulate the experience of memory.

It should be apparent from the foregoing that in the process of assessing memory we run the risk of modifying that memory. Such an interference between assessment and change has been noted before in psychological phenomena. For example, early conditioning therapists discovered that observing classroom interactions among children changed the nature of those interactions. This is known as the *Heisenberg Effect*, after the German physicist Werner Heisenberg, who discovered that observation of the motion of subatomic particles itself changed that motion. Thus, in assessing memory, we can never be exactly sure what we are assessing.

TYPES OF MEMORY

There are also different kinds of memories and memory systems. Early in the investigation of memory, scientists made a distinction between short-term and long-term memory. The former lasts only for a few seconds; the latter can last for years. To convert memories from short term to long term, a process known as *encoding* is used (Schacter 1996). In encoding, people associate the new learning with other meaningful data. For example, in learning a string of numbers, individuals may chunk the numbers into sections that are more meaningful; thus 3306727664 may be chunked into 330.672.7664. This is my office telephone number and I know (from prior learning) that 330 is the area code for my part of Northeast Ohio and 672 is the general prefix for Kent State University. Thus the only new information I have to remember is 7664. If I were to chunk the numbers as 33.067.276.64, they would be much more difficult to remember. Foreign telephone numbers are in fact often chunked differently from American telephone numbers, leading to recall difficulty of foreign numbers for Americans.

Because encoding makes use of prior knowledge, however, it can distort memory for the new information (Schacter 1996). Underencoding can lead an individual to recall two men who were short and had large mustaches as being the same person, thus resulting in misidentification. Encoding can also add information to the original data if the encoding is especially elaborative, resulting in overencoding. Elaborative encoding or overencoding occurs when new information is encoded into preexisting knowledge structures that are especially comprehensive. For example, if an expert on symphonic music listens to a piece of music, he or she may recall clarinets or horns if other similar compositions made extensive use of horns or clarinets. Devotees of the music of Gustav Mahler may recall horn calls in one of his works because Mahler made extensive use of horns in his symphonies. New memories may be influenced by old memories, leading to the saying, "We see what we expect to see." Thus the processes that enable memories to be converted from short term to long term may change the very nature of those long-term memories.

There appear to be two types of encoding processes, conceptually driven and data-driven. Conceptually driven processing refers to encoding activities initiated by the subject, such as generating, elaborating, organizing, and reconstructing (Fleming et al. 1992) and they act to increase recognition memory while reducing identification. This type of encoding is what has just been discussed. Data-driven processing, however, involves information presented without context and increases identification while decreasing recognition. For memory to occur with the latter form of encoding, we must first perceive the stimulus. Data-driven processing may be responsible for the experience of déjà vu, in which individuals experience a situation as familiar even though it has not occurred before. A phrase or idea may have triggered an implicit association (Schacter 1996) that results in the feeling that we have been there before.

A major advance in the investigation of memory was the discovery of multiple memory systems, specifically explicit and implicit memory (Schacter 1996). The ability to recognize, recall, or relearn information presented earlier is known as *explicit memory*. Such memory may be short term or long term, it may be deeply encoded or shallowly encoded, but it has been deliberately learned and can at least be partially recalled as having been learned.

Implicit memory, on the other hand, occurs when people are influenced by a past experience without an awareness of remembering (Schacter 1996). It is similar to what has been called unconscious processes, but that is so loaded with excess conceptual baggage that the former term should probably be used instead. Because it involves data-driven processing, which involves perception without context, we cannot recall the source of the information. We can recall the information but we cannot relate it to other information. The inability of implicit memory to be source-specific is an important point that will be discussed later.

Explicit and implicit memory appear to derive from the two types of encoding systems mentioned above (Dowd and Courchaine 1996, Fleming et al. 1992). Although there is overlap, in general, explicit learning derives from conceptually driven processing (memory as an object), while implicit learning derives from data-driven processing (memory as a tool). Thus implicit memory derives from the act of perceiving certain phenomena and leads to an identification without setting or context. It is similar to semantic memory and involves a tacit association of concepts and rules that form our knowledge of the world. It may lead to common experiences such as the feeling that two things are similar when we can't quite identify why and uncertainty whether an experience actually occurred or was imagined (Schacter 1996). For example, my son was once uncertain whether he truly remembered an often-cited childhood event. He wasn't sure, he said, whether he actually remembered it or simply remembered us talking about it. Repeatedly talking about it with my wife and me, as well as with others, however, would tend to embed this in his mind as a "memory" (Fleming et al. 1992).

Dowd and Courchaine (1996) have summarized the major attributes of implicit learning. Some that have particular relevance for this discussion are the following:

1. Implicit knowledge has been shown to be acquired faster than explicit knowledge, to be especially important in emotion-based knowledge, and to be more inflexible and resistant to change. Long-term, semiautomatic habits may be acquired by implicit learning (Schacter 1996)—and we all know how resistant to change they are!

2. Implicit learning may actually be more effective than explicit learning, especially in learning complex tasks. It occurs by the gradual induction of an underlying abstract representation that reflects the structure of the environment (Reber 1993). It's as if people learn by osmosis, by immersing themselves in the situation. They cannot report how they learned it or often where they learned it.

3. Implicit learning occurs through the tacit detection of covariation, that is, by unconsciously noticing which things or events go together. Behavioral theory has called this associational learning. If two or more events occur together, we assume they are related to each other. In the process, tacit (or unconscious) rules are formed (e.g., "When I trust people, I get hurt"). However, when faced with ambiguous situations, people tend to impose preexisting categories and rules on them, thus ensuring that they interpret new situations as similar to previous ones. They also can detect subtle covariations where none really occur. Thus people who expect others to be untrustworthy may interpret ambiguous interpersonal situations as reflecting a lack of trust-

worthiness in the other person and behave accordingly. They may detect small (and to other people inconsequential) behaviors as demonstrating this untrustworthiness.

4. The rules and associations developed by implicit learning are nonverbal (often preverbal) and therefore cannot be discussed verbally. Precisely because they cannot be discussed, they tend to be resistant to change. How, for example, can we decide to change what we cannot even put into words? However, implicit knowledge appears to be conceptually richer than explicit knowledge.

There are other ways to think about different memory systems. Williams (1996), for example, distinguishes among four different types of memory. *Fact memory* refers to the facts of our general knowledge and is what most people think of as memory. Dysfunctional attitudes and automatic assumptions are fact memories. *Behavioral memory* (or procedural memory) is the knowledge of how to do something and is often intact in amnesic patients. Emotional memories are partially encoded by this system and change can be fostered by deliberately focusing on the traumatic experience and reinterpreting these events. *Event memory* is the ability to recall or retrieve memories of, for example, traumatic events. It has been found that depressed individuals, though they know there was a time when they weren't depressed, often cannot recall any specific examples of such times. *Prospective memory* involves remembering to do future things—to keep appointments, for example. It may leave people with the uncomfortable (though often unspecified) feeling that they have something on their mind and may result in setting goals that are impossible to attain, such as being liked by everyone. These goals remain in the individual's memory system and interrupt and inhibit other tasks.

THE ROLE OF PRIMING

Think of priming as a form of hinting to enhance memory. For example, suppose I give you a list of words such as *woman*, *concrete*, *follow-up*, *employee*, and *jailhouse*. Later I ask you to fill in the blanks in the following words; *wo- - -*, *cl- - - - -*, *fol- - -up*, *su- -en*, and *conf- - -nce*. No doubt you could easily do this for the first and third words, but you would probably have much more difficulty with the second (*classic*), fourth (*sudden*), and fifth (*confidence*). There are in fact two correct answers for the last two. The reason you can fill in the blanks easier for the first and third words than for the others is that your memory for the first and third words has been primed by seeing them in the initial list (Schacter 1996). Priming helps you to recall words, ideas, or concepts by seeing them earlier, even in different contexts. Had *confidence* been included in the original list, it is much more likely that you would have recalled it than the equally likely *conference*.

Priming can affect what people think and how they interpret events. Kirsch and Lynn (1998) discuss evidence indicating that when participants read lists of names that included famous and nonfamous people, they were more likely to rate the nonfamous people as more famous when shown the list the following day. In other words, simply being associated with famous people may result in more ascribed fame for oneself, regardless of any real accomplishment. In this case, fame is inferred by association only. Kirsch and Lynn also discuss evidence suggesting that priming was noticeable when participants were asked to categorize ambiguous stimuli. When faced with ambiguous situations, we tend to impose our existing conceptual categories on them, ensuring that we will see the future as we see the past. Cognitive consistency is important to humans.

The interesting thing about priming is that it appears to operate largely out of consciousness or conscious memory (Schacter 1996). Although people are less and less accurate at recalling things consciously after greater lapses of time, the priming effect seems to be just as great later as it was earlier. Although older people tend to show memory deficits, they do not show deficits in priming. In addition, the priming effect is just as great whether or not people actually recall the original learning. The type of memory illustrated by priming effects is an example of implicit memory. Although the individual may not have an explicit memory of the original learning, he or she can demonstrate that learning did in fact occur. Not only that, but the learning does not appear to decay with time.

Priming occurs constantly throughout our lives (Schacter 1996). For example, we often recall things without knowing the source of our memory—sometimes plagiarizing a source in the process. We may tell a colleague or the boss about a new and exciting idea we have, only to hear that person tell us the same idea in a month or so, seemingly without knowing that we were the originator! It is easy to suspect duplicity, but priming may be the real answer. Some employees in fact may deliberately prime their bosses with ideas the latter may initially reject, hoping that they will later forget the source, think the ideas were their own, and implement them. The negative attributes of subliminal perception, when people are influenced by advertising too brief to notice explicitly, may be due to priming. The déjà vu experience, where we are certain we have experienced something before, may be due to priming from a previous similar experience. Gender, racial, and other biases may also be part of an implicit memory structure people are not aware of having, and their implicit negative views of certain groups may be primed by interactions with members of these groups (Schacter 1996). These people may be telling the "truth" (as they see it) when they say they are not prejudiced. Thus priming appears to be deeply implicated in human learning and memory and, as discussed earlier, implicit learning may be faster and more effective than explicit learning, though it may also be more resistant to change.

In implicit memory people often demonstrate an inability to remember the source of previously learned information (Schacter 1996). For example, we tend to discredit a message if we discredit the source, which is responsible for our dismissal of information from those on the other side of the political spectrum from us. But what happens if we forget the source of a previously discredited message? In that case we are more likely to accept the message in the future. This source amnesia in implicit memory can lead to memory distortions. We may remember that we have seen someone before but misremember where, leading perhaps to misidentification in a criminal situation. For example, we may incorrectly identify someone as a suspect in a crime but not recall that we actually remembered seeing him in another context. Source amnesia may be at the heart of what has been called the false memory syndrome.

Johnson and her colleagues (1993) have in fact argued that the ability to recall source information is what distinguishes memory from imagination. When we can recall the source and context of our memory, we can have more confidence it is real; when we cannot, we are more likely to confuse imagining and fantasy with the memory for real events. This is why it is so important to provide external corroboration for recovered memories of traumatic events.

USING PRIMING IN EVERYDAY LIFE

Besides being present in human learning and memory, priming can be used deliberately as well. The Freudian free association technique, in which individuals are instructed to say the first thing that enters their mind and continue likewise thereafter is an example of priming. Internal thoughts, feelings, and images act as the prime. Indeed, the whole point of free association is to encourage and enable people to report "unconscious" (i.e., implicit/tacit) memories and associations they could not otherwise recall and to bypass conscious and explicit resistance. It is likely that people are using internally generated primes when they repeatedly process words or images to themselves that trigger unpleasant or frightening memories and associations. The intrusive thoughts and images that characterize posttraumatic stress disorder may be seen as internally generated primes.

Primes can also be externally imposed and can be negative as well as positive. Devine (1989), for example, found that white students who were exposed to a quickly flashed list of words that suggested a stereotyped African American (e.g., ghetto, basketball, Harlem, busing, welfare) were more likely to rate ambiguous behaviors of an imaginary (and racially unspecified) male as more hostile than students who had been exposed to neutral words. In this experiment the words functioned as primes even though the subjects could not remember them. This is an excellent example of a negative prime that occurs in many different life contexts.

What might an externally imposed positive prime look like? Using Devine's (1989) experimental model, we might construct a list of positive words that suggest a stereotyped successful person (e.g., confident, energetic, forthright, successful, imaginative) and then expose subjects to them quickly. Later ambiguous behaviors of an imaginary person might then be rated more positively than those same behaviors might be rated by subjects who had been exposed to neutral words. It would be interesting to then specify the race of the imaginary person and see if the positive primes affected the ratings of the behaviors of the imaginary person.

We can use externally imposed positive primes in clinical situations too. Imagine that an individual, Joe, comes to a therapist for treatment of depression. All Joe has are negative thoughts about bad events. In Beck and colleagues' (1979) formulation he has negative views of the world, himself, and the future. Furthermore, Joe continuously indoctrinates himself, in a form of negative self-hypnosis (Araoz 1985), in his negativistic thinking by constantly rehearsing these negative thoughts and seeing (imagining) himself in negative situations. In other words, Joe constantly feeds himself negative primes with the result that he interprets ambiguous situations negatively. What will the therapist do to help Joe overcome his depression? First, assume that Joe has had some positive and happy experiences earlier in his life. No one has only unrelieved misery throughout life, though it may appear so at the time because depressed people remember depressing times and events better than they remember nondepressed times and events. In a simplistic formulation the therapist might quickly flash a series of positive and happy words to Joe (for example, *happiness, peace, ebullience, energetic*) and see if this triggers a change in Joe's subsequent automatic thoughts and mood. Now imagine the therapist saying these positive and happy words while Joe is in a trance and you will begin to understand the possibilities. The happy word primes may arouse associations to earlier times in Joe's life even if he cannot recall or explicitly perceive these words. Since the priming effect is not nearly as affected by the passage of time as explicit memory, the positive prime words may access former happy times that occurred quite a while ago. Of course, previous conversations with Joe might have given the therapist some indications of words, thoughts, and former events that Joe might have found mood-enhancing, so the happy word primes would have particular relevance for him. Generic positive primes may not be as effective as those specifically constructed for the person and the situation. In addition, the happy word primes may help Joe to interpret ambiguous situations more positively, much as Devine's (1989) negative primes fostered more negative interpretations in ambiguous situations.

This, in essence, is what Milton Erickson often did in hypnotherapy. He preferred not to suggest or add anything new to his patients' cognitive processes, relying instead on facilitating their ability to utilize and develop what they already have, that is, "taking the learnings that the person already has and applying them in other ways" (Erickson et al. 1976, p. 5). Later, Erickson and Rossi (1979) state that:

> The effective hypnotherapist learns to use words, intonations, gestures, and other things that evoke the patient's own mental mechanisms and behavioral processes. . . . Erickson liked to emphasize that hypnotic suggestion can evoke and utilize potentials that already exist within patients, but it cannot impose something totally alien. . . . [p. 19]

Erickson also reframed ambiguous situations so they could be interpreted in an unusual or alternative fashion from the client's current interpretation. But the unique associations triggered in the client's mind by the therapist's hypnotic suggestions can be seen as the effect of positive primes on reshaping the interpretation of past and subsequent ambiguous situations. Because the source of the original message cannot easily be remembered in implicit memory, it becomes more difficult to discredit the message by discrediting the source. The "divided attention" (Fleming et al. 1992) characteristic of the work of Ericksonian hypnotherapists contributes to the inability to recall source information. An example of divided attention in Ericksonian hypnotherapy follows:

> Your conscious mind may realize the experience of tenderness (memory used as an object [i.e., explicit memory]) while your unconscious mind relives that childhood experience (memory used as a tool [i.e., implicit memory]) from which it came. Or perhaps your

conscious mind will be aware of that childhood experience (memory as an object [i.e., explicit memory]) while your unconscious mind generates the feeling of tenderness (memory as a tool [i.e., implicit memory]). . . . [Fleming et al. 1992, p. 165, material in brackets added]

In this illustration the divided attention prevents the client from monitoring and evaluating the source of the explicit memory because he or she has more difficulty elaborating the cues available. The client cannot necessarily recognize items but can still assess familiarity of the item (Fleming et al. 1992).

THE "FALSE MEMORY SYNDROME"

Perhaps no psychological phenomenon today is as controversial and arouses such heated debate on both sides of the topic as the recovery of repressed memories of childhood sexual abuse, often by hypnosis. It is not my intent in this book to provide a detailed analysis of this controversy; it is available in other sources. However, I would like to describe some of the issues that have arisen as they pertain to memory distortion and reconstruction by hypnosis. These issues are important to an understanding of how memories can be modified by cognitive hypnotherapy.

The essential issue in the repression of traumatic memories is this: Is it possible for these memories to be so completely repressed that they cannot be recalled at all, even the very existence of the trauma? Furthermore, is it possible for these memories to be recovered, intact and with a high degree of accuracy, by psychotherapeutic, sometimes hypnotherapeutic, means? A related question is, Are there certain symptom clusters that tend to point to the existence of a repressed memory of childhood sexual abuse?

The proponents of this view argue that such repression is indeed possible for extremely traumatic events, and childhood sexual abuse is more common than is generally thought. They point to clinical evidence supporting the recovery of sexual abuse memories by psychotherapeutic means and argue that experimental analogues do not involve trauma sufficiently intense to cause the massive repression with which they are familiar. The more extreme views, put forth in such books as *The Courage to Heal* (Bass and Davis 1988), provide a list of symptoms that they consider to be indicators of abuse. Furthermore, if these symptoms are present, they often assume that sexual abuse occurred even if the individual cannot remember it. It is the task, even the ethical obligation, of the therapist to pursue it. As Bass and Davis state:

> Yet even if your memories are incomplete, even if your family insists nothing ever happened, you still must believe yourself. Even if what you experienced feels too extreme to be possible or too mild to be abuse, even if you think, "I must have made it up," or "No one could have done that to a child," you have to come to terms with the fact that someone did do those things to you. [p. 87]

The opponents of this view make use of several lines of evidence (Spanos 1996). They do not deny that childhood sexual abuse occurs, perhaps more often than we think, or that certain aspects of it can be forgotten. They do argue, however, that while certain aspects of the abuse may be forgotten or confused, it is highly unlikely that its very existence can be forgotten. Pointing to the analogous posttraumatic stress disorder in combat veterans, Spanos (1996) has stated that while PTSD combat veterans may forget or distort certain aspects of their combat experience, they do not forget that they were in combat at all. Indeed, these individuals generally experience unwanted and intrusive flashbacks rather than massive repression. The opponents see our current obsession with childhood sexual abuse as an example of social contagion, similar to the existence of witch (or communist) hunting in earlier cultures. The more we look for examples of a phenomenon, the more we tend to find them. Thus, in our present culture with all its publicity about childhood sexual abuse, it may be relatively easy for distressed individuals to begin to suspect they have been abused (Farrants 1998). The opponents are especially wary of suggestive psychotherapeutic and hypnotherapeutic procedures in uncovering repressed memories because they often involve strong demands by authority figures (in individual therapy) or group pressure (in group therapy) to come up with stories of sexual abuse in order to obtain group or therapist attention. They are more inclined to accept spontaneously recovered memories than those recovered by psychotherapy, but more than two-thirds of alleged abuses arise during therapy (Roe et al. 1994). They cite numerous studies indicating that suggestive experimental procedures can foster false memories (e.g., Loftus and Coan, in press, Loftus and Pickrell 1995), though the proponents argue that these procedures are not sufficiently traumatic. The opponents also cite evidence that hypnosis has not been shown to enhance the recovery of accurate memories, though it can induce false memories. Indeed, there is evidence that it is not the hypnosis per se that is important, but the hypnotizability of the subject that influences false recall (Brown 1995). Furthermore, Brigidi and colleagues (1998) found that traumatized individuals (regardless of the presence of an official *DSM-IV* diagnosis) may be more likely to generate false memories and that greater levels of anxiety, depression, and dissociation may be related to false memories. Finally, opponents point to the existence of bizarre recovered memories, such as satanic abuse and past lives memories, as evidence of the unreliability of those procedures. In any event, infantile amnesia would prevent the recall, by any means, of incidents prior to about three years of age.

Is there any middle ground in this debate? One of the problems is that most instances of recovered memories of sexual abuse involve retrospective accounts in which the individual is recalling events that occurred years ago. There is evidence that memories of past events can be shaped by present wishes, hopes, fears, and expectancies—and that the past can influence our memories in the present (Schacter 1996, Spanos 1996). For example, we often remember our participation in important events much differently after the passage of years, as anyone knows who has had to listen to an old veteran's war stories. The story of the Hungarian folk hero Hary Janos tells of his "memory" of defeating Napoleon singlehandedly. Thus retrospective accounts of childhood sexual abuse without corroborating evidence are suspect. It's not that they aren't true; it's just that there are no reliable procedures to determine which memories are true and which are false. We can't be sure without external corroboration. Another way out of this dilemma is to consider as accurate only recovered memories that arise spontaneously and are not the result of therapeutic procedures. All therapeutic procedures are suggestive to some extent, but some procedures are highly suggestive, especially where ritualized procedures are used by highly credible authority figures. In this regard Pope and Brown (1996) report data that indicate women who gradually and spontaneously remembered incidents of abuse were as accurate as women who had always remembered their abuse. Pope and Brown also report that the hypnotizability of the individual rather than the use of hypnosis per se is what increases the production of pseudomemories. Highly hypnotizable individuals produce more pseudomemories whether or not formal hypnosis is used, and social influence can produce more pseudomemories in highly hypnotizable people. Recall also that Brigidi and colleagues (1998) found that false memories may be related to such external variables as previous trauma and such internal variables as anxiety, depression, and dissociation.

THE SUGGESTIBILITY OF PSYCHOTHERAPY

As mentioned above, all psychotherapeutic procedures are leading and suggestive to some extent; it's one of the reasons why it's effective in fostering change. Even relatively innocuous therapist behaviors, such as leaning forward, looking interested, or saying, "Tell me more" when the client speaks of certain topics, or alternatively failing to respond when other topics are mentioned, can gradually shape the direction of the session. Therapists learn that they can help clients to explore certain sensitive areas by the encouragement and support they give and discourage them from exploring other, presumably less productive areas by disapproval or ignoring. For example, most therapists consider a simple recitation of the week's events to be therapeutically unproductive and would gently (or otherwise) steer clients away from this type of communication and toward an exploration of the meaning of these events

for them. Therapists also suggest to clients, at varying levels of direct-
ness, that they would profit if they explored areas in consonance with
the therapist's orientation. Thus psychoanalysts might suggest an exploration of the client's sexuality; behavior therapists might suggest a
discussion of reinforcing consequences in the client's environment.

Certain techniques are even more leading and suggestive. The belief among some therapists that all symptoms have trauma as their cause
may lead to false recall, as therapists urge their clients to "remember"
(Brown 1995). Some recovered memory therapists have been criticized
for using such statements as, "I've found through my extensive experience that people who show your symptoms have invariably been abused.
Even if you don't recall it now, I'm sure you can if you try hard enough."
Some reportedly have even said things like, "What did that bastard do
to you?!" Selective therapist attention itself can be a source of suggestion. Spanos (1996) has discussed the strong social pressure on clients
to generate memories of prior sexual abuse in order to obtain attention
from the therapist and other group members, a phenomenon well known
to those who have studied the social conformity process (e.g., Asch
1956). When guided over time by such therapist behavior, clients can
come to "remember" things that may or may not be "true."

Hypnotherapeutic suggestions can be especially powerful; indeed,
the definition of hypnosis according to the cognitive-behavioral formulation involves subject willingness to respond to suggestions and to therapist expectations in the context of an ambiguous situation defined as
hypnosis. Although it is a point of some controversy, there is evidence
that highly hypnotizable subjects (or clients) are more likely to follow
the hypnotist's (or therapist's) suggestions. Thus it appears that hypnotic suggestions, especially in ambiguous situations and for highly
hypnotizable individuals, may be especially powerful. Leading and suggestive hypnotic statements include "yes sets," such as, "It's interesting,
isn't it . . . ? You want to change, *don't you* . . . ? and truisms, such as
"Your problem can disappear as soon as your system is ready for it to
leave." "Yes sets" are obvious statements that encourage affirmative responses to subsequent, less obvious, statements. Truisms are statements
so obviously true that there is no possibility of disagreement (Erickson

et al. 1976). Other leading hypnotic suggestions (Erickson and Rossi 1979) include not knowing, not doing ("You don't have to do anything . . ."); open-ended suggestions ("You can begin to review your thoughts related to your problem but you don't know yet what you will find most useful"); embedded suggestions ("You don't know yet [implying you will] when you will begin to change, whether it will be in a day or as long as a week" [implying it will be no longer than a week]; or responses covering all possibilities, thus leaving no room for noncompliance ("You may first gain weight or lose it or remain the same as you learn really important things about yourself"). The important point, however, is that the hypnotherapist creates leading and suggestive statements designed to encourage the client to move in healthy directions.

THE RECONSTRUCTION OF MEMORY

I have now provided a theoretical and empirical context for the reconstruction of memories by psychotherapeutic procedures. Interestingly, however, these procedures are not new—though they are not commonly known. Hacking (1995) reported that Pierre Janet, an early collaborator of Sigmund Freud, replaced traumatic memories with pleasant but false memories in order to reduce trauma associated with the earlier memories. Janet often did this using hypnosis. Bandler and Grinder (1979), the creators of neurolinguistic programming, reportedly implemented false memories and even false childhoods in clients to make them feel better about themselves. They noted, "Made-up memories can change you just as well as the arbitrary perceptions that you made up at the time about 'real world events.' That happens a lot in therapy" (p. 96).

Indeed it does, and it's sometimes called *reframing*. Reframing is a quasi-paradoxical technique that has been defined as a reinterpretation of an event so that it is interpreted positively instead of negatively—or theoretically the reverse (Dowd and Trutt 1988). There is an implicit reframing component in Beck's cognitive therapy of depression (Beck et al. 1979) in that the therapist assists the client to examine the evidence against the interpretation of negative views of the self, world, and future, hopefully resulting in a positive reframing. Clients, however, engage in negative reframing, in that they consistently interpret positive or neutral events in a negative light. As an example of negative reframing, one client attempted suicide because her kettle of water boiled over. Her interpretation of this seemingly innocuous event was, "My God, I'm so bad I can't even boil water!" Cognitive therapists assist clients to reframe these types of negative interpretations positively.

One does not have to follow the more extreme views of Bandler and Grinder (1979) in attempting to implant entire false childhoods to use memory reconstruction. Often it is just a matter of helping the client to modify a certain aspect of his or her memory to reduce distress. Central to this approach is the idea, discussed in the first part of this chapter, that memories are often cognitive constructions that reflect a wide variety of wishes, fears, and motivations in addition to accurate facts. Furthermore, if we cannot determine the source of a memory, we cannot have the same degree of confidence in its reality that we otherwise could—though often we actually have more confidence in it. Thus, when clients bring us their memories of traumatic events, we cannot always distinguish the factual from the imaginative. Nor, for the purposes of psychotherapy, is it always necessary that we do so.

For an example of the use of memory reconstruction in the service of positive therapeutic change, let us look at Susan's experience. As 29-year-old Susan hurried home from the local convenience store, she shivered as a bitter January wind cut through the warmth of her coat. Feeling uneasy, she walked alone, accompanied only by the early darkness of the winter. With mind and body aching from the cold, she slowly climbed the stairs to her apartment. As her key slipped into the lock, she sighed with relief and opened the door. Suddenly, from out of the darkness, strong arms overpowered her and forced her inside. She heard the door slam shut as she clawed at the hand covering her mouth. Overwhelmed with fear, she struggled until a blinding pain in her face sent her crashing to the floor. As her head struck and her body went limp, she felt herself slipping away. Opening her eyes, Susan found herself in an unfamiliar setting with strangers hovering around her. As her thoughts began to clear, she understood and began to remember. She was questioned at length and on more than one occasion by the police about the incident. However, her memory appeared to be cloudy and with significant gaps and she felt a strong lack of trust in other people, especially men. Accordingly, she sought therapy from a well-known hypnotherapist. A cognitive analysis indicated the following beliefs:

1. I am/will always be powerless/helpless.
   a. I can't/will never be able to protect myself.
   b. I am/will always be vulnerable.
   c. I am not/will never be safe again.
   d. Every situation is dangerous.
   e. The world is not a safe place.
2. I should have been more careful.
3. I am dirty/I will never be clean again.
4. Men can't be trusted/I will never trust men again.
5. He will come back/He is watching me.

Her therapist, aware of the research on memory and learning processes, asked Susan exactly what she remembered of the situation and the incidents leading up to it. It is important that the therapist obtain as much detail as possible so that certain aspects of the memory can be reconstructed. Susan remembered primarily the helpless and powerless feeling, along with feelings of lack of trust in men, without many of the details described above.

Three memory phenomena may have been active in Susan's account of her rape. First, postevent information may have distorted her memory. This distortion occurs when postevent information, often in the form of misleading or inaccurate questions, changes the memory of the original event. For example, if people see a traffic accident in which a car ran a stop sign and are later asked about a yield sign, they may recall the nonexistent yield sign (Spanos 1996). Likewise, if they are told a story about a visit by a stranger and later asked about nonexistent behaviors by this visitor, they may begin to recall these behaviors even though they didn't actually happen (Schacter 1996). Because her power and control were taken from her and she reported this to the police (along with her lack of trust), she primarily remembered feeling powerless and untrusting.

Second, Susan had cognitively processed the situation to herself repeatedly before seeing the therapist. Research has shown (see Dowd and Courchaine 1996, Fleming et al. 1992 for a discussion) that the more events are recalled, the more confidence the individual has in that memory but the less accurate the memory becomes. Indeed, the most accurate memories tend to be recalled the least and the least accurate memories are often held with great confidence. Spanos (1996) reported that although people generally assume a strong relationship between the accuracy of a memory and the confidence with which it is held, the relationship has in fact been demonstrated to be quite weak (though apparently not negative). Repeated processing of a traumatic event can be healing, but the memory for that event may be changed in the process. By her repeated recollection of her helplessness and powerlessness during the event, Susan may have changed the memory of that event.

Third, Susan's memories of the situation may have been a combination of fact memories and behavioral memories. Her fact memory for the event had apparently been affected by the repeated questioning and repeated processing. Her behavioral memory for the event affected her in that she reacted to men and potentially dangerous situations differently than she once had.

Accordingly, the therapist constructed the following hypnotic routine to facilitate the reconstruction of Susan's memory. I should note that Susan required repeated hypnotic inductions and deepening before she felt comfortable going further with hypnosis. This type of repeated hypnotic processing is not uncommon with trauma clients and therapists must be patient. Each time, however, Susan was able to go a little further into a trance for a little longer. In the process she was slowly able to build confidence and trust in one person again. Because she was still emotionally affected by the incident, the therapist chose to use a distancing technique within the trance to help Susan reduce the emotion aroused. Had she been less emotionally affected, the therapist might have used age regression to increase the immediacy of the experience.

> Susan, I'd like you to remember the scene of the incident we talked about. Think back to the time you began to walk up the stairs to your apartment and see yourself in that setting . . . but see yourself from a

distance, as though you were looking down on yourself from higher up, seeing yourself smaller and farther away [distancing technique to reduce emotionality]. You don't need to feel quite as much . . . your feelings, just like you, are farther away and less intense. It's as though you were seeing and feeling from a distance—seeing less and feeling less—seeing smaller and feeling smaller. That's right! And you can relax yourself, just like we've practiced, as you see yourself beginning to walk upstairs. See yourself unlocking and opening the door; see yourself walking in; now, slowly, almost in slow motion, feel the hand upon your mouth.[Susan began to tense up, not an unexpected reaction. If it continued, the therapist might terminate the hypnotic session and return to it later.] You feel scared but it's happening very slowly, very slowly . . . and you can still be **in control of yourself** because you can decide to reduce your chances of being hurt. Now freeze that image in your mind, relaxing some of the tension away. Now let the image progress forward once again—toward the end of the incident. . . . Now slowly relax and think about what you have learned (*pause*). Now you can begin to imagine yourself becoming cleaner and cleaner [speaks to a distorted belief] . . . as the incident is over, you feel cleaner and cleaner, remembering the relief and happiness you felt afterwards and feeling cleaner as you feel more relaxed. And you can take comfort remembering that you did everything you could to stop it . . . were successful in not really being hurt . . . remembering that you weren't responsible for it . . . were as careful as you could be. Perhaps you can even remember locking the door as you first left [incorporation of possible new memory]. You remember too, don't you, that you have been safe, felt safe, in many situations before—and you will be safe again. You remember too, don't you, the many times you have **felt in control, felt strong and in charge**—and you will feel that way again. You remember too, don't you, that there was only one man . . . a different man would probably not have done that. Men are different too, aren't they, just like women . . . some can be trusted, some can't, the important thing is to know the difference. And you can begin to feel more comfortable with other men, knowing that men are different, do different things. . . .

Throughout this routine the therapist was constantly alert for signs of increased tenseness in Susan and stopped the image whenever it occurred. Had the tension continued, the therapist would have terminated the hypnotic session and discussed it later. It may take repeated processing before Susan is able to go all the way through the incident. During the hypnotic session there were repeated suggestions that she was not at fault, that she had been careful and had taken precautions to be safe. There were also suggestions of additional, possibly new, memories of having been in control in the past, of having trusted, and of feeling safe. Although I have included several suggestions for memory changes in this illustration, in practice it might not be wise to include them all in one hypnotic suggestion. Finally, although I usually have not identified therapist gender in this book, I would like to say that in treating female assault victims the therapist should likewise be female. There may be some advantage to a male therapist in that Susan could learn to trust at least one man again, but I suspect in this case the problems would outweigh the benefits.

For a similar example with a different hypnotic routine, let's consider the following case. Acquaintance rape is perhaps the most common type of rape; indeed, it is often not classified as rape at all, either by the perpetrator or by the victim. This very ambiguity can lead to memory distortions as the victim adjusts her memories to her definition of the situation.

Twenty-year-old Ann worked as a waitress at a small family restaurant in her rural midwestern town. The establishment's relaxed, comfortable atmosphere was enhanced by her warm smile and sparkling eyes. Her life seemed safe and predictable until one Sunday evening in late September. She had begun her day with a walk to work in the crisp morning air, accompanied only by the cheerful greetings of birds. Feeling fresh and energetic, she began a busy, yet uneventful, routine day. By the end of her shift she was tired, but eager to be surrounded by the soothing scent of honeysuckle and the tranquil serenade of lazy crickets during her walk home.

She had walked only a few blocks when the wind began to gust and the first drops of rain slapped at her face. The sudden darkness left her feeling uneasy and she quickened her pace as the drenching rain and howling wind took on force. The beep of a horn caused her to stop and turn around. She felt a sense of relief as John, her shift manager, motioned to her. Happy to see a familiar face, she ran to the car and jumped in.

John was an attractive, intelligent man of 21 whose charming personality provided laughter and small talk during the ride home. Through chattering teeth she invited him in for coffee. After changing into a warm, dry sweatsuit, she rejoined him in the kitchen. Suddenly, without a word, he impulsively came up behind her and slipped his arms around her waist. Surprised and confused, she tried to move away from him. His grip tightened as he bent down to kiss her. A wave of panic ran through her as she struggled to break free. As he pushed her to the floor, an overwhelming sense of fear and helplessness flooded her mind. For the first time in her life she felt completely powerless. After the assault, John casually got up and left without a word. Ann ran to the door, locked and bolted it, and fell to the floor. Pulling her legs tightly into her chest, she cried until there were no more tears.

When she came for therapy, Ann presented the following appearance:

- She wore unflattering, baggy clothes.
- Her hair was down and around her face in an attempt to hide.
- She wore no makeup.
- Her body language appeared protective.
- She had a dull glaze in her eyes and her facial expression was sad.
- Her manner was lethargic.

During the initial sessions Ann's therapist identified the following self-statements:

- "I never should have invited him in."
- "I should have seen signs."
- "I must have done something to lead him on" (e.g., a smile).
- "I should have driven my car instead of walking."

- "What is wrong with me?" (more generic).
- "It was my fault" (because he was not a stranger).

Ann also had several dysfunctional emotions, including anxiety, depression, embarrassment, and humiliation. There were also behavioral memories about not trusting men and situations that do not appear dangerous on the surface.

Ann's situation was different and more ambiguous than Susan's because the perpetrator was a trusted acquaintance and perhaps a friend. Whereas Susan may be helped by therapist attempts to change her memories of the event, it is more likely that she will believe that the assault was not her fault. Susan was clearly assaulted by someone she didn't know, so it would be more difficult for her to believe she was in any way at fault. Ann, however, may be more likely to believe that she had contributed to the situation because she knew and liked the perpetrator. There is a powerful and deep-seated cultural image, often tacitly accepted by both men and women, that women want to be forcibly seduced and therefore encourage men to do so. Tacit cultural assumptions are difficult to access and challenge precisely because they are tacit and hence not subject to the usual explicit evaluative procedures. As part of this culture, with tacit knowledge of its assumptions, it may be easy for Ann to tacitly assume that she in some way encouraged the situation—or at least be confused enough so she may not be sure what she *did* want. Over time, without therapeutic intervention, her memories may shift so that she may come to believe that she really did desire and encourage it. Feelings of personal worthlessness and degradation may then follow, although it is unlikely Ann will connect the feelings to the cognitions.

Accordingly, and because of the self-statements earlier identified, the therapist chose to shift Ann's memories of the event away from those implicating her culpability to those shifting the responsibility to John—where it belonged. Ann remembered very clearly what she had done immediately preceding the assault but had a great deal of difficulty remembering what John had done. The therapist focused initially on two of Ann's self-statements: "I never should have invited him in" and "I must have done something to lead him on" as a way of shifting her memories and changing cognitive assumptions of personal guilt.

The statement, "I never should have invited him in," can be understood in the metaphorical sense of "inviting" John to have sex with her as well as the literal sense of inviting him into her house. Ann's memory of the event may have included an invitation in both senses of the term; in any event, she clearly remembered inviting him into her house. Accordingly, the therapist used the following routine:

> As you think back over the **assault** [this time, because Ann may not define or remember the situation as a real assault, the therapist used the stronger word], you can begin to remember John's actions just before the **assault** [repeated use of the word will accustom Ann to thinking of it that way]. You can begin to remember him pulling up to the front door of your house and you inviting him in—or did he invite himself in? Which was it—did you invite him in or did he invite himself in? It's difficult to remember now, isn't it [yes set]—perhaps he invited himself in. And as you think about it more, perhaps you can begin to remember him inviting himself in. But even if you invited him, he accepted, didn't he? So either way, he's responsible, isn't he, for what happened? Perhaps you even felt you **should** invite him in—not a real invitation, is it? So the more you think about it, the more you can realize there are different degrees of invitation, aren't there? And it's difficult to know which came first, isn't it? Did he invite himself, did you invite him, did you invite him because you thought you ought to, did he invite himself because he thought you ought to [confusion routine; repeat several times if necessary]—and the more you think about it the more difficult it becomes to remember exactly what happened, isn't it? Perhaps he really did invite himself in—or he expected you to invite him. Expectations don't even have to be verbal, do they? They can be expectations only—so even if you invited him, he has to let you know he expected to be invited . . . maybe not by words, but expected nonetheless. . . . And there are also different kinds of invitations too, aren't there? [a shift of topic, from who invited whom to levels of invitation]. If someone is invited

for one thing, it doesn't mean he's invited for everything, does it? So someone can invite himself in [suggestion of new memory] without inviting himself all the way in. And you can keep him way out without keeping him out. It all depends on how far in you want to let him and how far out you want to keep him—and you can decide and have the right to decide. "In" doesn't mean "way in," does it? It's like gradually getting to know someone and trusting him to come in; you gradually learn to trust and gradually learn to get to know him—feeling the trust grow as you get to know him gradually—feeling comfortable knowing the trust will grow gradually—that different people can be trusted in different ways at different speeds [a suggestion that she will be able to trust certain men again]. Trust is individual, isn't it? Sometimes you can trust, sometimes you can't. It's difficult to know who and when sometimes, isn't it? But you can learn when to trust and when not to trust, whom to trust and whom not to trust by letting things happen gradually, so you can be more certain. The sense of trust can soak in gradually. . . .

The therapist also dealt with Ann's self-statement, "I must have done something to lead him on," connected with her friendliness and warm smiles. Female prosocial behaviors can be misinterpreted by some men, who may interpret them as sexual invitations. As a result, this area is fraught with ambiguity, with men often not knowing how to interpret such behaviors (or interpreting them other than intended, usually for their own purposes) and women wondering if they were behaving inappropriately and/or questioning their own motivations. Ann's subsequent unattractive clothing and appearance may have been an attempt to avoid behaving in any way that could possibly be interpreted as a sexual invitation. The therapist inferred that Ann's appearance at therapy might have been due to her memory and interpretation of her previous behavior as overly inviting. Accordingly, the therapist attempted to modify Ann's memory of those behaviors.

Ann, I'd like you to see yourself again talking with John—see yourself smiling and talking, talking and smiling. Notice how good it feels to talk and smile, how warm and happy you feel. You feel happy because you smile, don't you? And you smile because you feel happy. There isn't really any other reason, is there? All you can remember is how happy you felt and how you wanted to smile because you felt happy . . . and how smiling helped you to feel happier. That's really all you remember—or need to remember. Even now, right this instant, you can smile—right now (*Ann smiles a bit*) and feel a little happier. That's right! So you can feel a little happier when you smile . . . and you can smile even more when you are happy. That's really all you can remember or need to remember. Because you know deep within yourself what smiling really means, means to you; and what smiling really means to you is all that matters and all you want to and need to remember.

Note that the therapist never actually mentioned Ann's possible memory of her behavior as being perhaps invitational but referred only to the new memory she wanted to foster. To mention Ann's hypothesized memory of inviting John's assault could simply reinforce it—and the hypothesis could be wrong. It is better simply to suggest the new memory you want to encourage rather than attempt to eradicate a memory directly. In future sessions the therapist may wish to reattach new memories to attractive clothing as well.

Memory modification can be used in a wide variety of therapeutic situations; indeed, it is possible to think of psychotherapy in general as the process of changing memories, at least in part. Through interpretations, questions, and clarifications, therapists of different theoretical orientations attempt to change the way clients interpret events and even change the events they notice and think about. Therapist behaviors, such as verbal encouragement and postural changes denoting increased interest, may point clients in different cognitive directions; as they begin to dwell on neglected aspects of their lives, they may begin to remember different things or remember things differently. Leading therapist comments, such as, "You *do* remember that, don't you?" or "That *can't* be the way it happened!" or "Perhaps if you think about it more, other things will occur to you" may be especially powerful in fostering memory changes. In the process, memories for past events may be changed as clients begin to remember events they may have forgotten or remember events in a different way. For a completely different example of memory reconstruction, let's look at Arnold.

Arnold grew up in a dysfunctional family. His mother was an alcoholic and his father was preoccupied with his career and denying his wife's addiction. His mother provided him with sporadic though unpredictable attention; sometimes she was accepting and affectionate but mostly she was harsh and rejecting. Arnold found that the same actions would be accepted sometimes and punished at other times. Arnold's father provided him with predictably little attention but was not harsh, only absent most of the time. They did little together as a family. Arnold's two older brothers were ten and eight years older than he was and were involved in their own activities. Arnold was thus left essentially to raise himself. There was no lack of material goods, however, since his father was a high-level corporate executive.

Arnold was 20 when he came in for therapy at the urging of his girlfriend, who found him too withdrawn and self-absorbed for her taste. Although he didn't feel the need for therapy himself, he came to please his girlfriend, hoping it would satisfy her enough so she would stay with him. The therapist conducted an assessment of Arnold's early maladaptive schemas (Young 1994) in order to determine his cognitive structures. In order of prominence, Arnold's EMSs were emotional deprivation (especially deprivation of nurturance and deprivation of empathy), abandonment/instability, and (to a lesser extent) social isolation/alienation. Arnold's view of the world was that people would not be there for him, would not provide the nurturance and emotional support he craved, would not be willing to offer him guidance, and he felt he lacked strong relations with others. In fact, aside from his girlfriend, with whom he lived, he had only casual acquaintances. Arnold saw himself as different from other people in significant ways. The Beck Depression Inventory (BDI) was 11, indicating mild depression just over the normal cutoff score of 9. Arnold did appear mildly dysphoric to the therapist. Although interpersonally he was a loner, he was doing well in college and planned to become an accountant.

Arnold had been intrigued by hypnosis for some time; when he discovered his therapist practiced it, he was eager (at least for him) to try it. Arnold appeared to have few memories of his childhood, describing it as "a barren wasteland." What memories he did have were largely of his father coming home late and watching television and of his mother squirreled up in the kitchen drinking. Generally he ate dinner alone. He reported that he could not recall any family activities though he knew his grandparents lived in the same town and thought they must have gotten together during the holidays. Arnold said he didn't really "begin to live" until his graduation from high school at age 18; everything before that "was a dead loss."

Whether family events never occurred or whether Arnold didn't remember them is open to question. We generally remember those events that are consonant with our interpretation of reality or our view of ourselves. Thus, since Arnold saw himself as a loner possessing few interpersonal contacts, it is possible that his memory of family events had developed over the years to reflect this view. It is likely that his memory and his worldview had gradually become mutually reinforcing; since loners have few interpersonal contacts, his loner identification may have influenced his memories, but since those with few interpersonal memories are defined as loners, his lack of memories may have solidified his view of himself as a loner. Operating from the assumptions that no families are absolutely bereft of all interpersonal activities, the therapist decided to hypnotically foster some family memories in the hopes that this would break the "chicken-and-egg" cycle and gradually modify Arnold's cognitive structural view of himself as a loner. Whether the memories were strictly true is perhaps beside the point; they might be useful to Arnold. As previously discussed, memories do not have to be true in all details to be useful; they simply have to be plausible.

> Arnold, I'd like you to reflect back upon your early years—reflecting upon the times your family spent together [an implicit suggestion that those times in fact *did* happen without specifying what]. As we've discussed, memories are tricky; sometimes we forget what we know, sometimes we know things that aren't quite accurate [the therapist

had previously discussed with Arnold some of the ideas presented in this chapter]. Sometimes we can recall things that happened, sometimes what we recall isn't quite accurate, sometimes we can gradually recall things that happened earlier if we allow the memories to return [the therapist essentially covers all possible conditions of recall]. You've told me, Arnold, that you can't recall much from your earlier years—but of course *something* must have happened during those years . . . so it's just a matter of recalling, isn't it? So I'd like you to let your mind "lay flat" [a metaphor I use for emptying one's mind] (*pause*) and allow your mind to range freely over your past, picking up bits and pieces of memories of times your family spent together, did things together . . . as it goes, gradually putting these pieces together into a framework . . . incomplete framework, but a framework nonetheless . . . not really looking for anything in particular . . . just something, anything, memories of the times your family spent together (*pause*). When you have reached something interesting, raise the index finger of your right hand [ideomotor signaling]. That's right . . . now describe to me what's happening. . . .

In this routine the therapist allowed Arnold to conduct his own "search and discover" mission. Certain sections of this routine can be repeated and expanded as needed. Many clients are able to do this and in fact find the process fun. It is important, however, that the therapist set the stage prior to beginning this type of routine by discussing with the client the nature of memories, the slowness and difficulty of accessing them sometimes, and the use of ideomotor signaling. Initial preparation for hypnosis itself is also important, since some clients may think they are not in a trance if they are able to talk. If few memories are discovered (or constructed), the therapist may wish to try another type of routine. The advantage of client self-discovery is that memories more meaningful to the client may be discovered than if the therapist fostered certain standard memories, and client resistance may be reduced. The disadvantage is that not much may be discovered, possibly leading the client to think he or she has failed. Perhaps memories discovered by this procedure may be at least partially constructed, but if they are valuable to the client it may not matter. The therapist can shape the types of memories recovered.

Some clients prefer not to discover their own memories but would like more therapist direction. In that case the therapist may wish to directly suggest or foster certain types of "generic" memories. The advantage is that memories can be "recalled" more quickly and sometimes more easily than by client self-discovery. The disadvantages are that the memories so identified may not be as relevant to the client and therefore not as easily incorporated. Resistance might also increase. Therapists who use this method should have a good knowledge of the client's background in order to suggest relevant memories.

Arnold's therapist could use this technique by inserting a different ending in the previous routine. Because Arnold knew that his grandparents lived in the same town and thought they might have gotten together during holidays, the therapist used this as a memory base.

> Look especially for memories of times your family and grandparents were together over the holidays . . . perhaps all of your family, perhaps just you, your mother and father, and your grandparents . . . it could be all or a few . . . but the important thing is to see yourself together, around the Christmas tree, perhaps singing songs, opening presents, just talking. . . . That's right, just see yourself, your family, your grandparents in this setting [these are standard cultural images of Christmas]. As you see this picture, you can also hear their voices, smell the scent of the Christmas tree . . . and as you do so, you can feel the happiness of the season, the happiness of just being together, celebrating. . . . Just continue to let that scene play in your mind; seeing the sights, hearing the sounds, smelling the smells [it is helpful to engage as many senses as possible, in order to increase the reality of the scene], feeling good in yourself to be a part of this, feeling happy and contented. . . . Keep that scene in your mind, noticing how happy you feel to be a part of this family gathering, talking with your family, being involved with them in a happy occasion . . . feeling the warmth and pleasure. . . .

In this routine the therapist used standard cultural memories of Christmas to begin to suggest to Arnold that he had in fact had such an experience himself. Cultural images can sometimes be spontaneously experienced as real personal memories. It is important to keep the scenes as generic and time-nonspecific as possible to avoid suggesting something that the client will recognize as impossible (such as interacting with a relative who had died several years earlier). The therapist also began to suggest to Arnold that he felt happy being around his family and interacting with them as the beginning of suggestions that he might enjoy other people's company. It is important to repeat this scene with Arnold and eventually to suggest other happy times with his family or with other people. Any resistance on Arnold's part should be addressed immediately and therapeutic or hypnotherapeutic changes made if necessary.

The three examples of memory modification provided in this chapter are admittedly somewhat speculative, although they are derived from the experimental psychology literature on memory processes. However, memories—both good and bad—are a source of both human satisfaction and distress. Since it appears that memories are as much constructed as recalled, it might be important for an individual's psychological health to remember as many positive memories as possible. The work of Alloy and Abramson (1979) showed that depressives unfortunately are often more realistic than nondepressives in their perceptions. Perhaps a bit more of a "rosy glow" surrounding our perceptions and interpretations of reality might be helpful most of the time for people who are psychologically distressed and some of the time for the rest of us. In most instances the absolute reality of the memory is not important; if it is (as in legal situations), these techniques are of course not appropriate.

SUMMARY

Memory is a slippery phenomenon and memories are constructed according to our needs, fears, and wishes as much as they are recalled. There are several ways of assessing memories that lead to different results. There are different memory systems and encoding processes. Psychotherapy itself appears to be suggestive and therapists who use leading techniques may run the risk of assisting clients in constructing false or only partially accurate memories. Sometimes this memory construction can be problematical; at other times it may be beneficial. Contrived as well as spontaneous memory distortion can result in greater happiness and psychological health. Perhaps hynotherapeutic techniques, used judiciously, can shift memories toward more adaptive functioning in situations in which verification of the absolute truth of a memory is not necessary.

11

Cognitive Hypnotherapy and
the Enhancement of Life

Thus far this book has dealt with disorders and problems in living. Something is wrong and the client seeks therapy to fix it or at least to ameliorate it; in other words, to return to a previous state of psychological health. This is why most clients see therapists. For some of the more common psychological disorders, I have described principles and practices of cognitive hypnotherapy with illustrations that might be used to overcome these problems.

Now, however, I'd like to focus on the other side on the mental health equation. Sigmund Freud was reported to have said that the goal of psychoanalysis was to take human misery and turn it into ordinary human unhappiness. In an attempt to further reduce that ordinary human unhappiness, I'd like to discuss the use of cognitive hypnotherapy to enhance the enjoyment of life of already well-functioning people. These are people who might never seek therapy but who often have a gnawing sense of lack of personal fulfillment. They go through life reasonably happy much or most of the time, but are often painfully aware of significant gaps in their ongoing sense of contentment. They are, in other words, all of us. No intervention, psychological or otherwise, will make people happy all of the time, but certainly there is room for improvement.

What is it that makes people happy? Various answers could be given: more money, better love (or sex), success, many friends, and/or new experiences (among many others). Typically, however, these are external attributes: give me more things or better things and I'll finally be happy. But the acquisition of new possessions usually sets off a new round of wants (generally phrased as needs) as the standards are raised higher and higher. We can, of course, attempt to change our environment to make ourselves happier, but this is simply an inelegant solution (Ellis 1977). An elegant solution attempts to change irrational beliefs to more adaptive beliefs. Bernard (1993) has stated that, "The basis of a rational approach to happiness is that *change must first take place within you*" (p. II-23, italics original).

In describing and illustrating cognitive hypnotherapy for the enhancement of life, the basic cognitive therapy model remains the same. That is, the focus is still on the modification of cognitive events, processes, and structures that interfere with our enjoyment of life. While the use of the techniques described in the previous chapters may result in less negative self-talk (i.e., negative self-hypnosis; Araoz 1985), a reduction in negative cognitions or even their replacement with corresponding positive cognitions does not necessarily translate into optimal mental health (though it might result in better mental health). It may still be useful to foster a variety of positive cognitions that are unrelated to negative cognitions associated with psychological distress. Indeed, the former is an example of the "wellness" model, which actually subsumes the "illness" model (illustrated by the latter) rather than the other way around. Because habitual ways of functioning that interfere with optimal mental health are often schema-based, they will not change easily. Repetition and variation of the hypnotic routines to be presented are crucial to any long-term change. Thus I recommend that clients be given audiotapes of these routines to play at selected times during the day. Cognitive therapy has traditionally stressed the use of homework and this is an important example.

The role of redirected attention is important in enhancing the enjoyment of life (Walters and Havens 1993). All of us are presented continuously with vastly more incoming sensory stimuli than we can ever pay attention to. What we choose to ignore, tacitly or explicitly, and what we choose to attend to can determine how we view life. For example, many of the cognitive distortions presented by J. S. Beck (1995), such as selective abstraction, magnification/minimization, and tunnel vision, involve selective attention to certain details and ignoring others. Other cognitive distortions, such as dichotomous thinking, catastrophizing, and mind reading, involve interpretive mistakes. Taken together, problems in perception and interpretation likely account for the majority of cognitive errors. Hypnotherapy for the enhancement of life redirects attention from more problematic, negative aspects of life (which are often true) to more positive, adaptive aspects (which are also potentially true). There is even evidence that those individuals who engage in a moderate amount of positive cognitive distortions tend to be happier (Alloy and Abramson 1979).

Metaphors and stories are also helpful in enhancing the enjoyment of life. Inherent in them are powerful cultural messages that are part of our deep tacit knowledge. How we think metaphorically about ourselves and our activity in the world may have a great impact on how we feel and behave as well as on our self-perception. For example, if we view changes metaphorically as dangerous gambles, we are likely to respond quite differently than if we view changes metaphorically as exciting explorations and opportunities (Walters and Havens 1993). In essence, changing metaphors is akin to the principle of reframing (Dowd and Trutt 1988). Since these cultural stories and metaphors are so embedded in our tacit knowledge, using them in the change process can lead to less resistance and an immediate and tacit understanding of the hypnotherapeutic message.

Fostering more positive cognitions even has the potential to change our physical health. While it is commonly accepted that a negative physical state can affect our mental processes, the reverse is not nearly as well accepted. There is evidence, however, that optimism, humor, mastery, pleasure, and friendly social relations can affect physical as well as psychological health (Walters and Havens 1993). We have only begun to explore the extent and ramifications of the mind–body connection.

Bernard (1993) has listed ten rational attitudes and values that he thinks can help people become happier. Many of them are behavioral in nature; the following, however, are cognitive:

1. Don't blame others for making you unhappy. Take responsibility for making yourself happy.
2. Give yourself permission to make yourself happy—even if, as a result, others make themselves unhappy.
3. Accept the fallibility of others (and, I might add, yourself).
4. Don't take things personally.
5. See uncertainty as a challenge; don't be afraid of it.

The following topics are explored in this chapter: (1) overcoming hesitancy, (2) increasing goal-directed behavior, (3) enhancing optimism, (4) enhancing problem-solving, and (5) increasing interpersonal effectiveness. While I recognize that the number of life-enhancing activities is very large, these seem to cover most of the areas in which many of us would like our lives to be enhanced. The principles and illustrations presented under these five headings should be useful in assisting clinicians to generate hypnotic routines in other areas as well. In these illustrations I merge cognitive events, cognitive processes, and cognitive structures because this is the way clinicians typically conduct therapy. I separated them in previous examples for the purpose of illustration.

OVERCOMING HESITANCY

Why do people hesitate? Probably because they fear failure if they don't. From a cost/benefit point of view, they see the potential costs of moving ahead as greater than the potential benefits. It is possible to think of two basic motives here: the motive to achieve success and the motive to avoid failure. In hesitant people the latter motive may be stronger than the former. While it is true that hesitating or doing nothing will avoid failure, it is also true that it will not achieve success. But for some people that's safer.

Thus, as a general strategy, the negative cognitions (the costs) promoting hesitancy must be overcome by positive cognitions promoting moving ahead (the benefits). Attention is redirected from the benefits of hesitating to the costs; from the costs of moving ahead to the benefits. Hesitant individuals may have a schema of powerlessness, resulting in a feeling of "being stuck," which should also be addressed. For an example of overcoming hesitancy, consider the case of Abby.

At 33 Abby decided to seek treatment because of a growing dissatisfaction with her life. The births of three children before her twentieth birthday left her little time for her own needs. These children, now teenagers, were becoming more independent every day. Her increasing amount of solitude resulted in periods of uncomfortable reflection. She felt life was passing her by and change was unlikely.

Although she felt trapped in her job at the local factory, fear of the unknown prevented her from trying something else. She frequently indulged in fantasies of other occupations, only to crash back to reality as she talked herself out of various possibilities. Her life remained routine and unsatisfying, and she wondered if her future would ever be more than her present.

A cognitive analysis indicated that Abby had the following beliefs, which were subdivided into secondary beliefs:

1. Nothing ever changes!
   a. I can't change.
   b. I'll never be more than I am right now.
   c. I do not deserve anything better.
   d. I have no skills.
2. I am too old to try something new (i.e., take risks).
   a. I will fail if I try.
   b. All employers hire only young employees.
   c. I am too old to get another job.
   d. I am too old to go back to school.

   e. Everyone will laugh at me.

   f. Everyone will call me irresponsible.

   g. I look silly; I'm acting like a teenager.

   h. I am being childish.

   i. I will never be a real adult.

   j. I am being selfish (in thinking about improving herself).

3. I must have security.

   a. I will lose my benefits.

   b. I would be fired at another company.

   c. Things will be better when I get a raise.

   d. I can't make good decisions.

   e. I don't know what to do.

   f. I always make mistakes.

   g. I have bad judgment.

Besides these negative cognitive events, Abby's thinking processes were characterized by overgeneralization (seeing one negative event as all-encompassing), catastrophization (expecting the worst), and magnification of her negative qualities and minimization of her positive. She also had an early maladaptive schema of defectiveness/shame with secondary EMSs of self-sacrifice and vulnerability to error/negativity. Accordingly, the therapist developed the following hypnotic routine:

Abby, as you think back over your life, you may recall times when you moved ahead . . . and times when you didn't [somewhat of a truism; all of us have these times]. Sometimes you felt more confident than other times. Sometimes you tried new things, sometimes you didn't. So things were always changing for you, weren't they? Change is a constant, isn't it [a paradoxical statement]? We always change . . . whether we try to or not . . . whether we want to or not; we always change. Sometimes it's good, sometimes it's not as good . . . sometimes we like it, sometimes we don't [the previous statements are designed to loosen her distorted cognitive processes]. As you think back, you may begin to think about the times when you did move ahead [redirection of attention]; why you moved ahead . . . and why

you didn't. When we take risks, we can allow ourselves to move ahead
. . . to advance. That's right; risks can be good! Risks may work out
well, they may not work out well, they most likely will work out
partially well. But if we don't take risks, nothing can work out well—
nothing can work out at all. We do this all our lives, don't we? . . .
regardless of our age. Living itself is a risk, isn't it? We never know
how the day will turn out. It's easy, isn't it, to think about the problems in taking risks . . . without thinking about the benefits [redirec-
tion of attention]. So right now, Abby, I'd like you to imagine yourself moving out, standing straight [Abby had poor posture], looking
to the future, moving out and striding into the future [a metaphor
for overcoming hesitancy] . . . feeling more and more confident, taking comfort in your ability to "do what needs to be done" [a cultural
message from Garrison Keillor's *Prairie Home Companion* on what shy
people need to do]. Continue to see yourself striding into the future
as you feel more and more confident . . . and the more confident and
better about yourself you feel [addresses defectiveness schema], the
more you can stride into the future, trying new things, doing new
things, feeling increasingly comfortable in your ability to do many
good things much of the time [addresses magnification/minimization
and EMS of vulnerability to error/negativity]. And you can get these
good comfortable feelings anytime you want by seeing yourself
straightening up and striding into the future . . . knowing the future
is a good place, knowing that risk is a healthy part of life, feeling
increasingly comfortable in your ability to distinguish safe from un-
safe risks. And as you continue to think about the good risks, the
positive things that can happen if you take risks, you can begin to
see more clearly the benefits from taking good risks.

At a subsequent session the therapist decided to address Abby's
minimization/maximization cognitive distortion and the defectiveness/
shame EMS more directly by the use of a metaphor.

Abby, I'd like you to see all your good qualities in a small bag off to
your right [Abby is right-handed; this would be reversed for left-

handed clients] and all your bad qualities in a large bag off to your left. That's the way you normally think, perhaps; that your bad qualities are much larger and more numerous than your good qualities. Now I'd like you to see your large bag of bad qualities gradually shrink and become smaller and smaller . . . and see your small bag of good qualities grow larger and larger . . . the left bag becomes smaller and smaller . . . and the right bag becomes larger and larger [repeat several times]. Now you can see the right bag of good qualities is much larger than the left bag of bad qualities. Focus on how good it feels to see your bag of good qualities much larger than the bag of bad qualities. And you can have this good feeling anytime you want by visualizing the bags of qualities just this way; making the right bag as large as you want and the left bag as small as you want. . . .

Suggestions like these can be varied and repeated as much as necessary. Although in the first hypnotic routine I addressed several negative cognitive beliefs, cognitive distortions, and early maladaptive schemas in order to provide a comprehensive illustration, in practice it is better to pick only one or two cognitive distortions on which to focus, as I did in the second example. Otherwise the client can be easily overwhelmed by too much information and the central message may be buried. There is a difference between indirect communications and obscure, confusing, overloaded communications.

INCREASING GOAL-DIRECTED BEHAVIOR

Many people have difficulty setting directions in life. Although they can accomplish tasks set by others and often do them very well, they cannot set the directions themselves. Their lives are oriented toward short-term goals and short-term actions. There are also instances where individuals have successfully accomplished a great deal, only to be sidetracked or stopped by unanticipated life circumstances such as illness or injury. Sometimes these circumstances are sufficiently debilitating that they cannot get "back on track" or set new directions if that becomes necessary. Indeed, the ability to successfully surmount negative life circumstances may be one of the most important differences between those who ultimately succeed in life and those who don't. That and tenacity are more important than native ability in determining success.

For an example of hypnotherapy in increasing goal-directed behavior, consider the case of Ed. As Ed reclined comfortably in his chair, he spoke with pride about football and his life as a player. It was readily obvious he possessed not only natural talent but a genuine love of the game. His enthusiasm cooled as he described his career-ending injury and the apathy and lack of motivation that continued to smother him, even after two years.

As a child he had received constant encouragement toward athletics, not only by his family and friends but by his coaches and teachers as well. His assigned labels of "valuable" to the team and "star" had unfortunately led to grade inflation. It was during his junior year of college that his dream became reality. At age 21 he was signed by a professional football team for a six-figure salary. Just as his career was taking shape and he was making a name for himself, he suffered an injury that left him unable to play and no longer "valuable." Even after two years he continued to dwell on this misfortune.

A cognitive assessment showed that Ed's beliefs about himself were:

1. I should have snapped out of it by now.
2. I am now worthless, a nobody.
3. I can't do anything else.
4. I have lost everything.
5. My life is over.
6. I can't cope/I will never be able to cope.
7. I will never find another job so why bother.
8. No one cares about me anymore and will never care.
9. I am stupid—just a dumb jock.
10. Things will never get any better.
11. Why did this happen to me?

It is apparent that several of Ed's negative self-statements were characteristic of depression. However, the assessment did not show significant depression (his BDI was 12) and he had no history of depression. His cognitive distortions included catastrophizing, overgeneralization, tunnel vision, and labeling (himself as a "loser" and "no longer valuable"). In addition, Ed appeared to have primary schemas of unrelenting/unbalanced standards and entitlement/self-centeredness, with a secondary schema of undeveloped self. Such a pattern is not uncommon in well-known athletes. Accordingly, the therapist developed the following hypnotic routine for Ed:

> Ed, as you look back on your life, you have much to be proud of, don't you [a truism and a "yes set"]? You had a great time and career as a football player, didn't you [use of the past tense implies it's over]? And now you're wondering what to do next. . . . You worked hard for your success and felt you deserved it [speaks to the two primary schemas] . . . important things to you. But now, through a random event, through no fault of your own, you can't do that anymore, can you [speaks to the "why me?" belief]? What now? You don't know. But how can you use what you have already learned to set new directions for yourself, new goals? It's almost like a tunnel . . . you've lived your life moving through a tunnel, seeing your goal clearly at the end . . . but seeing nothing to the side. Now the end of your tunnel is blocked . . . where do you go, where do you look? Perhaps it's time to look off to the sides of the tunnel . . . but what will you see if you look there? Take a moment to look off to the side of your tunnel life (*pause*). Imagine what you can see there—so many things, so many possibilities. Take one or two possibilities and fix them firmly in your mind so you can talk about them later.

In this routine the therapist used the metaphor of "tunnel vision" to help Ed begin to examine other possibilities for his life direction and redirect his attention accordingly. Ed reported after the trance was concluded that that was exactly how his life seemed to him: a blocked tunnel with nowhere to go. The therapist also attempted to use Ed's schemas in the service of change rather than attempting to overcome them, an example of the utilization technique. In a subsequent discussion, Ed reported that when he had looked sideways in the tunnel, he had an image of himself as a radio or television sports announcer. Here, he thought, he could use the knowledge and talent he had to forge a new career for himself. In the next hypnotic session the therapist used the technique of age progression to help Ed see a future career as a sports-caster.

> Ed, I'd like you to move through time, into the future, to begin to see a new career for yourself. As I count, you will imagine yourself moving forward in time; one month for each count . . . one, two, three, . . . [the therapist counted up to fifteen, the approximate amount of time Ed thought it would take to make the contacts and obtain work]. Now we're fifteen months in the future. I'd like you to see yourself as a sports announcer . . . feeling the "rush," the excitement, the pleasant sensations you felt as a player. Notice the crowd hanging on your words as you describe the game [addressing schemas]. You know, don't you, that you have the ability to make the game more exciting by the way you describe it . . . to enhance the game in the eyes of the fans. It's a good feeling, isn't it? . . . to know you can create excitement just like you used to. Now continue to see yourself announcing the plays, letting the good feelings soak in, deeper and deeper, into your being . . . as you see yourself as a sports announcer. Now see yourself after the game, mingling with the players, talking with the coach, being a part of the action. Continue to play out that scene in your mind . . . (*pause*). Now gradually let that scene fade from your mind, but retain the good feelings about it. And as I count backwards from fifteen to one, you will gradually return to the present. Fifteen, fourteen, thirteen. . . .

In this hypnotic routine the therapist connected Ed's former positive feeling about his athletic ability and crowd adulation to his projected new career as a sportscaster. Hopefully Ed could then attain these positive feelings in another way.

ENHANCING OPTIMISM

Optimism is one of the most important, yet one of the least appreciated, of all psychological states. The level of optimism has an impact, for example, on depression, coping skills and problem solving, personal competence, susceptibility to disease, and physical health (Walters and Havens 1993). Furthermore, it doesn't seem to matter how accurate this optimistic perception is, at least within broad limits. Alloy and Abramson (1979) found evidence that depressed individuals were more accurate than nondepressed people in their perception of reality. Optimism itself, in a reflexive arc, may act as a buffer against depression (Abramson and Alloy 1981). Religious belief, which can be considered a form of optimism about ultimate (eschatological) things, is associated with better mental health. It does not, as Freud and Ellis thought, appear to be an aspect of neuroticism.

The perception of control over self and circumstances also appears to enhance our self-esteem and coping ability, even if little actual control is possible (Walters and Havens 1993). I have speculated that the necessity and desirability of personal control is a cultural core belief in North American and Western European societies (Dowd 1989), and that individuals who cannot exercise a positive form of control will choose a negative form (Dowd 1976). I suspect that one reason for much of the intergroup squabbling in many areas of contemporary American society is that people have learned that, though they may be powerless to foster positive change, they can at least exercise negative control. This may take various forms: enjoyment from blocking someone else, looking for the negative aspects of every idea, and a refusal to cooperate with anyone about anything. The tacit cognitive belief appears to be, "I may not be able to get what *I* want but at least I can stop you from getting what *you* want!" We can see the results of this cynical attitude from national and international politics down to marriage and family relations and risk ending up with a checkmated society.

Walters and Havens (1993) state that effective optimism is based on three beliefs: a positive view of the self, a belief that one can exert control over one's life, and a belief that life is meaningful. Apparently these beliefs don't have to be accurate to be useful, though there is probably a limit. People with highly debilitating illnesses are unlikely to convince themselves they are healthy, though they may be able to convince themselves that their suffering has meaning. The third belief, in fact, has historically been the special province of religion, although one of the values of psychotherapy is helping people to make meaning of their lives (e.g., Clarke 1993, Frank 1973). Erik Erikson (1963) noted that individuals who have difficulty finding meaning for their lives in the last stage of life may sink into despair and disgust. Thus optimism may be increased if people feel better about themselves, more in control of themselves and their environment, and convinced that life (specifically their life) has meaning.

For an example of hypnotherapy in enhancing optimism, consider the case of Sherry. On a warm, sunny June morning, 25-year old Sherry sat nervously in her first session of therapy. Although casually dressed, her body remained rigid, the dark colors revealing her pessimistic mood. Her hair, pulled tightly back, added to the tension already present in her face. Making minimal eye contact, she fumbled with an absent wedding band and struggled for words to begin.

In a strained voice she told of her four-year marriage to her high school sweetheart and the birth of a daughter within the first year. Her confusion became obvious as she vacillated between blame and denial. She began to sob as she recounted painful memories of the evening her husband had casually announced he was not happy and no longer wanted to be married. With shame she acknowledged her desperate pleading for another chance and the shock and devastation she felt as he coldly walked out the door.

For months she remained withdrawn from the world, uninterested in any kind of interaction. Although time had helped her wounds to heal, scars remained that she could neither understand nor penetrate. She reported that she was deeply pessimistic about her chances to attract another mate and to be happy; in fact, she reported she was pessimistic in general and had been so for as long as she could remember. She pictured herself living alone for the rest of her life.

Sherry seemed to have three major beliefs with several sub-beliefs in each.

1. It is my fault that my marriage failed.
    a. I should have made my husband happy; if I had, he would not have left me.
    b. It is my fault he was unhappy and left me.
    c. I wasn't a good wife; I'll never be a good wife.
    d. I will never have a successful marriage.
    e. I will be alone for the rest of my life.
2. I am a failure with all men.
    a. Men will always leave because I can't make them happy.
    b. No man will ever love me.
    c. I can't believe or trust any man.
3. I'm not good enough; there is something wrong with me.
    a. I'm not attractive enough.
    b. I'm not smart; I'm stupid.
    c. I'm not interesting; I'm a boring person.

Sherry had several cognitive distortions, including personalization, catastrophizing, emotional reasoning, and overgeneralization. In addition, she had several early maladaptive schemas in the disconnection and rejection area (Young 1994), including abandonment/instability, emotional deprivation, and defectiveness/shame. These seemed to account for her pessimistic frame of mind. Her lack of optimism appeared to be a long-standing attribute. Accordingly, the therapist developed the following hypnotic routine to increase Sherry's optimism.

> Sherry, I know you are full of doubts and bad feelings about yourself right now [validates her feelings and enhances the therapeutic bond]. You think you will never attract another man, don't you [establishes affirmative thought pattern through "yes set"]? You feel you failed, don't you? Perhaps you won't, perhaps you did (*pause*) . . . but perhaps you will and perhaps you didn't [answers Sherry's questions the way she would, then provides the alternative]. The second possibil-

ity is really difficult to think about right now, isn't it? You're so focused on the first. And perhaps you don't even want to think about it right now. So let me suggest you think of something else that may help you understand. . . . Think of a glass with water up to the middle. Is the glass half empty (*pause*) or is it half full? It all depends on the way you look at it, doesn't it? If you think it should be full, then it's half empty—perhaps this is the way you usually think, and you're disappointed. But if you think it should be empty, then it's half full, and you're pleased. Do you ever think this way? See, it's all in what you expect and how you interpret it. What would ever happen if you expected less? Would you get more? Would you feel happier? It's really interesting, isn't it, the possibilities. . . . Now let me tell you another story. You're very active in your church, aren't you [Sherry had recounted with some enthusiasm her long-standing interest in church activities]? What does that mean? How should someone interpret that? Suppose someone said, "Well, Sherry's very religious and spiritual and that's why she does that." How would you feel if you heard that . . . pretty good, wouldn't you? But suppose someone said, "Well, Sherry's involved in church activities because she wants to feel powerful and in charge." How would you feel if you heard that . . . pretty bad, wouldn't you? But it's the same activity, isn't it? You may know why you do something—though of course all of us can fool ourselves and often do. But how does someone else know? They have to guess, don't they? And how do they guess—they can't read your mind, can they? [Notice the repetitive agreement-enhancing statements.] So they have to use their own minds . . . if they think negatively, they'll explain things negatively . . . if they think positively, they'll explain things positively. But either could be true, at least in their minds. So, Sherry, what I'd like you to focus on is all the different ways we might explain something. If we explain it negatively, we'll feel bad; if we explain it positively, we'll feel good. It's difficult sometimes to know what's really "true"—and perhaps it doesn't really matter what's true, since there are many ways to be true . . . so very many ways. But you knew that already, didn't you? . . . it's just necessary to use your knowledge [activating her tacit knowledge]. And during the next week you can use this knowledge to learn more about yourself and how you think about things.

At the beginning of the next session the therapist asked Sherry what she had learned from the last hypnotic session. It matters little what the client remembers but the question requires a mental search and the answers need not be "true" but only useful (see Chapter 10). Via the utilization technique, whatever the client mentions can be used in the next session. In this case Sherry reported learning it was possible to think of the same thing in different ways (that possibility had apparently never occurred to her before). The therapist then used the following routine.

> Sherry, you learned important things last time [connecting to the previous session]. Now I'd like you to use that knowledge to learn more. You learned there was more than one way to see things, to think about things in different ways. Now let's think about new ways to think about your relationships. You feel abandoned, alone, deprived, don't you [speaks to EMSs]? You feel somehow deficient, don't you? But let's look at it another way . . . let's look at who's alone . . . you or your ex-husband? Who's really defective? Who's deficient? Is it you or him? Perhaps he's the one who's deficient . . . after all, he couldn't love you. Perhaps he's the one who's deprived . . . will he ever find a woman who he can love? Didn't you love him, cherish him? Isn't that good? Can't you use that knowledge of how to care, truly care, for a man to develop new relationships? Perhaps you can do this, as you did before . . . learning how to do it differently, learning how to control your relationships, how to develop your caring. And perhaps you know . . . after your new knowledge that you can look at things in different ways . . . perhaps you know now that because something happens once doesn't mean it will happen again. It might . . . (*pause*) . . . or it might not. It all depends . . . on many things that are different each time and that you can help control . . . not perfectly, but then there are few things that are perfect, aren't there? And as you are better

able to control, you can feel better and better about yourself . . . and the better you feel about yourself, the more in control you can feel. You can begin to feel new and important ways that you can decide to create relationships with others; not letting them happen to you [speaks to schema] but creating them yourself, with your newfound sense of control. It's a little scary to think about right now, isn't it? And you don't quite know how to do it. But you can learn—and you *will* learn, won't you?

In a subsequent session the therapist used the following hypnotic routine as a general optimistic enhancement that was designed to speak to her early maladaptive schemas.

Sherry, I'd like you to imagine that I've given you two pairs of glasses: one rose-colored and the other dark blue [these are metaphors for common cultural images of "looking at the world through rose-colored glasses" and "feeling blue"]. I'd like you to put on first the blue glasses . . . and notice how dark everything looks and how sad and pessimistic you feel. Now put on the rose-colored glasses . . . and notice how light everything looks and how happy and optimistic you feel. But it's the same scene, isn't it? The only difference is how you look at it, through what kind of lenses. If you look at things through dark lenses, you'll feel pessimistic . . . (*pause*). If you look at things through rose lenses, you'll feel optimistic. All you have to do is change glasses! And you can have this more optimistic feeling whenever you want by changing glasses.

This routine is a variation of the telescope technique described earlier in this volume. Changing a deeply entrenched pessimistic outlook is not easy or quick, and takes repeated exposures to this and other hypnotic routines, other forms of therapy, and different life experiences. However, hypnotic routines like these may start the change process so that Sherry may be more open to, and help create more optimistic life experiences (see Chapter 9).

ENHANCING PROBLEM-SOLVING ABILITY

Problem solving refers to the process by which people understand and formulate reactions to problems in living (Nezu et al. 1989). Problems are specific life situations that require additional or different responses from those the individual already has in repertoire. The solution is any coping response that reduces the emotional response and/or positively alters the problematic situation itself. Problem solving thus involves the creation of coping strategies to discover and implement a wide range of more effective behaviors. Effective problem solving has been shown to reduce depression (Nezu et al. 1989) and the model has also been applied to the reduction of anxiety (Miner and Dowd 1996).

Effective problem solving consists of five components: problem orientation, problem definition and formulation, generation of alternatives, decision making, and solution implementation and verification (Nezu et al. 1989). The first component includes attention to the problem and an examination of the set of assumptions and appraisals the individual makes regarding the problems in his or her life and his or her problem-solving ability. Essentially, these are a series of beliefs. The second component involves clarification and understanding of the problem, including a possible reappraisal of the implications of the situation for the individual's well-being—a sort of reframing. The third component requires the individual to generate as many solutions as possible (commonly known as "brainstorming") in order to maximize the possibility of finding a good solution. The fourth component involves a comparison of the viability of all the alternative solutions and the selection of the "best" one. The fifth component involves trying out and monitoring the chosen solution. While not all five components of the model may be equally treatable by hypnosis, the first two in particular should be amenable to hypnotic interventions. The remaining three can be handled by standard therapeutic techniques. Accordingly, this example focuses only on components one and two. Creative hypnotherapists may decide, however, to attempt hypnotic interventions with one or more of the last three.

People often see problems as insurmountable and their problem-solving ability as negligible. This is especially true when they are over-whelmed with a sudden catastrophe for which they are not prepared and for which their problem-solving skills are inadequate. In this case the first task of the therapist is to help the client approach the situation as a problem to be solved rather than as an overwhelming and unitary thing that defies solution. In other words, it is important to help the client move from a static view of the problem to a dynamic, process-oriented view. Nezu and colleagues (1989) describe the first component, problem orientation, as a motivational process while the remaining components consist of skills and abilities. The client brings to the problem-solving task a host of beliefs and assumptions, both about him- or herself and about the problem. The hypnotherapist's task is to change any maladaptive cognitions that are interfering with effective problem solving into more adaptive ones. For an example of how this might be done, we can examine Margaret's situation.

As she waited for her appointment, 45-year-old Margaret watched as a light April snow silently dusted the ground. Because her husband had assumed the responsibilities of head of the household, Margaret had been able to lead a simple, low-stress existence as a traditional wife and mother. For over two decades their marriage had survived and prospered, as each of them played out his or her specific family role. Suddenly, without warning, an unfortunate hunting accident left her widowed and alone. With a strong determination to protect and maintain her family, she struggled for months, only to find herself overwhelmed and frustrated in this complex and unfamiliar situation. Put simply, she had no idea what to do and did not seem to be able to take steps to learn. She viewed her life situation as more than she could ever handle.

A cognitive analysis showed her beliefs to consist of the following:

1. I can't bear this pain.
   a. I will always feel this way; this pain will never go away.
   b. I can't survive this.
   c. I will always feel afraid.

     d. No one understands or cares how I feel.

     e. Life is cruel and unfair.

2. I will always be alone.

     a. No one will ever love me again.

     b. I can never love anyone else again.

     c. I must have a man to take care of me; I'm nothing without a man.

     d. I am a failure.

3. I can't live without him.

     a. I can't do what he did.

     b. He was perfect; I am useless.

     c. He was strong; I am weak.

4. Everything is too complicated for me.

As can be seen, there is a static, unchanging quality about these beliefs that made it difficult for Margaret to see any way of actually solving her problem or indeed even seeing the situation as a problem to be solved. Her cognitive distortions seemed to revolve around catastrophizing, dichotomous thinking, overgeneralizing, and "awfulizing." Her early maladaptive schemas (Young 1994; see Chapter 5) were located in the impaired autonomy and performance area, primarily dependence/incompetence and enmeshed/undeveloped self, with a secondary EMS in failure. Accordingly, the therapist developed the following hypnotic routine for Margaret to address the first component, problem orientation:

> Margaret, you've suffered a severe loss, haven't you ["yes set" and fostering of the therapeutic alliance]? You don't know what to do or where to turn, do you [more of the same]? Sometimes when we don't know what to do, it's easiest not to do anything, isn't it? Doing nothing doesn't necessarily bring us rewards, does it? . . . But at least it may avoid doing the wrong thing. And sometimes people . . . and you might be one . . . see things as so bad that they don't ever see how they can ever get better! [speaks to catastrophizing] And sometimes people think . . . and you might be one. . . . that one bad thing means everything will be bad [speaks to overgeneralizing]. It's like the world

is divided into bad . . . and good, with no-thing in between [speaks to dichotomous thinking] . . . (*pause*). . . . But if you really think about it, you might see the flaws in that way of thinking. Let me show you how. Visualize to yourself a line graph with "bad" all at one end and "good" all at the other. Got that? Raise the index finger of your right [or dominant] hand when you do. . . . Good! Now see that the "bad" side is very large while the "good" side is very small. Raise the index finger of your right [dominant] hand when you do. . . . Good. Now see the bad side gradually become smaller and more spread out, moving toward the middle. Now see the good side become larger and more spread out—so they move toward each other; the bad becoming smaller and partly good and the good becoming larger and partly bad. As they continue to spread out, you can see them meet in the middle . . . but what do you do with the middle? (*Pause*.) What do you do with the middle, the place where things are partly good, partly bad . . . the good having some bad, the bad having some good? It's really confusing, isn't it? How can anything, some-thing, be both? But when you really think about it, that's true of many things, isn't it? Perhaps you can remember once upon a time [suggesting childhood] having difficulty making a decision [a truism; we all have them]. Perhaps you had difficulty making that decision because you had a conflict—what you wanted was partly bad, partly good. That's what makes it difficult to decide, isn't it? If something was all good or all bad, we'd have no difficulty at all [a reframing]. We'd know exactly what to do—and we'd do it. So really, when you think about it, most things are in the middle: confusing, hard to decide, both good and bad. So although you might be alone right now, that doesn't mean you will always be alone, does it? . . . Just like being together doesn't mean you'll always be together— and you know *that's* not true. So the more you think about life, the more you can realize that, just like that graph, most things are in the middle—where things are more confusing but more interesting.

In this example a metaphorical image was used to demonstrate and create a new way of thinking for Margaret, designed to address her dichotomous thinking and overgeneralizing. Margaret had been used to putting things in concrete conceptual boxes for years (another metaphor that might be used) and it will take her a while to begin to think in less tight and constricted categories. A confusion routine might be helpful as well.

To help Margaret address the second problem-solving component, problem definition and formulation, the therapist used the following routine:

As we've gradually clarified your assumptions about yourself that are part of your situation [not "problem"], you may begin to realize that you aren't even sure sometimes what you have to do, what you want to do. It all seems like such a big thing sometimes, doesn't it . . . without any resolution in sight? So perhaps the first thing is to decide what to do next . . . where to go from here. What is it you need most? Think of the things you need right now, such as money, a new mate, time with your children, a job, more self-confidence. And maybe something else, something more. Take a moment to run through your mind what it is you want, what it is you need. Think of the things I just mentioned and anything else . . . (*pause*). . . . Take your time, let the thoughts come to your mind, let your mind lay flat . . . (*pause*). . . . Now as I mention them again, think of them . . . and as I say them the second time through, raise the index finger of your right [dominant] hand as I come to the most important one. Remember, your unconscious mind knows what it needs, what it wants . . . you know more than you know you know—and you are wise in your knowing what's best for you [hint of a confusion routine, speaks to the undeveloped self]. You know what you need, at a deep level. So let your unconscious mind think as I mention money, a mate, time with children, a job, self-confidence . . . now let me say them again and let your index finger rise at the most important [finger rises at self-confidence]. Good, you've identified self-confidence as the most important thing. . . . Now let your mind lay flat and say the first additional thing you want that comes to your mind [therapist had earlier told Margaret she could talk in a trance]. Now say the first thing that comes to your mind (*Margaret says "strength"*). Good, now let's think about those two things: self-confidence and strength, strength and self-confidence. They go together, don't they? If we start to get one, we can start to get the other. But how do we start, how do you start? You already have much of what you need, you **know**? [Play on words.] So let me suggest something to you, okay? (*Margaret nods assent.*) Think of yourself standing alone, standing straight. Think of standing alone as good, as important . . . for it's only in standing alone and standing straight that we can really feel strong and self-confident [a reframing of her negative feeling that she would always be alone as well as addressing the enmeshed self]. Feel the strength flowing into you as you stand alone—fully in charge of yourself—and straight—ready to face the world, facing the world, looking the world in the eye, feeling increasing comfort in your ability to stand alone and feel self-confident . . . knowing that they go together, standing alone and feeling self-confident, feeling self-confident and standing alone. And you can have this feeling of strength and self-confidence anytime you want—by standing up straight and imagining yourself standing alone, facing the world with strength and confidence.

In this routine notice how the therapist helped Margaret identify where to begin to address her problem, to identify another area to attach to it and then to address it. Notice also how the therapist reframed the sense of aloneness from a problem to part of a solution. The therapist also attached, by repetition, feelings of strength, self-confidence, standing straight, and standing alone. Like many insecure people, Margaret's posture could be described as slumping. Standing straight is a simple behavior she can easily do, though not without practice, and its attachment to the others can be gradually fostered.

INCREASING INTERPERSONAL EFFECTIVENESS

Interpersonal effectiveness is a large and amorphous area that encompasses self-esteem, positive self-identity, finding positive inner strengths, and communication ability. It is generally advisable to discuss with clients in which areas of their lives they wish to become more effective and obtain from them some idea of what they have tried in the past. As is true in most therapeutic endeavors, a thorough history-taking is important. It is especially important here, however, because of the difficulty in focusing attention on appropriate targets for change. In addition, clients rarely enter therapy with the explicit goal of increasing their interpersonal effectiveness.

For an example of the use of hypnotherapy in increasing one aspect of interpersonal effectiveness, we can examine Matt's problem. Shortly after his fortieth birthday, Matt entered therapy to address concerns about the uncomfortable levels of tension he was currently experiencing at work. He described these relationships as "strained" and said they were affecting his ability to supervise others. As a result of the initial assessment, the therapist saw him as critical, inflexible, and highly sensitive to criticism. Similar problems at his former place of employment had caused him to quit, hoping for a fresh start in a new job. However, as is typical in these situations, he took himself with him, and the same problems surfaced in his new job. His rigid, protective body language eased as his angry tone became less defensive and more reflective. A heavy sadness came over him as he admitted that it hadn't always been this way. With pain in his voice he spoke of his former job and of several co-workers who had relentlessly ridiculed him because of his ethnic background. For over two years he had endured this increasingly bitter atmosphere until the stress began to affect his health. With embarrassment he expressed an overwhelming frustration at his inability to be the co-worker and supervisor he had once been. He said that the problems and the ridicule he had experienced in his former job had not occurred in his new position; nevertheless, he constantly expected it and was therefore always on guard.

A cognitive analysis indicated that Matt had the following beliefs:

1. I am not the person I once was.
   a. I have lost my ability to supervise.
   b. I can't change the way I am now/the way I feel now.
   c. No one likes me anymore.

2. I am different from other people.
    a. I am not as good as others.
    b. I don't belong/I'll never belong.
    c. No one likes me/never will.
3. I can't trust/get close to people.
    a. Everyone is too critical of me.
    b. I want people to leave me alone.
    c. I hate working with people.
    d. I have to attack others before they attack me.

Matt appeared to have the following cognitive distortions: dichotomous thinking, emotional reasoning, labeling, and overgeneralization. Because he had experienced real insults at his previous job and realized that he had not experienced them at his new job, he did not appear to be personalizing. Situations like this, in which there are real environmental problems, are always difficult to handle therapeutically. We want to help clients to learn how to handle problematic situations but in doing so we do not want to excuse the bad behavior of others.

Matt appeared to have two early maladaptive schemas that exacerbated his current problems: defectiveness/shame (perhaps responsible for his hypersensitivity to rejection) and, secondarily, mistrust/abuse (leading him to his expectation that others couldn't be trusted). In Matt's case there were real environmental reasons for these schemas (in truth, there probably are actual environmental reasons behind most EMSs), but these schemas exacerbated the environmental problems, which in turn were partially responsible for the schemas in the first place. Thus Matt was caught in a vicious circle (see Chapter 10) in which the schema caused by bad experiences then acts as a filter to constrain and channel perceptions such that schema-confirming data are admitted to the cognitive system and schema-disconfirming data are screened out.

Accordingly, the therapist developed the following hypnotic routine for Matt:

Matt, perhaps you have discovered throughout life that people are different from each other [a truism]. Different in many ways—sometimes by height, sometimes by weight, sometimes by hair color, sometimes by gender, sometimes by ethnicity, sometimes by skin color—different and yet the same in most ways [the therapist moved from trival differences—at least by our cultural standards—to more salient and significant differences]. For if you really look closely, you can see that people are more similar than different. We have the same hopes, the same fears . . . we all want good relationships with other people and we all want good things for our children. We all want to do a good job at work. But we are different in some ways . . . but the differences are only differences; not better, not worse, only differences. For example, you're different in some ways than I am but not better, not worse, only different [speaks to defectiveness/shame schema]. Imagine [or see] in your mind two different people standing side by side . . . not one higher than the other; not one lower than the other . . . but side by side—different but equal. So you can hold your head up [Matt tended to lower his eyes], knowing you are different and yet the same—the same and yet different.

To address Matt's lack of trust in other people, as reflected in his EMS of mistrust/abuse as well as his automatic thought that he could no longer trust people, the therapist used the following routine:

Matt, we discussed earlier how people are different in some ways—similar in many ways. Perhaps you've noticed that yourself. For example, you're similar to me in some ways, different from me in others. Perhaps you've also noticed [beginning formation of a "yes set"] that people differ in trust—and sometimes it's difficult to tell who can be trusted and who can't, isn't it? For example, can I trust you? You probably think I can—but how would I know? Conversely, can you trust me? And how do you know that you can? It's difficult, isn't it, to know for sure? And perhaps people differ on trust too, don't they? Sometimes they trust . . . sometimes they can be trusted . . . sometimes they can't trust . . . sometimes they can't be trusted . . . sometimes they change so they can trust, can be trusted . . . sometimes they change so they can't trust, can't be trusted [semiconfusion

routine suggesting constant change, to begin to break the rigid as-
sumptions]. So everything is in a state of change, isn't it? (*Pause.*)
Trusting, not trusting; trustworthy, not trustworthy—the important
thing is that people are different and continue being different, in different ways . . . not the same, not constant. . . . And the more you think
about that, the more it can gradually sink deeper and deeper into your
mind, suggesting new possibilities to you, always new and different
possibilities.

SUMMARY

This chapter has provided several examples of hypnotic routines that
can help enhance psychological functioning in fundamentally intact
people. Other quasi-hypnotic techniques used throughout the ages include prayer and meditation. All of us periodically have difficulties,
usually temporary, in handling certain aspects of our lives. While hypnosis will not and cannot remove all the pain associated with the human condition, it can reduce some of it at certain times. Other possibilities than those given in this chapter can be generated by creative
hypnotherapists using the principles derived from these examples.

12

Cognitive Hypnotherapy in Overcoming Resistance

THERAPEUTIC RESISTANCE

Resistance as a psychological phenomenon has both intrigued and baffled psychologists since the days of Sigmund Freud. Why should clients, deliberately or not, appear to resist the person, the therapist, who is trying to help them and in doing so undermine the very process designed to help them in achieving their goals? Why, even when they seek help in overcoming their psychological and behavioral problems, do clients sometimes appear to sabotage their own best efforts? Such seemingly paradoxical and self-destructive actions have been the source of much speculation by therapists from many different orientations. Psychodynamic theories have generally assumed that resistance is caused by unconscious conflicts and is a defense against the conscious awareness of repressed, unconscious material. Indeed, a fundamental psychodynamic therapeutic technique is the exploration of these conflicts and a gradual lifting of repression so the unconscious conflicts may be made conscious and relief thereby attained. This "hydraulic theory" of personality was derived from nineteenth-century science and assumes that resistance is an inevitable expression of neurotic conflicts. The healthier the individual, the assumption was, the less need there was for resistance and the less is expressed.

Behavior therapy either ignored resistance or attributed it to inadequate or inappropriate therapist techniques. Theoretically, resistance would be expected to mediate noncompliance with behavioral tasks, but it has been interpreted as due to faulty therapist techniques rather than to internal client variables. Meichenbaum and Gilmore (1984), in an information-processing view of resistance, consider it a reluctance to consider data that do not confirm one's existing worldview. They see as a major goal of therapy encouraging clients to view their cognitions as hypotheses to be continually tested against reality.

Cognitive-developmental therapy, which is strongly constructivistic in nature, carries this perspective one step further. It assumes that individuals actively organize and construct their perceptions of the world into cognitive schemas. Resistance is seen, according to this point of view, as arising from the occurrence of a specific schema-disconfirming event in which the meaning of that event cannot be incorporated into the individual's existing meaning structure or schema (Dowd and Seibel 1990). Resistance therefore is neither an expression of neurotic needs or inappropriate therapeutic techniques, nor a perverse unwillingness to consider alternative points of view. It is the expression of the fundamental human need to preserve core cognitive structures of personal meaning from too rapid change and to avoid the loss of a sense of personal identity in the process. As Mahoney (1991) has noted, the cognitive system quite appropriately and wisely protects itself from a too rapid change in its core constructs of personal meaning. The preservation of meaning structures lies at the heart of resistance (Liotti 1989). Liotti suggests that the resistance of a specific construct to change is a function of its past ability to predict events and its centrality to the individual's experience and self-definition. In other words, constructs that have proved to be useful in the past will be more difficult to change. The more the change process implicates more core cognitive constructs, the more this change will be resisted. Change involving more peripheral cognitive or behavioral aspects of the person, such as specific attitudes or tactical behaviors, will be easier and more rapid. An implication of this view of resistance is that it is caused not only by attempts to change core cognitive constructs but also by specific situations. In other words, resistance is situation-specific, appearing in some situations more than in others. As most people intuitively know, however, some people appear to be, in all or most situations, more resistant than others. Investigations into a related concept, *psychological reactance*, have shown that indeed this is true. Whereas resistance appears as behavioral manifestations of opposition, reactance is an internal oppositional potential that may or may not be behaviorally expressed.

PSYCHOLOGICAL REACTANCE IN THERAPY

The theory of psychological reactance was originally developed by Jack Brehm (Brehm 1966) and further elaborated by Brehm and Brehm (1981). They proposed that reactance is a motivational force that is aroused when perceived behavioral freedoms are eliminated or threatened with elimination. This motivational force is directed toward the restoration of those freedoms and can be expressed in a variety of direct or indirect ways. Thus people may engage directly in the prohibited behavior, may vicariously take satisfaction from observing others engaging in the prohibited behavior, may engage in a behavior similar to the one prohibited, or may aggress against the person who has prohibited the behavior. It is important to note that people do not actually have to engage in the prohibited behavior to reduce reactance effects but must only perceive the potential freedom to do so if desired. Therefore we speak appropriately of reactance potential. Dowd (1989) has proposed that reactance arises from a motivation to achieve or to regain control over one's self and situations in which we find ourselves. This motivation may involve a very powerful core cognitive assumption that in fact we ought to be in control of ourselves and situations. This core cognitive assumption may be especially powerful in the highly individualistic North American and Western European cultures, where cultural messages such as "take charge of your life" and "be your own person" are prominent, and less so in cultures where "fate" or "luck" are more prominent as cultural explanations for events. Indeed, Dowd (1976) has argued that if people cannot establish control in a creative and positive fashion, they may do so in destructive ways, thus explaining seemingly perverse, self-destructive individual actions.

Although reactance, like resistance, was originally considered to be situation-specific, a series of investigations has shown significant individual differences in reactance potential. These have been described by Dowd (1999). On the Therapeutic Reactance Scale (Dowd et al. 1991), reactance has repeatedly been shown to be normally distributed, and men have generally been found to be more reactant than women. Reactant people have been found to be more autonomous, dominant, somewhat intolerant and lacking in self-control, somewhat impulsive, not as interested in making a good impression on others, and not as nurturant of others or seeking nurturance from others. Among personality disorders the borderline, paranoid, antisocial, and obsessive-compulsive patterns were characterized by higher reactance levels while the passive-aggressive, dependent, avoidant, and histrionic patterns were characterized by lower reactance levels. Developmentally, reactant people seemed to have had difficulty resolving Erik Erikson's stages of trust versus mistrust (they were less trusting), intimacy versus isolation (they were more isolated), and ego integrity versus despair (they were more despairing). Reactant people appeared to have resolved especially well the stages of autonomy versus shame and doubt (they were more autonomous) and initiative versus inferiority (they took more initiative). In general, however, reactant people seemed to have less psychosocial health and a more negative resolution of the developmental stages as a whole. Reactant people also tended to experience more stress (or at least reported more). Dowd and Seibel (1990) hypothesized that reactance may be developmentally fostered by frequent physical punishment, inconsistency of discipline, use of coercive control techniques, threats of love withdrawal, and conditional acceptance (e.g., "I'll love you if you do this"). They also hypothesized that the development of a flexible sense of autonomy was critical to the development of an optimal level of reactance—neither too high nor too low, fostered by attachment figures of unconditional acceptance and safe separations with a secure support base when needed.

Given the personality variables associated with reactance, it might be expected that reactant people would prove to be difficult clients in therapy. There is some evidence that this is true. Reactance has been associated with greater symptom severity, with missing more appointments and coming late for sessions, with less satisfaction from therapy, and a less favorable view of therapists. Interestingly, however, reactant clients seemed to have as positive a therapeutic outcome as less reactant clients—at least as judged by the client! Therapists rated reactant clients as less improved, however, perhaps because they didn't like them as much. Reactant clients were also just as likely to comply with medical and psychological advice, though there was some indication that they reacted badly to negatively toned advice. In therapy itself, reactant clients were more concerned with distancing and maintaining strong boundaries from the therapist, although they were just as likely to engage in a collaborative therapeutic relationship as less reactant clients. In an analogue study, Dowd and colleagues (1992) found that high reactant individuals were more willing to see a therapist and thought the therapist was more willing to help them when absolute interpretations (e.g., "I think this is your problem . . .") were used. Low reactant individuals thought the therapist was more willing to help when tentative interpretations (e.g., "Could it be that this is your problem . . . ?) were used. Thus it appears that high reactant clients can benefit from therapy, although they may not relate as closely with the therapist and perhaps may be more difficult to handle. Different techniques may also be necessary.

It appears that resistance/reactant people can change as a result of psychotherapy, although this change may be slower and characterized by more conflict and distancing behavior, and be less satisfying. These are not the sort of clients therapists typically want or seek. Reactant clients may have more fixed and impermeable core cognitive constructs, especially those schemas concerned with power and control, that work against psychological change. The therapeutic situation is intrinsically unbalanced when someone of greater power and influence (the therapist) seeks to influence someone of lesser power and influence (the client). One can see immediately why therapy itself is likely to arouse reactance, especially in people already predisposed toward it. At best, core cognitive constructs change slowly; in reactant people they may change even more slowly.

WHY DO PEOPLE CHANGE?

I have described several reasons why people may resist changes, especially in therapy. The next question is, Why do they ever change at all? It's tempting, in view of the difficulty we often encounter in fostering psychological change, to reply, "They don't, at least not very much." Indeed, given the impermeability for new data of the human cognitive structure (Dowd 1997c), a more pertinent question might be, "Why *do* people change" rather than "Why *don't* they." But all of us know of instances of significant, often profound, psychological and behavioral change. Let me now describe why people *do* change.

Strong and Matross (1973) have argued that therapist social power is a major change-producing force. Therapist social power is based on legitimate power (documented, for example, by credentials, status differential, and social sanction), expert power (derived from perceived knowledge and skill), and therapist attractiveness (based on perceived similarity and interpersonal liking). These sources of power provide the therapist with credibility. Much research (e.g., Corrigan et al. 1980) has demonstrated that therapist expertness, attractiveness, and trustworthiness—at least as perceived by the client—are important aspects of the therapeutic change process. Therapists, or indeed any socially sanctioned healers, are more likely to foster change if they possess these attributes. To some extent, however, they work against each other. Expertness, as demonstrated by degrees, credentials, and a large knowledge base, is fostered by a status differential between therapist and client. Attractiveness, on the other hand, is fostered by perceived similarity. In the end, expertness seems to be more important than either attractiveness or trustworthiness. We should be cautious, therefore, about reducing therapist status. We may not want our authority figures to be too remote, but we also don't necessarily want them to be someone just like us—how then could they help us (Dowd 1997c)?

A major therapeutic change-producing intervention is *discrepancy* (Strong and Claiborn 1982). Discrepancy refers to the difference between the therapist's interpretation or explanation of a client's experiences and difficulties from the client's own explanation and is a way of fostering cognitive dissonance. For example, if the client attributes her emotional sadness to a lack of attention from other people but the therapist attributes it to her self-punitive nature and her original parenting, the discrepancy is likely to be great. If both the client and the therapist attribute it to a critical spouse, however, with their interpretations differing only with regard to the type of critical behavior, the discrepancy would be slight. Interpretations are important because there is a deep need in the human cognitive system to make meaning of events. Clients often seek therapy when their meaning system is seen as inadequate and therapist interpretation can provide alternative meanings.

Research on discrepancy has shown two important things. First, the content of the interpretation is less important than the discrepancy of the interpretation from existing client beliefs (e.g., Claiborn and Dowd 1985). In other words, it's not what the therapist says, it's how *different* it is from what the client already thinks that's important. Second, it appears that the greatest amount of client change is fostered by moderate discrepancy (e.g., Claiborn et al. 1981). Low discrepancy interventions are ineffectual because they add little or nothing to existing client beliefs; they do not challenge the client to see or interpret things differently. High discrepancy interventions appear too threatening and may challenge core cognitive beliefs too much and too quickly. The relationship between amount of discrepancy and psychological change therefore appears to be curvilinear.

Paradoxical interventions (Dowd and Trutt 1988) have been shown to be helpful in challenging cognitive assumptions and sometimes lead to what is known as "spontaneous compliance," compliance that seems to come from deep within the client rather than from the therapist or from an act of client "will." For example, insomniacs have sometimes been cured, not because they tried harder to fall asleep but because they stopped trying. They were given the paradoxical injunction to try to stay awake as long as possible, thus challenging the assumption that the best way to change something was to try harder. Spontaneous compliance was the result. Paradoxical interventions also seem to have a "sleeper" effect since clients exposed to them may continue to improve even after the interventions have ceased, often to their surprise. It's as if the interventions changed core cognitive structures that took some time to be affected. Paradoxical interventions may be especially valuable in challenging the tacit assumptions behind core cognitive constructs. The therapeutic and hypnotherapeutic techniques of Milton Erickson were often paradoxical in nature, which may have been why they seemed so mysterious and the subsequent improvement so magical to clients. Clients often could not explain what he did or said that contributed to their improvement and thus tended to ascribe the changes to themselves or to a quasi-magical effect. Erickson had the reputation of being a therapeutic magician, fostered in part by high degrees of expertness and credibility due to his previous reputation, and it is likely that therapists who possess unusually high social power and credibility can safely use more discrepant interpretations than ordinary therapists can. While discrepancy interventions in therapy have generally been thought of as verbal in nature, discrepant behavioral interventions—in which the client's expectations and assumptions are challenged by new behavioral data— can be especially powerful. Imagine, for example, the discrepancy and dissonance experienced by a client convinced he is not attractive to women when he suddenly obtains dates after trying a new behavioral experiment. He might eventually have to revise his view of himself as an "unattractive loser"—and this new image might be difficult for him to incorporate into his existing cognitive structure. We often become firmly wedded to our existing view of things, even if they are negative and self-disconfirming. Thus the use of behavioral assignments (homework) is an important nonverbal technique. New schema-disconfirming experiences, fostered by discrepancy between what the client expected and what actually occurred, can be important sources of data to be later discussed between the therapist and client. According to Hobbs (1962), behavior change precedes insight and this is an example.

WHAT TO DO TO HELP RESISTANT/REACTANT CLIENTS CHANGE

What recommendations might we give to therapists who are faced with high reactant clients? I would like to offer several, based in part on Dowd (1999).

First, use instruments such as the Therapeutic Reactance Scale to understand more about how clients might behave in therapy. Therapists might also wish to take the instrument themselves to understand themselves better and how they may interact with reactant clients.

Second, be aware that resistance may arise when implicit client therapy goals are seen as discounted or attacked. Reactant clients may be especially likely to interpret therapist actions in this manner. All clients enter therapy with implicit as well as explicit goals. Often they are contradictory; for example, a husband who explicitly enters therapy to improve his marriage but with the implicit goal of proving his wife to be "crazy" so he can justify leaving her. Therefore, it can be useful to spend some time initially thinking about and assessing implicit client goals.

Third, resistance may arise when an individual's cognitive system is forced to change too quickly. Reactant clients may be especially likely to possess cognitive structures that are relatively impermeable and change-resistant. Therefore, it might be best to begin with a series of low discrepancy interventions and gradually move to higher discrepancy interventions. This is similar to Milton Erickson's use of the "yes set" (Erickson et al. 1976), in which the hypnotherapist begins with questions or truisms that can always be answered in the affirmative and then uses these as a wedge to encourage affirmative answers to later, more discrepant, suggestions. Examples of the "yes set" abound throughout the hypnotic routines in this book. Indirect hypnotic inductions, long favored by Ericksonian hypnotherapists as techniques for bypassing conscious resistance, may actually be valuable as a general strategy for reducing resistance (Matthews et al. 1998). Again, many of the hypnotic routines in this book are at least partly indirect.

Fourth, and related, go slowly with reactant clients. At best, it takes time for discrepant material to penetrate the client's cognitive system; it likely takes longer with reactant clients. Interestingly, the use of tentative interpretations has been considered by therapist folklore to arouse less client opposition, although Dowd and colleagues (1992) found that *absolute* interpretations were preferred by reactant people.

Fifth, resistance is likely to be greater if the symptoms are consonant with the client's already-existing self-image (Dowd and Sanders 1993). In this situation clients generally do not see that they have a problem; rather, others have a problem with them. For example, an aggressive male client is likely to be more resistant to change if his aggressiveness is part of his core self-concept (i.e., machismo). To reduce this aggressiveness would be to lose an important part of himself and his identity. Often, input from other people, especially if these people have credibility with the client, may encourage the client to revise his or her self-image. Such multiple sources of input are found in group counseling and may be one reason why self-help groups (such as are found in the addiction field) are effective. A recovering addict is likely to possess more credibility than a therapist who "hasn't been there."

Sixth, use repetition. All people, but especially resistant clients, often do not hear and cognitively process discrepant material the first time it is presented—or even the second or third time. You may recall that many of the hypnotic routines in this book included notes for repetition. Recall from Chapter 10 that the number of times an event is recalled can manipulate the memory for that event, so material repeatedly recalled may be remembered with more certainty but with less accuracy. Therefore, it is important that the therapist repeatedly assist clients in recalling newly presented material to check how well and how accurately it has been remembered. The therapist might ask clients what they remember from the previous session, for example, or what they learned from the just-concluded session, to check perceptual accuracy. Memories and the act of recall can change over time so this aided recall may need to be done repeatedly. The difference between what clients remember was discussed in therapy and the meaning of that material, and what their therapists remember can be truly amazing! Even the memory of specific events that occurred can be different, as has been demonstrated by married couples who have very different memories of how many times a month they have sex.

Seventh, to avoid the memory distortions just discussed, ask the clients to write down important things they have learned in therapy. In a sense this is a variation of the last theme. Memory distortion is less likely to occur (though reinterpretation of changes can occur) if new and discrepant information is in printed form. The more discrepant the new information, the more helpful is this technique. Clients can place instructions for new behaviors or new interpretations on bathroom mirrors, refrigerators, and in other strategic locations. Cognitive therapists already use this principle when they ask clients to write down new and more adaptive self-statements to replace old, maladaptive ones. It even happens that later on clients don't recognize what they wrote (the press for cognitive consistency is very strong); though, if it's in their handwriting, it's hard to deny.

Eighth, allow the client to set the homework. Cognitive therapy has long advocated assigning homework, but this homework is often assigned by the therapist. Reactant clients may be less resistant if they are responsible for setting their own homework as well as for carrying it out.

Ninth, be content with small gains. As previously discussed, there is evidence that reactant clients tend to improve more slowly, to miss more sessions, and to engage less easily in the therapeutic process. Therapists with the best of intentions sometimes push their clients to accomplish a great deal in a short period of time. Reactant clients are more likely to resist those efforts.

Tenth, use metaphors. Ericksonian hypnotherapists have long advocated the use of indirect hypnotic routines and metaphors to bypass conscious resistance. Recently, cognitive psychotherapists have begun to use metaphor to access and change tacit knowledge structures as well

(Gonçalves and Craine 1990). Gonçalves and Craine, in fact, have stated that metaphors are especially useful in accessing and changing tacit cognitive knowledge and structures. Clients' metaphors are first identified and then modified by a variety of procedures. For example, for a narcissistic client who sees herself as the center of the world, a hypnotic metaphor speaking to the possibility of seeing things from multiple perspectives, such as the "Flatland Story" (Gonçalves and Craine 1990) might be useful. In this story the listener is presented with the description of a two-dimensional Square who cannot understand or communicate with one-dimensional Linelanders or three-dimensional Spheres. It's an interesting metaphor for understanding and accepting significant differences from one's own point of view. There are even studies (Gomberg 1996, Gore 1977) indicating that the use of metaphors was associated with nondefensive client self-exploration, lowered client resistance, and a higher level of the therapeutic alliance. Martin and colleagues (1992) found that clients rated sessions in which they recalled therapist use of metaphors as more helpful than sessions in which they recalled nonmetaphoric events.

Eleventh, use paradoxical interventions judiciously. There is some evidence that reframing and symptom prescription may be especially useful for reactant clients (Dowd 1999). In reframing, clients are presented with a perception or interpretation that is contrary to their usual way of understanding reality, such as (to a dysphoric client), "It's wonderful you have the ability to feel your emotions so well." Thus events or emotions that clients interpret as negative are given a positive interpretation in a variation of the old saying, "Is the glass half full or half empty?" Depressed clients, of course, often resort to negative reframing in which positive events are reinterpreted negatively. In symptom prescription clients are asked (or instructed) deliberately to perform the very symptoms of their problem. For example, anxious clients may be instructed to become even more anxious (or as anxious as possible), often resulting in less anxiety and/or more control over the anxiety. For more detailed descriptions and illustrations of paradoxical strategies, see Weeks and L'Abate (1982).

Milton Erickson's *utilization approach* may provide a more general way of dealing with resistant/reactant clients. While a detailed description of this creative set of techniques is beyond the scope of this book, an outline of its features and a few techniques may be helpful. In essence, utilization techniques make use of an individual's "own mental processes in ways that are outside his usual range of intentional or voluntary control" (Erickson et al. 1976, p. 19). What are used are the client's own associations and potentials as the hypnotherapist uses trance to alter "habitual attitudes and modes of functioning so that carefully formulated hypnotic suggestions can evoke and utilize other patterns of associations and potentials within the patient to implement certain therapeutic goals" (Erickson et al. 1976, p. 20). The utilization approach is thus highly idiosyncratic and does not use standard hypnotherapeutic techniques. Utilization involves behavior as well as attitudes and ideas.

The description of Erickson's utilization approach is often more complex than it needs to be. Essentially, it involves an acceptance of whatever the client happens to be doing right then or thinking right then as the best thing he could be doing or thinking, thus making resistance very difficult. Resistance is essentially defined out of existence. This action is then used in the service of future change. For example, when faced with a client who compulsively paced back and forth across the room, Erickson was reported to have paced with him and then gradually slowed down, allowing him to slow down with him and go into a trance. He used the pacing to facilitate trance behavior. Utilization is thus conceptually similar to reframing, in which a negative event is reinterpreted positively. When faced with a highly anxious client who thought she could not enter a trance, a therapist using the utilization approach might, for example, accept the anxiety and ask the client to use it to induce trance in her own way. A client who insisted on keeping his eyes open might be instructed how such behavior could be especially useful in going into a trance, perhaps as "alert hypnosis."

The utilization approach is as much a way of looking at things as it is a collection of techniques. In essence, it can be thought of as a form of therapeutic judo, in which the client's resistance is used in the service of ultimate change. Two examples of utilization techniques and an illustration are described below.

One important utilization technique is the truism. Truisms are statements about facts or observations that are so obviously true that they cannot be denied (Erickson et al. 1976). These statements then trigger associated processes within clients as they think about the statement and apply it to their own experience. Erickson and colleagues (1976) have provided examples of truisms, such as, "You already know how to experience pleasant emotions like the warmth of the sun on your skin" (p. 22), or "You can easily forget that dream when you awaken" (p. 21). Truisms can also facilitate trance behavior (e.g., "Sooner or later your eyes will close") and suggest symptom reduction (e.g., "Your problem will disappear as soon as your system is ready for it to leave" or " It probably will happen just as soon as you are ready"). It can easily be seen that it is very difficult to resist such suggestions; there is little to resist.

Another utilization technique is not knowing, not doing (Erickson et al. 1976). This technique allows the client's mental processes to occur naturally. People who are attempting to go into a trance often have definite ideas of how that should occur and try hard to "make it happen." Even if they don't know what to do, however, they often think they should do something. Like trying to fall asleep, however, attempting to go into a trance can result in just the opposite. When they stop trying and just allow it to happen, they generally find that trance "just happens." Suggestions such as these may be useful for allowing clients to enter and experience trance in their own way, at their own speed, and to begin to solve their problems.

- "You don't have to do anything in particular; you don't even have to keep your eyes open."
- "You don't have to know anything; your unconscious mind knows everything it needs to know, everything it wants to know, and will assist you with your difficulty."
- "You can find comfort in your own way, at your own speed."
- "You can experience whatever level (or depth) of trance you wish, in whatever way you want."

- "You can allow your arm to rise all by itself if you wish."
- "You can allow your problem to remain just as long as it needs to."
- "You can remain in the trance just as long as you want."
- "You can forget about your difficulty just as soon as you are ready."
- "You don't have to decide right now; you may find later that your unconscious mind has decided and has let your conscious mind know."

You are limited only by your own creativity in developing and modifying similar routines. It is important only that clients be encouraged and allowed to develop their own trance and solve their own problems without undue external direction. Although Erickson often used the term "unconscious mind," I would suggest that you view that term as a metaphor for tacit knowledge rather than a separate part of the mind. It has little or nothing to do with the Freudian unconscious.

For an example of a utilization technique, consider the case of Mike, a high-achieving, high-functioning professional who attempted to control everything in his life—generally with a great deal of success. He was very articulate and goal directed, set high standards for himself, and met them. Although he listened to and learned from others, his force of personality was sufficiently strong that his ideas generally prevailed over those of his co-workers and subordinates. He had obtained an executive position relatively early in life and there seemed to be no limit to how high he could rise. No limit, that is, until he developed an anxiety disorder that left him almost unable to function. In a panic, Mike sought therapy to help him over this hurdle.

Mike approached therapy like he approached everything else in his life—as a task to learn and as something to accomplish. An assessment showed that his reactance potential was well above average on the therapeutic reactance scale, reflecting perhaps his dominance and autonomy. He was a relative loner and had no friends with whom he and his wife socialized and only a few workplace friends. He tried hard to overcome his anxiety, but the more he tried, the more he failed. Admonitions from the therapist not to try so hard led to a blank, uncomprehending stare. Trying hard, and trying harder if that didn't work, was all Mike knew how to do.

Accordingly, the therapist discussed with Mike the use of hypnosis as an aid to relaxation and a lowered arousal level. Although Mike was receptive, he viewed hypnosis as one more task to learn and constantly evaluated how well he had done. After every hypnotic induction, he wanted to know, "Did I do okay, Doc? Was I in a deep enough trance? Did I do better than last time?" It became apparent that Mike's attempt to "do hypnosis" successfully was itself a form of tacit resistance. Therefore the therapist developed the following hypnotic routine:

> Mike, we've tried a number of things, haven't we [a truism]? And they haven't been what you wanted *yet,* have they [a truism with an implication that things might be different in the future]? So let's try something a little different. I'd like to ask you to use the knowledge you've gained so far [implication that there has been a gain] to enable you to further experience trance. You don't really have to do anything [not knowing, not doing]; you only have to allow things to happen. You can experience trance in your own way, at your own speed [not knowing, not doing]. You have been so successful in many ways in your life that you've already learned more than you know— you know?—which you can use to accomplish new things in new ways [linking his past success to the future]. New things in new ways . . . it's really interesting when you think about it, isn't it [a truism; most things are interesting when one thinks about them]? And you don't need to do anything special to think about it [not knowing, not doing] . . . all you need do is allow the thoughts to come to your mind . . . . you already know what to do. It's just a matter of realizing that [suggesting new ways of thinking]. New things in new ways . . . you might have thought of new things in old ways . . . or maybe old things in new ways . . . but what does it mean to think of new things in new ways [opening new possibilities in thinking]? It's really difficult to know right now, isn't it? . . . but you really don't have to—right now [not knowing, not doing], do you [yes-set]? Perhaps you can begin

to learn what that really means—new things in new ways—as your unconscious mind begins to use the knowledge it already has to realize new things that it already knows [suggesting a distinction between explicit and tacit knowledge] . . . (*pause*). . . . In the process, you may begin to develop new ways of learning, of thinking, of doing. But all these things can emerge gradually, by themselves, as you allow things to happen. We can't tell where the process will lead . . . which might be a bit uncomfortable at first but might also be exciting [reframing]. New things are often like that, aren't they . . . scary and exciting at the same time—especially new things in new ways, a double scare/excite. They're scary because they're new . . . and new things can upset us. They're also exciting because they're new . . . and new things can challenge us. And in the past you've had many exciting challenges, haven't you? So learning new things in new ways is just another exciting challenge, isn't it [using past associations]? The only difference is how to do it. Rather than *making it happen*, your best strategy might be *allowing it to happen*. You already know how to *make things happen*, don't you? But how do you *allow things to happen*? It's opposite from what you learned. When you learn to make things happen, you *take steps*. But when you allow things to happen, you *step back* [using past associations to build new learning]. So you see, you step in both cases . . . but instead of stepping forward, you step back . . . you step back, allow your mind to lay flat, allow things to happen. It's new and different, isn't it? And for that reason perhaps scary . . . but also full of challenges. And you can learn to use those challenges to learn to do new things in new ways, just like you learned to do old things in new ways and new things in old ways [using past learning to build new learning].

This routine was used to overcome Mike's resistance (which was based on his rigid cognitive style) and to suggest new learning and possibilities to him. These new possibilities were hooked to his former learning style and framed as an extension of it. The next step would be to use hypnosis to help Mike reduce his anxiety level, according to the principles and techniques found in Chapter 5.

SUMMARY

The human cognitive system is deeply conservative and tends to interpret incoming data according to the existing cognitive structure. Indeed, the appropriate question should be why people change at all, not why they don't change. The more the incoming discrepant data implicates core cognitive constructs, the more resistant to the new data the individual is likely to be. In addition, certain people appear to be especially characterologically resistant to change and we may call them psychologically reactant. Acting against these forces for stasis are therapist social influence variables that foster change. Several suggestions are offered for dealing with this characterological resistance as well as an example of a hypnotic routine in overcoming resistance.

Epilogue

We have come to the end of our hypnotherapeutic odyssey. In this book you have learned about the various models of cognitive therapy and hypnotherapy, and been given examples and illustrations of creative ways in which the two might be linked together in treating a variety of psychological disorders. You have also learned a few ways in which hypnosis might be used to foster more optimal psychological functioning. However, no book can do more than give you a few examples. Hypnotherapy is a very creative endeavor and it is now up to you to apply these principles and use these illustrations to build and develop your own hypnotic routines for treating the clients you see, in all their idiosyncratic glory. Clients are like snowflakes; no two are ever alike—and the hypnotherapeutic routines you will generate to treat them will likewise be idiosyncratic. So if you plan to use hypnotherapy in your professional practice, I would advise you to attend workshops, read extensively in the specialized hypnotherapy literature, and join one or more of the hypnosis societies. Division 30 (Psychological Hypnosis) of the American Psychological Association is a special interest division for those interested in the topic. There is also the Society for Experimental and Clinical Hypnosis (SECH), the American Society for Clinical Hypnosis (ASCH), and the Milton Erickson Foundation in Phoenix, Arizona. The latter has offshoots around the country. In other words, get involved and constantly extend your learning!

Hopefully, you have also learned that hypnosis is not a magical intervention that can remove psychological distress and enhance psychological functioning without significant client effort. We all want that, don't we? As clients and as humans. But hypnotherapy, like any other aspect of human functioning and change, is in part a learned skill that improves with practice. While some people seem to learn better and faster than others, in the end we can all benefit by diligent practice. There isn't any free lunch and there aren't any shortcuts to health, happiness, and good functioning.

So I wish you happiness and good functioning as you continue to extend your knowledge in and practice of cognitive hypnotherapy.

> And you can continue to grow and develop, becoming more and more confident as you continue to try new techniques, becoming more comfortable in your ability to learn and to grow . . . feeling more confident as you become more comfortable . . . feeling more comfortable as you become more confident . . . being more willing to try new techniques, new interventions, new and creative ways of thinking about your clients and yourself, as you become more confident and comfortable . . . as you grow and develop, develop and grow . . . so that in the end they all merge together, as you become the best professional you can possibly be. For none of us can ever be any better than we can possibly be, can we? But we can be that good!

References

Abramson, L. Y., and Alloy, A. B. (1981). Depression, nondepression, and cognitive "illusions": a reply to Schwartz. *Journal of Experimental Psychology* 110:436–437.

Alford, B., and Beck, A. T. (1997). *Cognitive Therapy: An Integration of Current Theory and Therapy*. New York: Guilford.

Alford, B. A., and Norcross, J. C. (1991). Cognitive therapy as integrative therapy. *Journal of Psychotherapy Integration* 1:175–190.

Alloy, A. B., and Abramson, L. Y. (1979). Judgement of contingency in depressed and non-depressed students: sadder but wiser. *Journal of Experimental Psychology: General* 108:441–485.

Araoz, D. L. (1985). *The New Hypnosis*. New York: Brunner/Mazel.

Asch, S. E. (1956). Studies of independence and conformity: I. A minority of one against a unanimous majority. *Psychological Monographs* 70: (9, Whole No. 416).

Bandler, R., and Grinder, J. (1979). *Frogs into Princes: Neurolinguistic Programming*. Moab, UT: Real People Press.

Bandura, A. (1977). Self-efficacy: toward a unifying theory of behavior change. *Psychological Review* 84:191–215.

Bass, E., and Davis, L. (1988). *The Courage to Heal: A Guide for Women Survivors of Childhood Sexual Abuse.* New York: Harper & Row.

Bates, B. L. (1993). Individual differences in response to hypnosis. In *Handbook of Clinical Hypnosis,* ed. J. W. Rhue, S. J. Lynn, and I. Kirsch, pp. 23–54. Washington, DC: American Psychological Association.

Beck, A. T. (1987). Cognitive models of depression. *Journal of Cognitive Psychotherapy: An International Quarterly* 1:5–37.

Beck, A. T., and Emery, G. (1985). *Anxiety Disorders and Phobias: A Cognitive Perspective.* New York: Guilford.

Beck, A. T., Freeman, A., and Associates (1990). *Cognitive Therapy of Personality Disorders.* New York: Guilford.

Beck, A. T., Rush, A. J., Shaw, B. F., and Emery, G. (1979). *Cognitive Therapy of Depression.* New York: Guilford.

Beck, J. S. (1995). *Cognitive Therapy: Basics and Beyond.* New York: Guilford.

Benson, H. (1975). *The Relaxation Response.* New York: Morrow.

Bernard, M. E. (1993). A rational approach to happiness. In *The RET Resource Book for Practitioners,* ed. M. E. Bernard and J. E. Wolfe, II 22–II 25. New York: Institute for Rational-Emotive Therapy.

Bolocofsky, D. N., Spinler, D., and Coulthard-Morris, L. (1985). Effectiveness of hypnosis as an adjunct to behavioral weight management. *Journal of Clinical Psychology* 41:35–41.

Bowers, K. S. (1976). *Hypnosis for the Seriously Curious.* New York: Norton.

Brehm, J. W. (1966). *A Theory of Psychological Reactance.* New York: Academic Press.

Brehm, S. S., and Brehm, J. W. (1981). *Psychological Reactance: A Theory of Freedom and Control.* Orlando, FL: Academic Press.

Brigidi, B. D., Zoellner, L. A., and Foa, E. B. (1998). *False memory in PTSD.* Paper presented at the annual meeting of the Association for Advancement of Behavior Therapy, Washington, DC, November.

Brown, D. (1995). Pseudomemories: the standard of science and the standard of care in trauma treatment. *American Journal of Clinical Hypnosis* 37:1–23.

Bugelski, B. R. (1984). Memory. In *Encyclopedia of Psychology*, ed. R. J. Corsini. New York: Wiley.

Channon-Little, L. D. (1994). Accentuate the positive: a development of Spiegel and Spiegel's technique. *Australian Journal of Clinical and Experimental Hypnosis* 22:161–163.

Claiborn, C. D., and Dowd, E. T. (1985). Attributional interpretations in counseling: content versus discrepancy. *Journal of Counseling Psychology* 32:188–196.

Claiborn, C. D., Ward, S. R., and Strong, S. R. (1981). Effects of congruence between counselor interpretation and client beliefs. *Journal of Counseling Psychology* 28:101–109.

Corrigan, J. D., Dell, D. M., Lewis, K. N., and Schmidt, L. D. (1980). Counseling as a social influence process: a review. *Journal of Counseling Psychology* 27:395–441.

Clarke, C. (1993). Creation of meaning in incest survivors. *Journal of Cognitive Psychotherapy: An International Quarterly* 7:195–203.

Crasilneck, H. B., and Hall, J. A. (1985). *Clinical Hypnosis: Principles and Applications*. Orlando, FL: Grune & Stratton.

Crawford, H. J., and Barabasz, A. F. (1993). Phobias and intense fears: facilitating their treatment with hypnosis. In *Handbook of Clinical Hypnosis*, ed. J. W. Rhue, S. J. Lynn, and I. Kirsch, pp. 311–338. Washington, DC: American Psychological Association.

Devine, P. G. (1989). Stereotypes and prejudices: their automatic and controlled components. *Journal of Personality and Social Psychology* 56:5–18.

Donovan, B. S., Padin-Rivera, E., Dowd, E. T., and Blake, D. D. (1996). Childhood factors and war zone stress in chronic PTSD. *Journal of Traumatic Stress* 9:361–368.

Dowd, E. T. (1976). The Götterdämmerung syndrome: implications for counseling. *Counseling and Values* 20:139–142.

———— (1989). Stasis and change in cognitive psychotherapy: client resistance and reactance as mediating variables. In *Cognitive Psy-*

chotherapy: Stasis and Change, ed. W. Dryden and P. Trower, pp. 139–158. London: Cassell.

———— (1993). Cognitive-developmental hypnotherapy. In *Handbook of Clinical Hypnosis*, ed. J. W. Rhue, S. J. Lynn, and I. Kirsch, pp. 215–232. Washington, DC: American Psychological Association.

———— (1996). Hypnotherapy in the treatment of adolescent enuresis. In *Casebook of Clinical Hypnosis*, ed. S. J. Lynn, I. Kirsch, and J. W. Rhue, pp. 293–310. Washington DC: American Psychological Association.

———— (1997a). The evolution of the cognitive psychotherapies. In *Handbook of Cognitive Psychotherapies*, ed. I. Caro, pp. 25–36. Barcelona: Paidos.

———— (1997b). The use of hypnosis in cognitive-developmental therapy. In *Practicing Cognitive Therapy: A Guide to Interventions*, ed. R. Leahy, pp. 21–37. Northvale, NJ: Jason Aronson.

———— (1997c). What makes people really change: and what keeps them from changing? Symposium presentation at the XXVII Congress of the European Association for Behavioural & Cognitive Therapies, Venice, Italy, September.

———— (1999). Toward a briefer therapy: overcoming resistance and reactance in the therapeutic process. In *Current Thinking and Research in Brief Therapies: Solutions, Strategies, Narratives* (Vol. III), ed. W. J. Matthews and J. Edgette, pp. 263–286. New York: Brunner/Mazel.

Dowd, E. T., and Courchaine, K. E. (1996). Implicit learning, tacit knowledge, and implications for stasis and change in cognitive psychotherapy. *Journal of Cognitive Psychotherapy* 10:163–180.

Dowd, E. T., Milne, C. R., and Wise, S. L. (1991). The Therapeutic Reactance Scale: a measure of psychological reactance. *Journal of Counseling and Development* 69:541–545.

Dowd, E. T., and Pace, T. M. (1989). The relativity of reality: second order change in psychotherapy. In *Comprehensive Handbook of Cognitive Therapy*, ed. A. Freeman, K. M. Simon, L. E. Beutler, and H. Arkowitz, pp. 213–226. New York: Plenum.

Dowd, E. T., and Rugle, L. G. (1999). *Comparative Treatments of Substance Abuse*. New York: Springer.

Dowd, E. T., and Sanders, D. (1993). Resistance, reactance, and the difficult client. *Canadian Journal of Counselling* 28:13–24.

Dowd, E. T., and Seibel, C. A. (1990). A cognitive theory of resistance and reactance: implications for treatment. *Journal of Mental Health Counseling* 12:458–469.

Dowd, E. T., and Trutt, S. D. (1988). Paradoxical interventions in behavior therapy. In *Progress in Behavior Modification:* Vol. 23, ed. M. Hersen, R. M. Eisler, and P. M. Miller, pp. 96–130. Newbury Park, CA: Sage.

Dowd, E. T., Trutt, S. D., and Watkins, C. E. (1992). Interpretation style and reactance in counselor's social influence. *Psychological Reports* 70:247–254.

Eisen, M. R. (1993). Psychoanalytic and psychodynamic models of hypnoanalysis. In *Handbook of Clinical Hypnosis,* ed. J. W. Rhue, S. J. Lynn, and I. Kirsch, pp. 123–150. Washington, DC: American Psychological Association.

Ellis, A. (1962). *Reason and Emotion in Psychotherapy.* Secaucus, NJ: Lyle Stuart.

———— (1977). The basic clinical theory of rational-emotive therapy. In *Handbook of Rational-Emotive Therapy,* ed. A. Ellis and R. Grieger, pp. 3–34. New York: Springer.

———— (1993). Rational-emotive imagery: RET version. In *The RET Book for Practitioners,* ed. M. E. Bernard and J. E. Wolfe, pp. II-8–II-10. New York: Institute for Rational-Emotive Therapy.

Ellis, A., and Dryden, W. (1997). *The Practice of Rational-Emotive-Behavior Therapy.* New York: Springer.

Erickson, M. H., and Rossi, E. L. (1979). *Hypnotherapy: An Exploratory Casebook.* New York: Irvington.

Erickson, M. H., Rossi, E. L., and Rossi, S. I. (1976). *Hypnotic Realities: The Induction of Clinical Hypnosis and Forms of Indirect Suggestion.* New York: Irvington.

Erikson, E. H. (1963). *Childhood and Society,* 2nd ed. New York: Norton.

Evans, M. D., Hollon, S. T., DeRubeis, R. J., et al. (1992). Differential relapse following cognitive therapy and pharmacotherapy for depression. *Archives of General Psychiatry* 49:802–808.

Farrants, J. (1998). The "false memory" debate: a critical review of the research on recovered memories of child sexual abuse. *The Counselling Psychology Quarterly* 11:229–238.

Fleming, K., Heikkinen, R., and Dowd, E. T. (1992). Cognitive therapy: the repair of memory. *Journal of Cognitive Psychotherapy* 6:155–174.

Frank, J. D. (1973). *Persuasion and Healing*, rev. ed. Baltimore: Johns Hopkins.

Golden, W. L., Dowd, E. T., and Friedberg, F. (1987). *Hypnotherapy: A Modern Approach.* New York: Pergamon.

Golden, W. L., and Friedberg, F. (1986). Cognitive-behavioural hypnotherapy. In *Cognitive-Behavioural Approaches to Psychotherapy*, ed. W. Dryden and W. L. Golden, pp. 290–319. London: Harper & Row.

Gomberg, D. S. (1996). *The function of metaphor in psychodynamic psychotherapy.* Unpublished doctoral dissertation, Long Island University.

Gonçalves, O. F., and Craine, M. H. (1990). The use of metaphors in cognitive therapy. *Journal of Cognitive Psychotherapy: An International Quarterly* 4:135–149.

Gore, N. S. (1977). *Psychological functions of metaphor.* Unpublished doctoral dissertation, University of Michigan.

Guidano, V. F. (1987). *Complexity of the Self: A Developmental Approach to Psychopathology and Therapy.* New York: Guilford.

Guidano, V. F., and Liotti, G. (1983). *Cognitive Processes and Emotional Disorders.* New York: Guilford.

Hacking, I. (1995). *Rewriting the Soul: Multiple Personality and the Sciences of Memory.* Princeton, NJ: Princeton University Press.

Hobbs, N. (1962). Sources of gain in psychotherapy. *American Psychologist* 17:741–747.

Hollon, S. D., DeRubeis, R. J., Evans, M. D., et al. (1992). Cognitive therapy and pharmacotherapy for depression: singly and in combination. *Archives of General Psychiatry* 49:774–781.

Johnson, M. K., Hashtroudi, S., and Lindsay, D. S. (1993). Source monitoring. *Psychological Bulletin* 114:3–28.

Kelly, F. D., and Dowd, E. T. (1980). *A comparison of cognitive and behavioral strategies in the treatment of depression.* Paper presented at the annual meeting of the American Psychological Association, Montreal, August.

Kirsch, I. (1993). Cognitive-behavioral hypnotherapy. In *Handbook of Clinical Hypnosis*, ed. J. W. Rhue, S. J. Lynn, and I. Kirsch, pp. 151– 172. Washington, DC: American Psychological Association.

Kirsch, I., and Lynn, S. J. (1997). Hypnotic involuntariness and the automaticity of everyday life. *American Journal of Clinical Hypnosis* 40:329–348.

———— (1998). Social-cognitive alternatives to dissociation theories of hypnotic involuntariness. *Review of General Psychology* 2:66–80.

Kirsch, I., Montgomery, G., and Sapirstein, G. (1995). Hypnosis as an adjunct to cognitive-behavioral psychotherapy: a meta-analysis. *Journal of Consulting and Clinical Psychology* 63:214–220.

Kroger, W. S. (1977). *Clinical and Experimental Hypnosis in Medicine, Dentistry, and Psychology*. Philadelphia: Lippincott.

Krupnick-McClure, C. (1994). Altered states of consciousness: trance as an adaptive coping mechanism for chemically dependent people. Doctoral dissertation, Antioch University/New England Graduate School, 1994. *Dissertation Abstracts International* 55/04, p. 1670.

Lankton, S. R., and Lankton, C. H. (1983). *The Answer Within: A Clinical Framework of Ericksonian Hypnotherapy*. New York: Brunner/ Mazel.

Lazarus, R. S., and Folkman, S. (1984). *Stress, Appraisal, and Coping*. New York: Springer.

Leahy, R. (1996). *Cognitive Therapy: Basic Principles and Applications*. Northvale, NJ: Jason Aronson.

Levitt, E. E. (1993). Hypnosis in the treatment of obesity. In *Handbook of Clinical Hypnosis*, ed. J. W. Rhue, S. J. Lynn, and I. Kirsch, pp. 533– 554. Washington, DC: American Psychological Association.

Liotti, G. (1989). Resistance to change in cognitive psychotherapy: theoretical remarks from a constructivistic point of view. In *Cognitive Psychotherapy: Stasis and Change*, ed. W. Dryden and P. Trower, pp. 28–56. London: Cassell.

Loftus, E. F. (1993). The reality of repressed memories. *American Psychologist* 48:518–537.

Loftus, E. F., and Coan, J. (in press). The construction of childhood memories. In *The Child Witness in Context: Cognitive, Social, and Legal Perspectives*, ed. D. Peters. New York: Kluwer.

Loftus, E. F., and Pickrell, J. E. (1995). The formation of false memories. *Psychiatric Annals* 25:720–725.

Lynn, S. J., Neufeld, V., and Maré, C. (1993a). Direct versus indirect suggestions: a conceptual and methodological review. *The International Journal of Clinical and Experimental Hypnosis* 41:124–152.

Lynn, S. J., Neufeld, V., Rhue, J. W., & Matorin, A. (1993b). Hypnosis and smoking cessation: a cognitive-behavioral treatment. In *Handbook of Clinical Hypnosis*, ed. J. W. Rhue, S. J. Lynn, and I. Kirsch, pp. 555–586. Washington, DC: American Psychological Association.

MacFarland, W. L., and Morris, S. J. (1998). Are dysphoric individuals more suggestible or less suggestible than nondysphoric individuals? *Journal of Counseling Psychology* 45:225–229.

Mahoney, M. J. (1991). *Human Change Processes*. New York: Basic Books.

Mahoney, M. J., ed. (1995). *Cognitive and Constructive Psychotherapies: Theory, Research and Practice*. New York: Springer.

Martin, J., Cummings, A. L., and Hallberg, E. T. (1992). Therapists' intentional use of metaphor: memorability, clinical impact, and possible epistemic/motivational functions. *Journal of Consulting and Clinical Psychology* 60:143–145.

Matthews, W. J., Conti, J., and Starr, L. (1998). Ericksonian hypnosis: a review of the empirical data. In *Current Thinking and Research in Brief Therapy: Solutions, Strategies, and Narrative*, Vol. II, ed. W. J. Matthews and J. H. Edgette, pp. 239–264. Philadelphia: Brunner/Mazel.

Matthews, W. J., Lankton, S., and Lankton, C. (1993). An Ericksonian model of hypnotherapy. In *Handbook of Clinical Hypnosis*, ed. J. W. Rhue, S. J. Lynn, and I. Kirsch, pp. 187–214. Washington, DC: American Psychological Association.

Meichenbaum, D. (1977). *Cognitive Behavior Modification*. New York: Plenum.

———— (1979). *Cognitive Behavior Modification Newsletter, No. 4,* January, University of Waterloo, Ontario.

Meichenbaum, D., and Gilmore, J. B. (1984). The nature of unconscious processes: a cognitive-behavioral perspective. In *The Unconscious Reconsidered,* ed. K. S. Bowers and D. Meichenbaum, pp. 273–298. New York: Wiley.

Miner, R. C., and Dowd, E. T. (1996). An empirical test of the problem-solving model of depression and its application to the prediction of anxiety and anger. *The Counselling Psychology Quarterly* 9:163–176.

Murray, E. J., and Jacobson, L. I. (1971). The nature of learning in traditional and behavioral psychotherapy. In *Handbook of Psychotherapy and Behavior Change,* ed. A. E. Bergin and S. L. Garfield, pp. 709–747. New York: Wiley.

Nezu, A. M., Nezu, C. M., & Perri, M. G. (1989). *Problem-Solving Therapy for Depression: Theory, Research, and Clinical Guidelines.* New York: Wiley.

Page, R. A., and Handley, G. W. (1993). The use of hypnosis in cocaine addiction. *American Journal of Clinical Hypnosis* 36:120–123.

Peterson, C., and Bassio, L. M. (1991). *Health and Optimism.* New York: Macmillan.

Pope, K. S., and Brown, L. S. (1996). *Recovered Memories of Abuse.* Washington, DC: American Psychological Association.

Reber, A. S. (1993). *Implicit Learning and Tacit Knowledge: An Essay on the Cognitive Unconscious.* New York: Oxford University Press.

Resnick, R. B., and Resnick, E. (1986). Psychological issues in the treatment of cocaine abuse. National Institute on Drug Abuse: Research Monograph Series, Mono 67, pp. 290–294. Washington, DC: National Institute on Drug Abuse.

Roe, C. M., Schwarz, M. F., and Peterson, F. L. (1994). Memories of previously forgotten childhood sexual abuse. *Behavioural Sciences and the Law* 12(3):279–298.

Schacter, D. L. (1996). *Searching for Memory: The Brain, the Mind, and the Past.* New York: Basic Books.

Schwartz, R. M., and Garamoni, G. L. (1989). Cognitive balance and psychopathology: evaluation of an information processing model of positive and negative states of mind. *Clinical Psychology Review* 9:271–294.

Selye, H. (1956). *The Stress of Life.* New York: McGraw-Hill.

Spanos, N. P. (1996). *Multiple Identities and False Memories: A Socio-cognitive Perspective.* Washington, DC: American Psychological Association.

Spanos, N. P., Mondoux, T. J., and Burgess, C. A. (1995). Comparison of multi-component hypnotic and non-hypnotic treatments for smoking. *Contemporary Hypnosis* 12:12–19.

Spiegel, D. (1993). Hypnosis in the treatment of posttraumatic stress disorders. In *Handbook of Clinical Hypnosis*, ed. J. W. Rhue, S. J. Lynn, and I. Kirsch, pp. 493–508. Washington, DC: American Psychological Association.

—— (1996). Hypnosis in the treatment of posttraumatic stress disorder. In *Casebook of Clinical Hypnosis*, ed. S. J. Lynn, I. Kirsch, and J. W. Rhue, pp. 99–112. Washington, DC: American Psychological Association.

Spiegel, H., and Spiegel, D. (1978). *Trance and Treatment: Clinical Uses of Hypnosis.* New York: Basic Books.

Strong, S. R., and Claiborn, C. D. (1982). *Change through Interaction.* New York: Wiley.

Strong, S. R., and Matross, R. P. (1973). Change processes in counseling and psychotherapy. *Journal of Counseling Psychology* 20:25–37.

Teitelbaum, M. (1969). *Hypnosis Induction Technics.* Springfield, IL: Charles C Thomas.

Vandamme, T. H. P. (1986). Hypnosis as an adjunct to the treatment of a drug addict. *Australian Journal of Clinical and Experimental Hypnosis* 14:41–48.

Wachtel, P. L. (1977). *Psychoanalysis and Behavior Therapy: Toward an Integration.* New York: Basic Books.

Wadden, T. A., and Anderton, C. H. (1982). The clinical use of hypnosis. *Psychological Bulletin* 91:215—245.

Walters, C., and Havens, R. A. (1993). *Hypnotherapy for Health, Harmony, and Peak Performance.* New York: Brunner/Mazel.

Weeks, G. R., and L'Abate, L. (1982). *Paradoxical Psychotherapy: Theory and Practice with Individuals, Couples, and Families.* New York: Brunner/Mazel.

Weishaar, M. E. (1993). *Key Figures in Counselling and Psychotherapy: Aaron T. Beck.* London: Sage.

Williams, J. M. G. (1996). Memory processes in psychotherapy. In *Frontiers of Cognitive Therapy*, ed. P. M. Salkovskis, pp. 97–113. New York: Guilford.

Wright, M. E., and Wright, B. A. (1987). *Clinical Practice of Hypnotherapy.* New York: Guilford.

Yapko, M. D. (1993). Hypnosis and depression. In *Handbook of Clinical Hypnosis*, ed. J. W. Rhue, S. J. Lynn, and I. Kirsch, pp. 339–356. Washington, DC; American Psychological Association.

——— (1995). *Essentials of Hypnosis.* New York: Brunner/Mazel.

Young, J. E. (1994). *Cognitive Therapy for Personality Disorders: A Schema-Focused Approach*, rev. ed. Sarasota, FL: Professional Resource Exchange.

Zaragoza, M. S., and Mitchell, K. J. (1996). Repeated exposure to suggestion and the creation of false memories. *Psychological Science* 7:294–300.

Index

ABOUT THE AUTHOR

E. Thomas Dowd, Ph.D., ABPP, is currently Professor of Psychology at Kent State University. He has previously taught at Florida State University and the University of Nebraska. He has authored or co-authored more than 100 publications on cognitive behavior therapy, hypnosis, psychological reactance, paradoxical interventions, and social influence processes, in addition to other topics. He edited *Leisure Counseling* (1984), co-edited *Case Studies in Hypnotherapy* (1986), and co-authored *Hypnotherapy: A Modern Approach* (1987). Dr. Dowd was founding editor of the *Journal of Cognitive Psychotherapy: An International Quarterly*, is currently North American Consulting Editor for the *Counselling Psychology Quarterly*, and serves on several other editorial boards. A Fellow of the American Psychological Association in the divisions of Counseling Psychology and International Affairs, Dr. Dowd was also President of the International Association for Cognitive Psychotherapy and is President of the American Board of Behavioral Psychology, Inc. He has served on the Board of Trustees of the American Board of Professional Psychology. Dr. Dowd holds diplomates in Behavioral Psychology and Counseling Psychology from the American Board of Professional Psychology, Inc.